QUEST *for* PEACE
Star Quest

JEREMIAH NICHOLS

iUniverse, Inc.
Bloomington

Quest for Peace
Star Quest

This is a work of fiction. All of the characters, names, incidents, organizations, and dialogue in this novel are either the products of the author's imagination or are used fictitiously.

iUniverse books may be ordered through booksellers or by contacting:

iUniverse
1663 Liberty Drive
Bloomington, IN 47403
www.iuniverse.com
1-800-Authors (1-800-288-4677)

ISBN: 978-1-4502-9251-1 (sc)
ISBN: 978-1-4502-9252-8 (ebook)

Printed in the United States of America

iUniverse rev. date: 01/24/2011

Jeremiah Nichols has one amazing daughter Katherine Grace Nichols. His parents are Lee and Paula Nichols and they all reside in Monahans, Texas. Jeremiah is a graduate of Monahans High School in 1996 and he graduated from Texas A&M in 2003 with a Bachelors in Industrial Distribution. While he is not writing books he writes songs, poems, sermons, and sometimes preaches on Wednesday nights at Grace Fellowship Church in Monahans.

Contents

Acknowledgements

This book is inspired by God and dedicated to my daughter Katherine Nichols and also to my faithful and supportive parents Lee Nichols and Paula Nichols.

I would like to thank God for everything, my savior Jesus Christ, Special thanks go out to my family: my beautiful, amazing daughter Katherine Grace Nichols, inspirational and loving parents Mom and Dad Nichols, wise Uncle Dexter Nichols, Aunt Kathy Nichols, Lexie, Caleb, Judy, and Scott Nichols, sister Leah Nichols Cavitt, John Cavitt and the boys Shepard Jamison Robert and Regan Cavitt, sister Alyson Myers and all of the Myers family, Aunt Bonnie and Uncle Orville, Bryan and Billy Kidd, Kathy Hannah and Keith Norris, Kelsy Aaron and the new baby Brown, Chyenne Cody Norris. Lorrie and Donna Tramell and their families.

I would also like to thank the following people for being such a good friend: my amazing pastor Mark Bristow, you and I put the we in awesome Lisa Bristow, listener Ron Long, friends the Carrells, hilarious Eddie Day, very funny visionary Chuck Rogers, jokester Sid Scarboro, Rueben Browning, Peyton Beard Ashley, Billy Beard and his family, Dianna and Wendel Harkey, Joe and Lana Flores, Holly Harkey Beggs and Jonathan and Kennedy, Jackie Jeffery and Judy Harkey, the Woody's, Zeke Dawdy and the Dawdy's. Matt Wittie and his family, Marcos Sanchez my neighbor, Becky Calder my other neighbor, The Dendy's, The Bean's,, Amber and Hannah Benad, JoClare McCurdy, Brandon and Gail Wade, Melinda and Melissa Wade, Misty Mayhall, Paige White, Paige Tamplin, Jenn and Jeramy Montgomery and the

Monty's, Sandra and Wally Meeks, Becca Curtis Terry and Steve Steen, Jennifer and Jeremy Jacob, Connie and Jake Jacob, the Dewey's, Sabrina Chase and Elizabeth McAdams, Don and AnnaRae Brown, Wanda Lemons, Everitt Hewett,, The Nussey's, Waylon Wilcox and all of the Wilcox's, Tregg Passmore and all of the Passmore's, Jon, Leeland, and Big Ed Day, all of the Collins' family, Kathy Mike Shelby and the Corneilieus family, Sammy and Zain Carrell, Matt Sammy and Sarah Carrell, Roy and Zeida Young and all of the Young's, Big Phillip, Amy, Phillip, Jay (we will see you someday), and Brandon Bell, Shannon Huckabee, Ryan and Mark Valenzuela, Keith and Bridgett Bilski, Ana Castillo, Ali Covington, Jami Carter, Jena Tisdale, Cody and all of the Stocktons, Danielle Tyler Brandon and the Lee's, Tres and all of the Thomas's, Miss Jones thank you for all your support, Mrs. Thomas (we will see you someday), The Heinz's, special thanks to Janell and Jay Kelton, Lisa Savage Hack and Denny Savage, Big Denny and Libby Savage, Jason Larissa and the Pittman's, Hector Hernandez, Cheno Sonya and the Navarette's. Ryan Reagan and the Williams', Crystal Swenson, Kelley Cooke, Abbie Watts Hubbard, Amy Morgan and Nicole and the Hammonds, Athena Jessica Jenny and Linda Johnson Jerry (we will see you someday) Dustin Johnson, Bianca Watson Foley, Melissa Allen, Chad and Heidi Branham, Chris Morris, Lilly and Gatan Patel, Scott and Tonya Taylor, Debbie Coffee, Regina Fuentez, Regina Juan and the Popaleo's, Michael Philbrick, Jesse Bejaran, Michael and Laura Defranco, Coach Ward, Mark Moore, Coach Moore, Coach Cliff, Tonya, and Mrs Gardner, Coach and Mrs. Curry, The Weavers, Coach Curley, The Teinerts, Kevin and the Swanners, Will Karen and the Kempers.

Introduction
to Quest for Peace

The state of Ionious United is not united anymore, they have found themselves in a continual state of disarray and in division. The entire Zeus mountains were destroyed and the element Nivio was demolished with it. While the South were in the midst of constructing an answer to their energy needs the mountain range was attacked and depleted the entire supply of Nivio. This would force the North to find new deposits on the other side of the planet and also on another planet.

While their efforts were successful, this left them in a state of vulnerability for several months, in which they decided to attack the South for their attack on them or so they thought. God revealed Himself to Ezekiel Epsilon as he was in a coma in a hospital bed not knowing if he would live or die. Jesus appeared and told the Southern General Isaiah Omega that He would be giving Ezekiel a dream, and Isaiah followed that dream and had it recorded and then gave it to the North as proof. They should have seen that he did not give the order to destroy the North's deposits of Nivio their lifeline for all of Ionious, but they fail to believe and this has proven to be their downfall.

The South obeyed their God and found the culprits that were responsible for the attack and are in the process of dealing with their crimes against humanity. In the meantime the North have attacked the South in a training camp and countless casualties have been the result. A new General has arisen in the South to compliment Isaiah Omega in their Quest to stave off the consistent attacks of the North.

Seeking peace the South pleaded with the Northern Council to believe the dream that God gave Ezekiel Epsilon but they refuse to believe, so onward they press in vain to destroy the South. They attempt also to regain control of the planet's energy supply source and the power of the South's position in Congress so that they may have their way on Ionious.

Quest Starships (Quantum Universal Energy String Transports) have been patrolling the Ephesian Galaxy relentlessly for months after the last attack. A new attack has arisen and the South must deal with this nemesis threat, to their culture and society, which has been created from their lack of belief. Revelation 22:13 says, "I am the Alpha and the Omega, the beginning and the end." As Aaron Alpha began his attack on the Southern State of Ionious United, General Isaiah Omega had to thwart off a clandestine operation that was from a formidable foe and one that was once his friend. DreamStream Interactive has shown many new found mysteries revealed through God's mighty hand and now the Americans are able to access these technologies as they too wage war against their rival the dreaded Muslims a continent away. Several SWORD object and food generators were also given to the Americans to help sustain their efforts against their religious counterparts.

The civilians from the USA enjoy the comforts that Ionious technologies bring as they seek refuge on the planet. Some have chosen sides and decide to fight for either the North or the South. They know that the war is wrong from any way that they look at it, and they think that they can make a difference and bring peace back to this utopic planet. The Americans have made such great progress in their fight as millions of people have given their lives to Jesus and have moved to Ionious to live a life for God as all that do on the planet. Ezekiel Epsilon was given a prophecy from God and here it is:

There was a gleaming light in the distance,
It was the end but yet a beginning,
This bitter journey and all circumstance,
Captive and obedient to feeling,
The presence of Jesus when I couldn't feel,
Before I saw the road there was a light,
Before the light there were flickers so real,
Flashing so bright of what I knew was so right,

Blasting the darkness into an unknown truth,
Refreshing sweetness fallen then building,
Attack and victory shown as the proof,
God moves gently and the spirit revealing,
The glory resonates that was felt by eyes that couldn't see,
But they shake in awe the light growing brighter,
Their roads before them as darkness flees,
The light is there but you have to be a fighter,
Laying all of yourself down to pick up the dream,
To dare to believe and dare to walk with the upright,
Taking hold of the word and to the knowledge that brings,
Peace in the first step of faith to walk towards the light.
Your quest to see God in the light,
Knowing that this path is right,
Will bring you to revelation,
A reason in Jesus for celebration,
For someday we will fly to him in the sky,
A glory surrounding Jesus face so bright,
To revel in his presence all will be worth the path,
Traveled to see what is waiting for us on his behalf,
We praise with wilted eyes not seeing his full presence,
But someday to our surprise all will be revealed in essence,
We will worship with complete clarity and vision,
And see Gods face, the glory, the light, the revelation.

…Thus begins the next adventure in the Epic of Star Quest: Quest for Peace.

Chapter 1
A Beautiful Day

"Things to Consider"

You might know that I have a daughter Katherine Grace Nichols, what you don't know is that she is the sweetest, most beautiful, and amazing daughter I could ever ask for. She is my world and I would do anything for her. So think about some of the best times that you have had with your children and how you can remind them of how amazing they are to you.

In this chapter I talk about the story of how Daniel met Zeph at church camp one summer. This story is reflective of my experience in church camp in the fourth grade where I met and dated the most beautiful girl Camille McCune. The camp was Roaring Springs and there was a river near the camp that we went to on the last day. Peyton Beard was also at this camp and I did everything I could to please her by giving her boyfriend my shirt and having him get cleaned up to see her. If I couldn't date Peyton I wanted her to have the best boyfriend that she possibly could so I became friends with him and gave him good things to say to her and compliment her on. I had been in love with Peyton for over a year. Think about the way that you met your wife or husband or significant other and how you can thank them and relive the story by telling it to your children.

Chapter 1
A Beautiful Day

His house was built for worship, and that is what he instilled in his children and his wife supported his vision for what God had in store for them. Daniel was a very loving man kind and gentle in nature, and always wanted God's will for his family in every situation. His duty was to his God first, then to his family, and if he had enough time and if it called upon him his country. Daniel was there in the living room reliving a dream that his daughter had the night before. They were bonding in ways that they never could have when he was on Mars, and this was his joy of his life, to be spending it with his beloved family.

DreamStream was something that his daughter loved to do as much as he did, and to share their feelings together was something that Daniel had always dreamed of. In the dreamstream dream application, they were in a scene where she was playing in the meadow and her friends had invited her to go to Jerusalem while her Dad was calling out her name she heard him from a distance, and she had to decide her friends or her Dad. She had been missing her Dad so much and longed to be in his presence and laugh with him again as they had done before the war.

Daniel always had a way of making her laugh and he loved to play games with her whether in DreamStream or in reality. Daniel was out picking blueberries in their back yard underneath their tall beautiful trees. Sariah was playing out in the field next to Daniel behind their house. So when she heard her Dad's voice say, "Sweety," it was the

7

sweetest music she had ever heard. She then decided to go to him as she ran back to where her Dad was in the meadow on a beautiful landscape, that was full of grass up to her ankles and trees that brimmed the horizon with a mountain peak of crested purple's majesty. All capped with snow glistening in the mid-day afternoon sky, speckled with patches of bright white clouds that caught her glimpse as her head turned in her run to Daniel's arms.

Finally through the greenest grass high stepping the last trods to pounce with both legs in a bounce that leaped into his arms. In the dream she heard his strong but gentle voice rejoicing in her return to him. "Honey Pumpkin, Baby Girl, oh how I have missed you."

She took her face back from being stuck to his uniform and looked in his eyes and told him. "Daddy, you're here, you're here." Then she returned the side of her face back to being planted in his AIIA uniform and squeezed his chest with all of her might.

A tear trickled down her other cheek as she said, "You have been gone so long, promise me you will stay forever, and never leave."

A smile consumed his face as jubilation overtook his emotions and he told her, "My dear, I promise." As he pulled her away from his chest and looked in her eyes. Standing a quarter mile away from the house in grass surrounded by a narrow row of Mulberry trees.

"Now ice cream for the one who makes it back to the house first." She was brought down gently to the ground as she quickly took her running stance with one hand raised and one behind her and one leg forward and one back. She then directed her attention directly towards the house looked down at her stance and then back up again intensely. Daniel then gathered himself and said, "On your Mark, get set, GO!"

They both took off with a blazing speed bounding with the first step then settling into a comfortable pace to a trot. Daniel got a late start because of his joyful laughing, she was several steps ahead and looked back then dug in and put in her all into her run. Her head turned ever so slightly with every step with eyes focused now on what was their back porch patio chairs.

Slightly by slightly she edged towards the goal, the back porch surrounded by Ionic columns and Ivy that grew on the paralleled terrace. She was halfway there and her Dad was getting winded, trailing, as running was something that he hadn't done since the last time that they played in the meadow.

As she neared the marble floor of the porch she looked back at her Dad who was trailing by a considerable length. So, out of love for her Dad she slowed to a stop and waited for a second, for him to catch up with her. "Daa-aaddy, are you ok?"

She was a good ten yards away and she ran with all her might and made it to the marble flooring first, she then planned for them to get to the kitchen to the SWORD to get Ice Cream together.

As he finally got there she put her arm out to reach around his back for support then Daniel reached out his hand and tagged her and said, "You're it!" then he ran his fastest and made it to the door first.

Then he said, "Honey, Baby Girl, I'll make the first bowl for you. And tell me something how did you get so fast?" She just laughed thinking he was really winded; to herself she thought goodness I love my Dad.

"Daddy I got my speed from Mom you know that." He chuckled with his head to the sky bright and shining.

"Baby, God made you that way."

He then returned his eyes to her and said, "Lets get Ice Cream. I know you're first. Go ask your brother if he wants some Ice Cream too, and where is my babe?"

They were now back in reality and in the house making their way into the kitchen as he made his last statements loud enough for all in the house to hear.

Zeph was in their room exercising in her intellichair and heard his voice calling out to her as a smile and purpose came over her. She quickly arose and ran into the kitchen where his voice was coming from. "Oh Sweetness, did I hear Ice Cream?" As she made it into the walkway of the entrance of the kitchen their eyes met as if they hadn't seen each other in days and then they were glued to one another as she fixed them on him and intently took each step showing off her new figure to him and met with a hug and a kiss.

Their son just came waltzing into the room and said, "I heard Ice Cream, Sis I get next on the SWORD."

She looked over to him and said, "Ok, I am getting chocolate chunk."

Her brother said, "I don't know what I want. Dad where is your Scroll?"

Daniel took his clutch from Zeph glanced over and said, "Its on the table Zedakiah."

Daniel then looked back to Zeph and said, "Sweets, what kind do you want? Any kind I'll get it for you, just say the word."

As he was walking over to Zed to see the flavors she grabbed Daniel's hand and pulled him back within a breath away and said, "Do you remember the mountains of Odyssey and that Ice Cream Parlor that we went to where they made it from real snow?"

He took his head back and got a good look of her amazing green eyes, "Of course I remember you ordered Cookies and Cream."

She smiled something big, and tilted the front of her head down and looked up with her big green irresistables batting and all and said, "Yes, sweetness that's what I want."

He quickly said as if he couldn't get it out fast enough, "I'll do it then, its yours." Then he took his head back to the side at an angle to her and wanted to know, "Any toppings?"

She took both of his hands and swayed them side to side and said cravingly with a wrinkled top of her nose, "Chocolate Chips," as if they were dancing.

She was already seated at the table and enjoying the food and the time that she had just had with her special Dad. Sariah loved him so much because she knew how special she was in his eyes and she respected all that he does for her family. She saw how Daniel was treating Mom as if they were on a first date or something and to realize that they still had that sparkle in their eyes as he went to get her some Cookies and Cream. This made her realize how God had blessed her with such amazing parents and she thought I want my life to be like that someday.

Sariah was lost in utopic thoughts and was wondering, as they all now were at the table eating different types of Ice Cream, "Daddy, could you tell me again how you and mommy met?"

Zeph and Daniel locked eyes and just laughed, "Okay, sure honey dumplin, I'll tell you, Zed are you staying around for this too?"

Zed had pink all over the sides of his lips. "Of course I want to know how y'all got together."

Daniel then prepared his Scroll for their clips to go along with his story that would be played on the walling. "I was just out of school that year and I was hanging out at the Temple walls with all my friends and I came home to your grandparents. They told me something dreadful, I had to leave my friends at the Temple and go to some revival Camp for one week. I wasn't happy needless to say, but with rebellion in my heart I went with crossed arms."

A scene from his parent's house popped on the screen and he was very skinny wearing some kind of glowing shirt with bags around each shoulder. The particle stream materialized and he stepped through to a room with a ton of bunk beds and a camp counselor that was telling all of the arriving to put their belongings under their beds.

"There I was unhappy in the middle of nowhere and I was hating every minute of it wishing I was back at the Temple wall just hanging out. However somehow I made the most of it and went along with all of their things that they had to do for us. The camp counselor was a pretty good guy, come to find out he was a surfer, and there was a spring that lead to a river that lead to the ocean. I thought that we would all go surfing by the end of camp so that made me excited."

"We all had to put on our best Sunday clothes and go to dinner then to a church service. I put trunks on underneath and I followed along with everyone else just waiting for the word to go surfing. I even wore a surfing wristband and I found out that at the concession stand that you could rent surfboards. So before dinner I went to the concession stand to see if I had enough money to rent one for a day, and there she was."

"She had a surfboard in her hand wrapped around her arms I saw her eyes, green as can be, peek out from behind an enormous surfboard twice as big as her. At first I didn't pay that much attention to her, as I was just concerned with how much the boards were. So I got up to the window and this guy came out with a wave of a hair-do, and said the boards are 50 a day. I didn't have near that much and she was still standing there and I stood there for a minute wondering what I was going to do."

"So I just stood there and good thing that Mom isn't shy because she had noticed what was going on with me and she asked the question, "Do you want to go surfing?" And that was the sweetest voice that I had ever heard, my heart leaped inside and I just blurted out, "Yeah, I don't have enough money though." I edged around over so I could see her better out from behind the board and she was even prettier than her voice lead on, as I saw her entire sweet face. She looked me up and down and said, "You can go with me." I perked up and smiled really big and said to her, "When are you going?" She looked down then up and said, "Now, if you want to go with me we could share the board." I stood there and thought about it for a minute knowing that everyone else was going to the service and to dinner. She then saw he was not sure. "Only if you want to?"

I said, "I have to go eat dinner and to service, my camp counselor said that we might go on Friday." She felt like she wanted to do something nice for him. "You know you're kind of cute, and I think you're brave if you go." That was all it took, "Okay, I'll go, we have to be careful though, that no one sees us leaving."

She looked around and noticed where all of the campers were going and said, "Look, they are all in line at the mess hall so if we go now they will never notice. Let's run towards the spring. Okay?" I was all for it and I said, "Okay, lets go." We looked at each other, "Ready, Set, Go!" Then we took off running as fast as we could both holding one end of the surfboard across the meadow down to the spring. And that's about it."

Sariah was just in awe but she had a question, "Daaad, mom told me something." Daniel replied, "What is that? Sweets what did you tell her?" Zeph winked over to Daniel and said, "You know when we..." Then Sariah jumped in and let out a big, "Kiss!"

Daniel was embarrassed, "Honey did you tell her that? I am not telling her that story you will have to tell it." Zeph smiled and sighed, "Alright I'll tell it, it's a wonderful story, you know that don't you?" Daniel just said, "Yes sweetness I remember it very well."

She then began to tell the rest of the story, "Okay we had just run past the camp site down to the spring where no one could see us. When we made it to the spring he wanted to stop and get a drink of water so we both knelt down and began to drink, he made a cup with his hands and drank as much as he could then I saw this huge wall of water coming towards me.

I got soaked, he was such a joker, so I grabbed the board and splashed him back with an even bigger wall of water. Now I thought that was really funny, luckily so did he. So after our splash in the spring we trodded the wet clay in water up to our shins out to the river."

"Still, we carried both ends of the board until we got to the river and it was a flowing. So we just jumped on, he got on in front of me just in case we saw a crock or something; he was being the brave one. We paddled down to the end of the river to the delta where the clay met seawater and the glorious ocean."

"We made it to the beach and there was a sunset only God could have painted, it looked a lot like the sunsets over our snowcapped peak in front of the house. I didn't know this at the time but he had never been surfing before but you could never tell by how brave and confident he was in three-foot waves."

"I was a pro, I had been surfing before I lived near a beach. He said that he would go first, just in case there were any sharks. So without ever surfing before he went out there and gave it his all, there were no sharks, and he was not afraid, he had seen surfers before and he did it just like I did."

"He paddled out a good ways, then paddled in and stood up at the crest and he rode the wave all the way into the beach. By the time the board hit the beach he was so tired that he just fell over into the mush being silly. I was clapping the whole way but when he fell over to make me laugh I just had to giggle. I thought he was trying to make me laugh but he didn't get up and I got very worried and ran over to him."

"I shook his back and he didn't move, so I rolled him over on his chest and checked for a heartbeat and it was beating but he wasn't breathing. So I did what I knew to do and started to give him mouth to mouth resuscitation."

"When my lips touched his he kissed me back and I just hit his chest and said, "I thought you couldn't breathe. You scared me to death." He straightened up and said, "Oh, I am so sorry I was just wanting to kiss you." I got over it and we both watched the most beautiful sunset I think that I have ever seen. And that is our story."

Sariah was almost in tears, "Oh, Mom that is so romantic, tell it again, please." One peaked just underneath her left eyelash and strolled halfway down her cheek before her index finger caught it. She then used her other hand clinched to wipe any potential tears from flowing from her other eye. Such humble browns with greens of depth and understanding filled with a watering tenderness that could only be felt by someone who had a heart for her parents and something so pure.

Her mom, Zeph, knew that she had such a tender heart and one that was susceptible to sappy love stories, not to diminish their story in any way but just to bring light to her pure heart. With a softness she asked Sariah, "Honeybear, are you okay?"

Honeybear looked up with her big browns and pushed her finished ice cream aside, "Maaooom, I am fine its nothing no really its nothing it must be that particle catcher I think a breeze just shot through here and dried out my eyes that's all."

Zeph then leaned over to her and whispered, "You know you are sweet, even when you were a baby, you were sweet to everyone, you always poked Dad's dimples and you loved my bunny rabbits, they were your favorite. And they wouldn't just snuggle up with anyone but they sensed your heart and they knew you were special just like your Dad and I know you are special."

Sariah kind of shyed away and pulled her self back in her chair, "Maaoom, I know you think I am special but the boys at school don't think that I am special."

Her mom was sensing a moment of wisdom coming on here, "Honey, did you know that the only opinion that matters is God's and he says in Isaiah 43:4 You are precious in his sight and you are honored and because you are loved by God He will do anything for you. So you just pray and after a while they will see what God already sees in you. Just remember man sees the outside and God sees your heart. The seed of the righteous shall be mighty in the land."

Sariah just perked up taking in all that her mom had to say, now she was very intelligent she didn't know all about what her mom was saying but she did understand what her heart was saying, and made her feel a lot better.

Daniel was sifting on his scroll and he found something that looked pretty cool for Sariah to do, "Baby girl, did you know that I just found a Medina and Ruth princess Dream Catcher on DSI and it's the latest and I know that you don't have this one yet and if you want I'll play the King. How does that sound?"

She dismounted from the intelli-chair and jogged over to where her Dad was to see what he was talking about, all smiles, "No way, you got it? For real? Okay, I'll play if you want to Dad." Before you knew it they were in the entertainment room and lost in an intriguing fantasy dream.

Zeph said, "Be good, if I jump in there better be no mischief."

14

Taken away by the game Sariah responded, "Okay, Mom, no monkey business." Then they were away to conquer new lands.

While they were in the entertainment room Zed was in his room downloading the latest from the Sacrifice of the Lamb. This was suggested to him by his youth pastor and he normally played all of those games so this was going to be a new experience for him with the Lamb. Zeph was busy cleaning the house and several hours later Daniel came running into the living room to tell her of what had just happened.

Zeph was expecting another princess story however this would not be about any DSI stories. "Honey, I have to go there has been an attack and they need me there. They said that the Eastern gate was destroyed and that they need a reinforcing shield to combat the onslaught."

Zeph knew that this wasn't good she ran to get his scroll and noticed that he already had it on his hip he was ready for this one. "If you must, then go Daniel."

He hugged her then got out his scroll and typed away. "I'll be back soon, I am praying that this shouldn't take too long. I love you." Zeph looking at a picture of the family on the wall said, "I love you too." Then he was gone.

Chapter 2
A Reason for Praise
Worship in Song

"Things to Consider"

If you're wondering what is going on in this Chapter I jump into poem mode when telling the story, it is just a creative thing that I like to do since I write so many poems. I also love to sing and you will find this out throughout the book as I write many songs in the book. There is always a reason for worship and praise I think, whether you have just accomplished a great goal or if you are in the midst of a storm. There is always a reason to sing, I praise my savior always no matter the situation. As you breeze through this book think of your favorite songs and also about songs that you would like to write or just sing about. Maybe there are certain subjects that you like to sing about the most. If you want you can make up your own melody and sing the songs that I have written in the book to help you take it all in.

Chapter 2
A Reason for Praise
Worship in Song

Daniel was ready, "You have the coordinates? I am there."

Titus was already on location where they were needed and he piped over to Daniel who received the transmission in his office. "Do what you can I'll be there in a moment."

He was calibrating some instrumentation equipment that he would need and then he saw the herd swift past his door. There was a great commotion that he was picking up from his ears and his transcomm, everyone was needing his help and pronto. With the tools in his hand he slammed his drawer shut typed in a lock and sped through the PAST.

"Titus when I give the signal will you be ready?"

Titus was typing in code as fast as the human body would allow he was also coming over to Daniel simultaneously. "I am in a bind man you have to bring the trilateral array, we are gonna need it."

Daniel was already one block away from Titus' position and there was a heavy crossfire in the way that was preventing his forward progress to enter at the drop spot. He inched his right eye past the corner of a dimly lit scroll-walling exterior and felt something sharp plow right into his right wrist. Jerking it back immediately he saw blood gushing from it. He had been hit. He tore a piece of clothing around his collar off to make a tourniquet.

His heart was jumping out of his chest as his head rested about three feet from the edge of where he had been shot. Glancing over at the edge he couldn't tell if it was a disrupter blast that had got him or if it were a piece of shard from the walling that had lunged into his wrist.

Nonetheless, he was in pain and needed to be about a block down from where he was, and he couldn't see a means of getting over there at this time. "Titus, I have been hit. I'll be there in a minute." Titus could sense the pain in his voice.

"We need that array system with out it they are going to just infiltrate at will. I have one and we will need at least two more to stave off the attack. Can you make it here?" Daniel surveyed his surroundings and got a good grasp of where he was.

There was a PAST way about one block to the East of where he was. It was some kind of medical pharmacy and across the street there was another PAST way that was much closer but he would have to risk getting hit again if he decided to venture across the street. Decisions, decisions.

"There will be an opening in precisely one minute if you run at full blast you will make it." The holy spirit was talking to him and for all he could tell there was no way that he could ever make it across the street.

This would be much faster and he knew this, however actually having the strength to make it across was another thing. "You can do all things through Christ Jesus who strengthens you." Jesus was there for him too, giving him an encouraging word, to assure him that he would make it if he decided to go.

Jesus had never been wrong; he was the only perfect man to ever live so why would he doubt him now. The blood was gushing out of the tourniquet and his legs were weak from the DSI game as king, inside he felt like there was no way that he could make it.

While he was plotting the best scenario, a blast shattered the walling beside him, and a piece of shrapnel caught his leg. He saw the piece in some sort of slow motion that had fragmented frames that allowed for the dust from the side wall to be plunging towards him in segments. He was now standing a good three yards away and when he got hit he limped further down the sidewalk. One leg in front of the other blood trailing down his leg. "Thirty seconds and you can make it to Titus."

Daniel backed into a PAST way that hadn't been in use for at least a decade, and as he lounged his back into the cubbie hole a mouse came running right past his new boosts and brushed against his new AIIA cloaking suit. It was the bottom edge of his pant leg that was shifting from a jade to meridian blue to back his surroundings in case there were any Alphas peeping his way.

A sudden sound burst aloud in the blast,

He reached for ammo praying this wasn't his last,

With a feel on the hip he knew that he would have to go through the PAST,

Looking up, with courage disrupter clinched, the southern flag was half-mast,

Confidence grew in his heart, 10 seconds countdown, with his disrupter a burst,

He heard from the Holy Spirit and took a heed to the call which wasn't his first,

One second away from a step of faith, his blood was a cauldron boiling in his veins,

He heard "GO" so running he did his wrist bleeding and as his leg was in pain,

This faith was adrenaline pumping with each pounce dodging shots and sounds,

He ducked as one whirred by, disrupter clinched in the left he let out a round,

Up ahead was safety and refuge a clearing was where he slid to the ground,

With the last blast he was out and as he slid into the wall guess what he found?

Beneath the particle stream glittering pinks there were rounds that someone had just thrown out,

Sight-noise blasters and ammo galore with a pill that he took to ease the pain that was ever so stout,

Daniel keyed in intently the address of Titus covered by a wall that blocked the fire of the enemy,

He landed uncovered and bare with shots ablazing overhead there was a wall that protected the entry,

Where Titus was getting ready for the array to arrive he then saw Daniel running in stride,

The wall was exploding from pinpoint hits right behind him to Daniel's left side,

When he arrived he threw out an umbrella shield that was twelve feet wide,

To protect their work as they set up the trilateral array to back off the fight.

Two were setup at the base of the wall the third was thrown up at the height of the arch,

Daniel was then ready to set it aglow of as he pressed it, it started and the soldiers did march,

Around the light purple and pinks the energy glow was electric and a sight to see,

They then both went back through the PAST tending to his wounds as safe as can be,

Ever so thankful for the heeding to his call our God all parts of the three,

What a government so perfect and whole who could stand against the Holy Trinity,

With God on our side who can be against us not the Zyahth or the Muslims and not the,

North that hasn't one shield engineer so give thanks to the Lord that gives us blessings.

Daniel then began to praise as he saw victory from his hand, "Oh Lord how great are you,

How great are your blessings and your words of direction that saved me through,

(Mark 13:11) "For it is not a man who spoke but the Holy Spirit" giving me instructions anew,

(Psalms 22:26) "Those who seek him shall give praises to the Lord and giving thanks" unto,

The Lord God of Israel (1 Chronicles 16:35) "to give thanks to your Holy name,

To triumph in your praise" Rejoicing in your victory with my hands I raise,

Lifted to you (Ephesians 3:20) "who is able to do exceedingly and abundantly,

Above all that we think or ask, through your power in us" which is so mighty,

(1 John 4:4) "For he that is in me is greater than he that is in the world,"

(Daniel 3:4) "To you it is commanded O peoples and nations cried the herald"

(1 Chronicles 16:29) "O worship the Lord in the beauty of the holiness""

And Daniel made his praises resound to the Lord with loving-kindness.

His eyes were a spring all the tears in praise welling up,

When God opens one for us and to them one is shut,

He has delivered us from our certain destruction,

And made a way for us as we created our construction.

(Genesis 15:1) "Do not be afraid for I am your shield your exceedingly great reward."

Gods voice rained down to remind them that in all things I am here and I am your Lord,

"To the North, believe in me, and in Ezekiel's dream, if you don't, it is something that you cannot afford,

You will not last or sustain your attack against my people I warn you this is my word."

God's voice was heard from above to the North's soldiers that were attacking at the East gate,

"Your opportunity to believe is drawing near so believe now before it is too late",

Seeking peace Daniel praised the Lord what I sow might be small but with God the harvest is great,

Until all have heard the gospel then Jesus will come back for his desire is to save.

"Glory be to God Daniel I would be praising Him if I were you." General Lambda transcommed over to Daniel and Titus as he was drafting some plans for a FOLED campaign over Olympia to support peace.

John Lambda was undertaking his first projects from Isaiah and wanted to remind Daniel to keep praising the Lord for the victory that they had just received. Daniel who was glowing with Gods presence and had a smile of confidence and thankfulness with some sweat still pouring from his forehead after the last adrenaline filled sequence where God had just delivered them.

21

"With all the energy that I have left after that release I am giving God all the praise, you better believe it John, congratulations on the promotion."

A set of fans popped out from the intellichair that Daniel was sitting in as it sensed his plethora of vital signs that required a general cooling.

GRRRUMPH! His stomach growled as hunger was bubbling up, "John I think that the SWORD is calling out to me."

John was panning through various maps and flight plans on the scroll walling in the central command room with a sundry of officers and ranking officials giving their input. "Blessed are those that hunger and thirst after righteousness for they shall be filled. I suggest the infilling of the Holy Spirit and thirst after faith like Abraham and you will be filled with righteousness."

"There is something that we need to talk about in 10 minutes at the Chronos room, we have new intel, and we need Daniel and Titus, with Jacob and your twelve advisers in attendance. Can you make this happen? Pray as you go. Peace be with you. Peace is on the way." Isaiah broadcast this to General Lambda and the recipient's transcomms simultaneously.

General Lambda hit the side selection that brought up a screen on the scroll walling that viewed from the scrolls of all of the intended recipients. "We need a UAV run through on this district at this hour for a potential extrapolation and simulation of this event. Jehovah Jirah."

There were two minutes remaining before all of the assembled were supposed to be there in the Chronos room and Daniel, Titus, and Timothy were already there talking about the possibilities. "This could be about our PERSON's project you both know of the potential that his could bring for peace."

Timothy was the liaison between the engineers and the strategists and he knew most of what Daniel and John knew, however this was from Isaiah, and he knew that it could be anything. "Could be, also this might be about the FOLED sails John was just preparing flight plans when I left the command room." Timothy was smoothing out a wrinkle on his AIIA suit on his chest.

The man that was seated and in much pain looked to his scroll to find anything to discover what this meeting could be about and said, "God knows things that we could never imagine and when he reveals himself to Isaiah like he has in the past we know that this could be something of great importance to our pursuit of peace."

They all knew that it was time for the meeting and they saw Isaiah walk through the PAST and take a seat near the head table. Then Jacob and his followers proceeded through the gateway and they all took their seats waiting on the message at hand. Isaiah then put his Scroll on his hip while enduring much pain in the other hand. John Lambda then walked through the PASTway and sat next to Isaiah and whispered something into his ear, Isaiah nodded and the meeting began.

Isaiah then arose from the table and began to speak, "So these people that were once part of us choose to attack us. Who do these bozo's think that we are? Do they think that we are just going to lay down and given them our precious elements? I don't think so. I don't think that they know whom they are dealing with. We are Ionious United and if they choose to break away and attack us we will fight back. Can I get a witness?"

"So these bozos decide to attack us at our weakest fortified gate, well what happened? We were ready and thanks to Titus and Daniel we staved off and thwarted their attack. Thanks to our own engineers that took the time to develop a shield that is resistant to the Nivio technology. We are superior and we will remain superior as long as I am a General. There is nothing that they can do that we will not resist and overcome."

"They hit us with a jab, we will counter with a cross hook. They start throwing punches, and we will retaliate. Mark my words we will seek peace according to what God has instructed us to do. There is no backing down this is our city this is our land and they will not defeat us on our own soil."

He was giving an inspiring speech with arms flying and pacing all the while. "As I have said before in other wars "We will not be breached!" "We will not be over taken!" When we fight we not only fight for ourselves, we fight for their future as a United Ionious."

A roar entered the room with applause following. "Our goal is peace as instructed by our God and we will do anything to achieve it. There is no place on Ionious that they can attack us where we will not fight back. There are no depths that they can go where they will not feel the presence of the calling that God has placed on our lives. We fight not only for ourselves, we also fight for our future and the future's of our families."

"We fight as the south, and as the south we will fight for the future of the North as well because when we attain peace we are attaining it not only for the south, and also for the north. They cannot see this yet, they think that someday they will be the ruling party and our fight within us will subside. However the only thing that will subside in us is our faction, is our will to start a war against them. This is a war that we do not want, however if we want peace we must defend our freedoms. And if that means fighting so shall we fight."

"There are other means that we can pursue to achieve our desired end and that does not include fighting. We serve a God of peace, and diplomacy is our only way out of this melee. So I will pray and ask God to deliver us from our enemy. Dear Lord in the name of Jesus we come before you knowing that you see us where we are, knowing that you are so great that you see out from our very eyes, and know our struggles, you hear through our very ears and you know our battle."

"We praise you for all that you have done for us in the past and now we humbly come before you to ask for the guidance that only you can give. Show us a way that will bring the northern army to their knees begging us to resolve this diplomatically. You hear our prayers as we seek your direction for you are the Lord of all Lords and the creator of the Universe."

Isaiah then sat down in his chair and awaited the response of God if there was to be any response at all. One minute went by and nothing, in the next minute they all sat around looking at one another. Then the Scroll walling began to open and there were many images coming on the screen all at once. They then saw a woman that was in a church that appeared to be one of the churches in the north.

The vision allowed the crew to see the emblem of Apollo in the corner of the stained glass windows on the Scroll Walling. Jacob the Prime Minister said, "There it is the sign of the Apollo." This was the indicative marking of the North after the war had begun. This was part of their propaganda schemes to justify their attacks that was instituted by Aaron Alpha himself.

Isaiah Omega noticed the pews and the altar that, "This is definitely in the North I have been to this Church before it is called The Cathedral of the Branch. Aaron Alpha goes there."

In this church, before the service had begun, there were many pews and this woman walked towards her seat and sat down next to Aaron Alpha's wife Sharon. This woman then said something to Sharon and then they both proceeded to type in something on the intellipew in front of them.

Directview then took over from the Sharon's eyes and the team saw what they had been searching for on the screen. It was the DreamStream rendition of the scripture Hebrews 1:3 that says, "who being the brightness of His glory and the express image of His person, and upholding all things by the word of His power, when He had by Himself purged our sins, sat down at the right hand of the Majesty on high."

The screen then went holographic and it showed a hurricane of light conflicting with darkness and things representing sin all whirling around in this hurricane. Eventually the light overpowered the darkness and a glorious image was revealed right in front of them and Jesus sat down on the right hand of God.

He was clothed in majesty with silver linings on the sides of his outline all enveloped in light. This radiated the power that Jesus had over sin as his smile brought warmth to the both women that were watching. Sharon then spoke, "I have never seen this scripture, this is incredible, what about it were you wanting me to see, Kedar?"

In the room Daniel and the entire group heard this and he had never heard of her before. "Who is this Kedar that's her name right? And what does she have to do with us?"

Immediately Isaiah had a flash of memories that brought him back to his days in the Academy and it was all clear to him about who she was. "When I was in the Academy there was a man that you might know named, Tophet Tau, and at the time he was dating a woman named Kedar that he told me about in one of our classes. We were the best of friends and I saved his life during an AIIA suit boost drill. He owes me and if we need this woman, his wife now, I know that I could depend on him to come through for us."

A look of shear joy overtook Daniel's face as they all gained a greater knowledge of what the Lord might be doing here. "Should we watch the rest of it General?" Isaiah then said, "Of course, proceed."

The Directview then took over; "I was wanting you to know that the sins that Aaron has committed with the attacks will all be overpowered by Jesus when we are called up into glory. The sins of the South also will be omitted for their destruction of the Nivio. This verse shows this in a great way and this is why I wanted to talk to you after church. If that's alright with you?"

Sharon then took her hand and covered her mouth as it opened as wide as a river delta. "He has not sinned, God told him to attack the South it is what had to be done. You know that right?"

They were practically inseparable and Kedar then said, "I just want to talk to you about some things that the Lord has been putting on my heart. Okay?"

The hand of Sharon then patted the leg of Kedar with understanding as she said, "Sure, we can talk after Aaron and I eat lunch unless you would like to join us again today?"

Kedar then said, "Sure, that would be nice."

They met up just as planned and the conversation was going fine and Kedar was getting closer and closer to getting the passcode getting to know Sharon even more and getting in better with Aaron.

Time elapsed and she obtained the passcode and brought it back to Isaiah. "I know you saw me in Directview and you already have them by now so is there anything that I can do now?"

"We are going to need for you to keep back from their situation and let us do the work from here on out. If the passcode changes we might need you to go in again."

It was time for them to put the passcode into use and when they did everything went according to plan. A week later after the attack Aaron Alpha shuttered to think that he had been defeated and became very paranoid and accused many people of stealing his private passcode that someone gave to the South. He then remembered the situation with Kedar and decided to take action upon her.

General Alpha said to his hitman, "Kedar is the spy do whatever it takes, kill them all."

The hitman that he was talking to asked, "Are you sure?"

"Yes, her whole family." He was terse, succinct, and unremoreseful, then General Alpha walked away.

"What we are seeing here today has not taken place yet, this is the future people and we need to talk to my friend Tophet about his ties to his wife's friend." Isaiah spoke with authority, as he sat down to collect and enter his thoughts into his Scroll.

Then Jesus began to speak to Daniel; "Kedar will be of great use to you in the future with the war that is at hand. She can attain critical data from Aaron and Sharon that you can use to fend off attacks in the wars ahead. Know that I am God, and this can be used to further peace among your people."

Sitting in an intellichair the legs of Daniel just went straight as he arose to speak, "It is obvious to me that she is not on either side, and if we could talk to Tophet and get him to side with us. Then we could use Kedar to be a spy for us, and gain important information about Aaron. Information that only his wife would know, or even better information that only Aaron knows. I think that we have something here."

The clinched fist of Titus went from the resting-place on his chin to the table in front of him, he had something to say, "And Daniel said it best, I think therefore I think I am? Or we think that we can win this war by guessing what they are going to do next? Or I know therefore I am, and I know that this war belongs to us."

"Knowledge is the key here people if we could know what Aaron was doing before he does it. It could be paramount in out efforts to bring peace back to Ionious. How do we do that? If we had information like say... Aaron's passcode to his Directview from the DTR, then we would have the essential ingredient to some victory cake."

"To stop Kedar from getting killed we must plant an aware trojan horse in his Scroll that will track any changes to his pass-codes as he changes them. There is always the chance that she is in danger so lets hope that Ezekiel can create a fool-proof system."

Ezekiel nodded, "With God anything is possible he will protect his people and so will I."

Starring at the screen that was fixed on the last image before they paused the feed Timothy was lost in thought and he felt the urgency to speak what he had found. "We could just get Ezekiel or someone to override the passcode at the DTR and then we could most certainly acquire the passcode and access to Aaron's Directview. What if this woman won't side with us? You all know this; the DTR is on our land we own it and we can use it any way that we want. They would be blind out there if we had control of it."

The intellichair of Isaiah was in the upright position, with both arms on the table before him he spoke, "That's a great idea however I think that it's a matter of morals here. We could do that and take away their entire order system and they would be analog. We have to do what we are planning to do and not let them know that anything is going on. Stealth people. They will never know what hit them." Isaiah then leaned back in his seat wondering if the DTR takeover wasn't such a bad idea. We don't even know if this will work.

The hands of Jacob were resting on his head as they went to his side he had an opinion that he wanted to share, "What if this doesn't even work? The DTR would be a sure thing and we could break up the pattern and use intermittent takeovers only when we need the information to gain key insights into their plans. We could make it stealth, Ezekiel can program anything, Macro, Micro, A.I. anything."

Scratching his head and looking to the walling he had an answer. Isaiah wanted to remind them that, "When we get a visitation from God telling us to use the DTR then we will. We got this from God and last time I checked God is in control and he knows what the best method is to use so I think that we have the upper hand here. God is the sure thing, He knows our future and he spoke to John and I so lets use our faith here and put some trust in God. Let Him direct our paths and we will succeed."

The voice was resounding and John knew whom it was at the first word, "Remember the promise that I made to you and Isaiah, I will direct your journey, and no matter what you go through I am the Alpha and the Omega and I will see you through this. Peace is out there you just have to trust in me and you will find it." It was God.

John's hand was pointing at the Scroll walling going up and down, "Psalm 9:10 says, And those who know Your name will put their trust in You; For You, LORD, have not forsaken those who seek You." "Matthew 21:22 says, All things, whatsoever you ask in prayer, believing, you shall receive. I think that we need to pray about this people. Isaiah?"

He nodded his head as they all bowed their heads in reverence and Isaiah prayed, "Oh Lord, we have seen your glorious works, we have seen your majesty and splendor, we know that you are all knowing and all powerful. We thank you for all that you have done for us, together we come asking and believing that you will make yourself known to us. We ask in Jesus name that you show us the right road to take as we are presented with many options and we seek you as you have instructed us to do. Knowing that you will answer, we give thanks, for yours is the power and glory forever."

Then the power of the Lord came upon Daniel and he began to sing much like he was singing to his wife only this way he was trembling under the power of the Holy Spirit. His hands were raised to the heavens and his face was turned to God.

He began speaking in other tongues then his song erupted. The Scroll walling was showing pictures and video of God on his throne in Heaven and the angels began to sing and give a tune to which Daniel began singing. The song was this:

Holy Holy is the Lord God Almighty,
Who was and is and is to come,
Heed my voice and listen to me,
For the battles have yet to be won,
When you fight I will be on your side,
Take Kedar and make her your sister,
When you talk to her make sure and hide,
I will use her to make you a winner,
She is key to your success in the war,
I will lead her to the information you seek,
She will be on your side I give you my word,
Take this knowledge to ponder and think,
I will direct your ways so listen to my Holy Spirit,
I will use him to give you critical information,
When you find the treasure in the field bless it,
As you seek peace so shall you find it is my proclamation,
Go in peace not that you have already attained it,
Go onward towards the goal where I have called you,
I have delivered you before from the enemies stinging hits,
I will deliver you until there is peace and this war is through.

There were tears in Daniel's eyes as his beautiful song ended. He then dropped to his knees overcome by the presence. All of the other men in the room were still worshiping in the presence of God as some were standing and others were also on their knees listening to the beautiful and melodic tune and words of promise that they received. Some had their eyes opened so they could see what God was doing on the walling and others had their eyes closed intently concentrating on their worship to God.

They all worshiped in the presence for a while longer singing along with the angels that were on the walling and singing in the spirit. After the angels had stopped singing the men returned to their seats and began to think about what the Lord had instructed them to do in the song.

The hands of Isaiah were laid upon the table and he rose his head up from prayer and said to the men, "I will talk to Tophet, and from what I have gathered so far I think that God has already spoken to him and he will be ready to hear from me. In the meantime pray for Tophet and Kedar that God would show them wisdom and make them ready for what their role is going to be with us."

Chapter 3
Kedar's Role

"Things to Consider"

DirectView is something kind of new in this book and it is used to see into the future as well as see the present of any persons senses and thoughts. Have you ever been given the opportunity to stand up for something that you know is right even though the general consensus is against what you know to do. Well, Kedar gets her chance to stand up for peace and find a way to make a difference in this war. There are a ton of things in our world that are really messed up so I would like for you to think about what you would stand up for today that is going on in this world that you know just isn't right. One person can make a difference as Joan of Arc did for France. Think about the things that you know that God has chosen for you to do that you would like to take action on and really make a difference.

Chapter 3
QUEST for Peace
Kedar's Role

In the house of Tophet Tau he had many rooms, some for every different thing that his family enjoyed like the Directview room, where they watched the latest DVS (Direct View Show) stories unfold in a holograph. This room was equipped for every sense that one could experience during a DVS show.

It had sound from the corners of the Scroll wallings and a holograph projector that must have cost a fortune. This was surely given to him from the military for his research in the field of visual communications that they used in the North. Tophet was an officer in the Army and his goal for the day was to relax with his wife and son, and spend some of their day in the Directview room.

Tophet's son Shallum was in his room sporting some serious competition on the Eye 2 Eye game on his portable DVS holographic program of the Nephalim Chronicles 2. He was linked to several of his school buddies that were all gaming with him and Shallum was in the lead. He had already unmasked three conclusions to the first part of the show in a record time of 39 seconds.

All partakers must have never seen the show before competing in the Eye 2 Eye interactive competitions. "King Zed takes the scrolls to all of his guards and orders all babies of the Nephalim to be exterminated." Shallum guessed at the next scene and he was right once again. A few minutes into the next scene he stumbles across the thoughts of one of the guards and projects kindness with his eyes to the holograph as a guard rares back his hand and then drops it to tell the woman not to consort with the giants.

"Honey could you put up the sound shield when you are playing those games." Kedar could hear him talking with the blasting speakers of the DVS all the way in the kitchen. She knew how intense he got when he was competing and she didn't mind him playing at all, she just wanted some quiet time while she was watching her favorite scriptures in the Bible unfold.

This was her time to unwind in the nice cold air blowing intellichair that she hovered into the kitchen from the living room. The south walling was holograph equipped to play all of her favorite scriptures from the bible and she was in lala land worshiping aloud along with some of the Psalms. Later on in the evening Kedar and Tophet liked to relive Songs of Solomon in their room while everyone else was sleeping.

They would put up the sound shield to their PAST way and just get to know one another even more. The compliments and flattery was like none other that could be found in the bible and this book was made for the intimacy of a husband and wife. There were several ways to experience the bible, one was to hook up to the DreamStream and relive it and interact with it.

Another way was to interact with it in the Eye 2 Eye application on a holograph. And if you just wanted to soak it all in you could just watch the bible in stunning clarity of the holograph Directview mode. They would choose what suited them best based on their mood of the day.

Today her mood in the kitchen was to soak in the brilliance of the holograph Directview mode she was just a singing as loud as David was in some of the verses. When Shallum and his friends would walk in while she was worshiping this would embarrass him and they would run to the Directview room for entertainment.

Right now Tophet was in the Directview room reliving last Sunday's sermon from the Cathedral of the Branch. Pastor Mark Mu was eloquent and could weave a message into your heart like no other and to relive this was something that Tophet liked to do when he wasn't working.

"God's hand is always upon you he never let's go even if you do." Pastor Mark was preaching and a reaching people and suddenly Isaiah Omega's face was right in front of him on the holograph, and Tophet got a transmission.

"This is Isaiah Omega, I was wondering if we could talk sometime today?"

Images of the last time that they had spoken to one another were playing in his head as the sermon was paused for a later time. "Isaiah how are you? My goodness its been so long."

Tophet had a congenial sense of familiarity with Isaiah after all he did save his life. "The Candera Mission March of 2024, deep space Axis reconnaissance they had no idea what hit them."

Isaiah was glad that even with all that they had been through they still had it. That spark in the conversation, that whoa, in a dynamic conversation program, it was still there and this was something that he had to have.

"I know, it was like living in a trailer house with no Doppler radar, no TV and bam! A tornado hits them full force. They never saw it coming, man, those were some moments to remember. There is nothing like a well deserved victory."

Tophet said laughing quite convulsively. In front of him was Isaiah's face and man was he laughing too. They chuckled for a while and then Isaiah got a serious look on his face. "Is it okay if I PAST over right now? You know, while we are already talking there are some other things that we need to discuss, face to face."

Tophet didn't have anything against it he just knew that he would have to shut down all communications and receptions while he was there. This was a precautionary measure due to the war of course. If any of his comrades found out about this he would be in deep trouble, so precautions must be invoked. "Sure, come on over I'll send it out to let you in, anywhere is fine, I am in the Directview room." In a flash the PAST was sparkling and Isaiah was in the Directview room.

There would be much to talk about and things to discuss that were on Isaiah's mind, he had something to accomplish and it would take skill and precision. Tophet never was the defector type and he knew it might come down to talking to Kedar alone, and this was something that he didn't know how to accomplish, he must find a way though.

So with God at his side, the DTR was still broadcasting even in the

North to Isaiah, he sought out to find a way. He was worrying about his trace ability if he were to get a message from God the North would detect it and it would show up on their radar. Unless, unless Tophet had a shield up or that he could put up so that no one could detect him there.

Isaiah just hoped that his next conversation started and ended faster than a message could come flying in to his transcom. Now to start talking and talking with brevity and terseness, "You must be fast, they have found your location, you must get back to Athenia Isaiah."

It was too late the Holy Spirit was seeing something that Isaiah couldn't see. Forget about the shield for now and get Kedar on his side or schedule for another time for Tophet and Kedar to go to Athenia where they would be safe. Now just get them to agree to it.

"I have to go now, is there any way that we could schedule this for another time." Isaiah said with conciseness as he held out one hand with a scroll in the other, standing up.

"Isaiah it was good to see you again however brief it might have been, and yes we can reschedule. The Holy Spirit has been telling me that you don't have much time for the window."

Isaiah was confused so the Holy Spirit was now talking to him about me too. "What window?"

The address was already keyed in and he was ready to go. "The widow that is passing right now, you have ten seconds to cross the border. Go now."

The PAST was already streaming this time the bright sparks were saying different words trickling down from the top. Isaiah then started to walk from the projector towards the door and the words stopped. He has enough time ten seconds hasn't passed by yet. He ran towards the door and he was gone. The stream stopped and the PAST was back to normal in the Tau household.

Pitch darkness is all that Isaiah saw. "Where am I?" He was thinking to himself.

Gotta talk to Daniel he would know. "Daniel you there?" Daniel was at a blank, PAST unstreaming he couldn't see past it only the next room that was in the base.

"Its me General. Where are you?"

Isaiah was then fumbling around to find out what he could with the light of his scroll. It looked like a supply closet of some kind ammo here guns over there he was at home. As he got to looking around he noticed that the Guns weren't green, they were red, or at least had red North logo's on them. "I don't know where I am Daniel you are going to have to find me on your Scroll okay?"

Daniel the professional that he is, "Yes Sir, will do. While I am tracking you can, you try to key your way back to my address."

Daniel's address popped up on Isaiah's Scroll however it was to no avail because the link has already been defeated. Some hacker that has access to the DTR already got there before we could get to him. Isaiah then typed in the other similar addresses that were around the base. Ath17BSE10R109... nothing still he stood in a darkly lit place that only shined from the glow of his Scroll. Directly in front of Isaiah's face there was the North Euclid red stripe's edges that had a metallic outlay sparkled in the glowing hue of the blue screen on the Data Pad.

"Okay, Isaiah I found you, and whatever you do you have to find a way out of there quick. There is a barrage of North soldiers coming your way. There is a 51% probability that they will enter the room that you are in. Any ideas?"

Isaiah's blood started to boil and he was getting a little tempered, "Find Ezekiel, he has got the clearance and start praying brother."

There was seriousness in Isaiah's voice that caught Daniel off guard. He actually caught a glimpse of what would happen if they reached him and Isaiah was killed. Deep breaths, solid focus, tamed thoughts, brevity; these are the next thoughts that went through Daniel's head after this vision of sorts.

Proclaiming help from God internally he voiced over to Ezekiel, "The chief is in the fire, Zeke we need you."

Ezekiel was programming a new module of an Eye 2 Eye application as he answered the call; "I'll go now. Send me the details."

Glitter, Stream, a hand and a leg, Ezekiel was there at Daniel's office. An intelli-chair hovered over to the side of the table that Zeke was on and the two men took their places hacking away like they were 19th century loggers waiting for a timber. Timber would come soon only would it be the right log? They needed to bypass the block that the North had on their PAST system.

"Ezekiel is here with me and they are approximately 33 seconds away from reaching your position. Have you been able to find a shield to prevent their entrance?"

Isaiah was getting quite frigidly nervous about this however he did have a disrupter, that he had just modified with the Scroll, to take out more than one at a time if he had to. "I am working on a shield right now, and please step in gentlemen if you can break this code that they have over here. Its some kind of new encryption that they have and I can't bypass it for anything. 23 seconds. I can hear them."

Daniel was working on one encryption that had to do with getting them over to where Isaiah was and Ezekiel was on the other encryption that would allow Isaiah to get over to where they are, and on a shield to block the intruders. "We will yell timber if we get anything over here you'll know when the glitter stream glows. 16 seconds." Daniel said to Isaiah optimistically.

The new set of codes were like nothing that Ezekiel had seen before and he had no clue as to who the mastermind was behind all of this. Both men were hunched over their Scrolls in glaring light as a bead of sweat poured down from Ezekiel's alabaster brow. Ezekiel had a response, "Sir, I just bypassed the next crypt and I am seconds away from getting you a shield so just hold on. One way or another we are going to get you through this. 9 seconds sir."

The soldiers were all watching their data pads as they encroached upon Isaiah's location. Step by step they inched closer to an inevitable disaster the red and yellows from the thermal scans were growing closer and closer towards the target location. In one window the soldier could see Isaiah breathing, all Isaiah could do was continue to hack and pray that God delivers him. One of the soldiers spoke up; "There it is I can see the door, come on now let's run men. He is in there and we have a code."

Isaiah heard them talking and now he had to pray, "Dear Jesus, please deliver me from this situation and make a shield form around this PAST."

God then heard his prayer and responded Genesis 15:1, "Do not be afraid, Abram. I am your shield, your exceedingly great reward."

The soldiers were outside the door and Daniel and Ezekiel could see them too and Zeke had something if it wasn't too late all he had to do was finish typing it in. Would he finish in time? That is the question.

He was keying it in as fast as he could possibly type his fingers danced over his pad and the sounds were almost melodic. Now was the time and Daniel could see the soldiers opening the door.

The soldier that opened the door had a huge grin on his face and he laughed when he saw Isaiah standing there in the glow of the Scroll in the back corner of the room. All of the soldiers were sporting their latest weapons that begged the intruder to weep on till he surrendered. Isaiah also had one of their weapons in his hand as well as his disrupter in the other.

It was a standoff, whoever shot first Isaiah would die. That is if they had been instructed to kill him on the spot. He was no match for all of them and their weapons, if they did fire he could get out a few rounds at most. He needed something supernatural to happen.

A soldier blurted out, "We have you now General and you're gonna pay, we have orders to take you all the way to Alpha, you don't have a chance. Looks like God is on our side now General Omega."

The soldiers that were standing around now prepared to drag him out of there, and then one of them reached out his hand. The man holding out his hand had a small disrupter in it and he fired at the heart of Isaiah. As the other one said Omega, suddenly a shieldstream parted and fell to the floor, his hand was severed in half, chopping it as it fell to the floor.

The shot fired hit the ceiling and Isaiah was saved. Isaiah Omega just looked at the pathetic soldiers once gloating in his presence and said, "Do not be afraid, Abram. I am your shield, your exceedingly great reward. Whose side is God on now boys?"

Zeke had done it and saved Isaiah Daniel thought as Zeke spoke up, "I don't know what happened sir, the shield went down before I could even finish typing I still had a whole nother page to go. It wasn't me sir it was God." And just like that they all witnessed a miracle it was God who had saved Isaiah and now they needed another miracle before the soldiers could break the code on the PAST.

All of the soldiers dropped their weapons and grabbed their Scrolls they were trying to hack into the PAST to get an unlock code for the shield that had just appeared. The one handed soldier just took off running to the nearest office that had a SWORD. Daniel then said, "Looks like we're not out of the woods yet General, we need another miracle."

The General had dropped his weapons too and started doing what he could to get past the security on their PAST system. He needed to open a link to the south anywhere in the south would work, only how could he bypass their codes?

He said to Zeke, "Ezekiel, man, I don't know where you were on that shield and I think that you were pretty close to breaking past their lock on travel through the PAST to the south. Work with me here can you get me outta here before these Bozo's get to me? Do what you can and I am gonna pray."

"Sir, I will do my best to get you outta there. I think that God needs to intervene on this one too. This could take a while on my part again. I'll be praying for you." Zeke said to Isaiah with a sigh at the end there to ease the tensions or either to just release some.

The prayers of Isaiah were always poignant and terse with all respect to the creator so then he began, "Father in the name of Jesus, you see my position and you know my needs. I will tell them to you anyway just to be specific. I need to break past these codes to get to the south in the PAST system that just isn't letting me right now so please make a way for me, in Jesus name I pray."

The scroll that Isaiah was holding suddenly became a holographic projector and a verse from the bible popped up and God started speaking.

Isaiah 43:19 "I am going to do something new. It is already happening. Don't you recognize it? I will clear a way in the desert. I will make rivers on dry land." In the holograph there was a vast and bleak desert void of all water and vegetation it was just dirt, dry dirt. As God got to the part where he said, "rivers" the dry desolate landscape was engulfed by a rush of waters as blue as the sky, torrenting towards the viewer until there was a wild rushing river running right through the desert.

Just as the river rushed into the face of Isaiah another stream came particling down in new colors blue and green all sparkling like fresh waters. Isaiah realized that he must go for it before the soldiers could get any further in their cyber attack on the PAST so he ran for the PAST knowing that if it wasn't a stream to the south he would just hit the shield with a blunt force. So he ran and run he did right into the back of the hovering chair of Zeke. He was back on base and more importantly he was back in the South.

"To God be all the glory! He has delivered me once again from the jaws of defeat. He is my rock and my pillar of strength, my safe refuge he is everything to me. And heal the hand of the injured soldier Lord. Glory be to God who reigns in Heaven."

Isaiah and the men were ecstatic they couldn't stop doing fist pumps and leg jumps. Ezekiel is a very tall man and on one of the jumps he almost hit his head on the ceiling.

The soldier that had his hand cut off by the energy shield ran to a room that was empty and in the corner he noticed a SWORD. He then typed with one hand as a cup of water and bandages were created by the Dynamatoms. He quickly made a tourniquet and bandaged up the bleeding nub that was once a hand.

After Isaiah disappeared into the PAST the soldiers had access to get into the room and one of them reached down and picked up the fallen bloody hand. The man with the hand ran with it transcomming his friend and they linked up. "I've got your hand Jason. Where are you? I'll bring it to you."

Jason heard this call and told him that, "I am in the room with the open door and the lights on, on the left. Hurry I need help."

His prayers could be heard by all the guys so they followed his cries. Jason prayed, "In Matthew 12:10 it says that Jesus said to the man, "Hold out your hand." The man held it out, and it became normal again, as healthy as the other. Lord you healed a man with a paralyzed hand and I know you can heal my hand. Whatever I bind on earth will be bound in heaven, and whatever I loose on earth will be loosed in heaven. Lord Jesus Matthew 18:18 I loose healing because I know that there is healing in heaven."

Just then the soldiers came running in with the hand and as soon as he said heaven the hand levitated to his arm that was bandaged up and formed a seal. Jason got the water out as the cloths fell he poured out the water and it made a fizzing sound as bubbles came rising on the severed area.

God had healed his hand, it was whole and complete and was as good as new even better than it was before. Jason moved his wrist around and his hand went in a revolving motion and there were no pains. It was a miracle God had saved the day for the South and for the North. It doesn't matter what side that you're on God is no respecter of people if he can see your heart and that you need a healing and you pray with conviction God will answer your prayers.

The south know that God is on their side just as much as the North knows that God is on their side. What the North can't see yet is that God is for peace and they both need to find and create measures to attain peace. Unfortunately the South is the only side that is seeking peace and that is why God is moving more on their side.

The moments that Isaiah spent with Tophet and Kedar were not enough to accomplish his goal, so to reach out to them now has become his goal, and as they both press onward Isaiah seeks a time where they all can speak freely to each other, on the southern side of the planet.

Still reveling in the victory to overcome all obstacles, Daniel was just praising God as silently as he could. The occasional claps could be heard by Isaiah who was in the room and was listening to some worship music from Jeremiah's Cathedral Choir. He was rehearsing and preparing himself to speak with Kedar and this music brought peace to him and allowed him to turn his thoughts to God.

Isaiah prayed silently to himself, "In the name of Jesus, I ask you to give me the eyes of Jesus to see things the way that he would see this situation, God I want the mind of Christ in all things. Give me the wisdom of Jesus to know what to say. Bring all things past to my remembrance and give me the discernment to know what and how to say what you will put upon my heart to say. Above all things Lord give me the mind of Jesus."

God heard his prayer and began giving him a series of scriptures that would provide a foundation to give him the mind of Christ.

Matthew 22:37 "Jesus said to him, 'You shall love the LORD your God with all your heart, with all your soul, and with all your mind.'"

Matthew 5:9 "Blessed are the peacemakers, For they shall be called sons of God."

Matthew 6:3-4 "But when you do a charitable deed, do not let your left hand know what your right hand is doing, that your charitable deed may be in secret; and your Father who sees in secret will Himself reward you openly."

The voice continued to give him many more important scriptures as he prepared to talk to Kedar. Isaiah consulted with Ezekiel about how to get a link to Tophet. "What is the best way to do this?"

Ezekiel thought for a minute and then responded with an answer, "I can bypass the codes if you are ready to talk I'll get a location on them and we can get started, this might take a few minutes."

Isaiah decided after hearing from God that he was ready. "Whenever you are, let's do this."

Ezekiel was typing swiftly from the sides of his Scroll pants and the support station was holding up the screen in front of him as he was sitting in an intellichair across from Isaiah in his office. Daniel was getting a lock on their position and Ezekiel was getting past the codes. Dynamic conversion was happening between the characters and then there was an "Okay" from Daniel.

And an, "I'm ready" from Ezekiel. Ezekiel got out a, "All systems are go."

The tone of Isaiah's voice at first was somewhat rattled and shaken, "Tophet, you would not believe what I have been through my friend."

Tophet replied, "I guess that is a major reason for this war in the first place isn't it."

Isaiah then assured himself God would be there for him when he didn't know what to say, "It would take to long to explain what all happened so if we could just get down to business?"

Tophet laughed and said, "Sounds good to me."

Isaiah then proceeded, "There are some things that I need to speak to you and Kedar about and it can only be done here on our continent so that nothing breaks out again over there. Any of us are susceptible in enemy territory. So at your earliest convenience could you take a PAST over to my office with your wife. God has spoken to me and I know that I am in his will when I ask this of you. It concerns the peace of our planet."

The response of Tophet was delayed, it took him a while to sort out everything concerning his role with the North and what it would mean if he just PASTed over to the South continent. If anyone finds out he could be killed and his family would be in Jeopardy.

Tophet finally spoke up, "I am not sure about this Isaiah, do you know the ramifications of my actions if someone were to find out that I was consorting with you about anything right now? There are assassins that would love a shot at your head and there is a bounty out for your capture."

He continued, "As a soldier of the North, I am not sure if you gave those orders or not. As your friend, I know that you wouldn't do a thing like that, however the person that I know wouldn't have given that order and I am under oath to fight for my Army and not side with you or anyone in the South. I am for peace and want this war to end as much as you do."

The prayers and talks from God would be of great assistance here and Isaiah knew it so he thought of what Jesus would see in this situation and God made a way for him, "Tophet, if you PAST over here I can prove to you and show you the dream and prove that I didn't give those orders if that is your only concern. If you have other concerns I have Ezekiel Epsilon with me here and he can make your every move stealth and unnoticed by the North Army's detection. God has spoken to me and we have to discuss this here."

The beginning of Tophet's response was staggered, "I, … I, … I think that wouldn't be very wise of me Isaiah and I hope that you understand. I shouldn't even have agreed to see you at my house, that put your life in jeopardy and that was wrong of me to do that."

In an unconscious response Isaiah said, "Matthew 6:3-4 "But when you do a charitable deed, do not let your left hand know what your right hand is doing, that your charitable deed may be in secret; and your Father who sees in secret will Himself reward you openly. Stealth Tophet, this is Ezekiel here you can trust him. And put your trust in God."

The presence of God was moving over Tophet as he received those words from his friend. He was moved to respond accordingly, "Okay, just tell me what to do."

Isaiah and Ezekiel talked for several minutes getting all of the details ironed out and after several dances across the sides of the keyboard on Ezekiel's pants they found a way.

Ezekiel then began speaking to Tophet. "In precisely 18 minutes you and Kedar will see a particle stream glisten in your Directview room. Do not go through it! This is the decoy, so throw something through the stream, then 30 seconds later there will be a green particle stream, and this is the one that you want to go through. Proceed through it, and you will be here, in Isaiah's meeting room. We, then, will have 22 minutes to talk and then you must go back to your house during the North's scheduled PAST maintenance routine. Do you have any questions?"

The information seemed pretty clear to him. "No! I will be there," said Tophet, as he had some amount of ambivalence in his heart towards his reluctant decision.

He knew what his objections were, and they seemed to pale in comparison to that of God's calling upon his life. If it was that, a calling which he hoped it was, and he still had thoughts of backing out.

However, he decided not to, due to the fact that the promises far outweighed the negative possibilities of the situation. At the same time he was looking forward to fellow-shipping with his good friend. This administered him to be at ease with his decision to some degree.

All of the specifics were a quandary to him however, what if he made a mistake and went through the first one, or what if there was a glitch in the system, or even worse what if they were tracking their conversation as they were at his house.

Did they have that ability? He most certainly wouldn't put it past them in any form or manner. He could just see it now Aaron was tracking their entire conversation and he was waiting with his own solution to the problem and probably he would be burned at the stake. He would be burned alive for the first offense, much less this whole debacle.

What was he thinking? All of this would not matter if none of this was really happening he now only had 10 minutes and he hadn't even spoke to Kedar about it and there was no time to waste. There is no better time than the present to present your best to God and follow his calling, and by this time he had realized that, yes, this was his calling. There was no one who would stand in his way from attaining whatever Isaiah had to say to him, or whatever he had him to do.

As devout as he was to the North's military in his heart he knew what they were doing was wrong, and there was nothing that he could do about it. Until now, he jerked out his Scroll and started giving Kedar the instructions on where and when to meet him, and then he would divulge the rest to her once she got there.

With much conviction he typed the directions to her and waited on her response. His last words were: "Come now I need you here this is of great importance. Love, Tophet." He then, in faith waited tapping out his favorite worship song on the left side of his Scroll Datapad keyboard with his fingers. In his head he was singing the words and you could hear a faint tune every now and then creep out from his lips.

In his head you could hear if you were on Direct view,
"You are with me always,
my redeemer in time of need,

when others leave you stay,
by my side and always see me,
through my struggles every day,
and I will rejoice in what the Lord has done,
and I will sing of how the war was won.

His mind was lost, not even thinking about the task at hand. When he got to the part where he was singing about winning the war he jumped out of his chair and hit the keyboard to see what the time was. They only had six minutes and there was no response from Kedar. He wondered what the problem was.

Was she in trouble was there some holdup on her end? Or did she not even want to go? She had to go this all hinged on her being there with him. He then logged in and keyed in her passcode to her Directview to see if she had even whipped out her Scroll. The thing should alert her transcom with every message from him. There had to be something going wrong with her or she would have answered by now.

Logging into Directview wasn't always that easy even when it was your wife. It always had a ton of questions to ask you before you could get into seeing. There was four minutes left by the time that he was into her view. She was talking to someone and the conversation seemed pretty heated.

He didn't know who the man was that was talking to her and all he could see was this closeup of his face, nothing more. Maybe she could backup and walk around so he could get a better look to see what he was dealing with here. Tophet was getting un-nerved at the tone of voice that the man, not gentleman, was using with her. Kedar's head then turned to the side and he caught a fleeting glimpse of where she was.

Wherever it was he had never been there and this was not one of the places that she talked about to him. Was she having an affair. His blood began to boil at the thought of it, maybe this was some kind of lovers quarrel. He was irate and he didn't even have any proof. He then began to think about the last fight that they had gotten into and it made him wonder if she was getting disinterested in him as a companion.

Tophet then said aloud, "What am I thinking?" He realized that this was not on any grounds of fact it was shear paranoia and he purged it from his thinking. Now to discern what is really going on here. He

45

looked at the clock and they had two minutes to get there. This was not looking good at all how would he get her attention?

With all of this technology there had to be some way that he had overlooked. Unless… Unless she had blocked him from the transcom. That would explain the extra questions when he logged onto Directview, he thought that he would never get through that.

The Holy Spirit was prompting him, "The peace of the planet. Trust in your God." This brought back images of what was going through his head when Isaiah spoke those words to him.

He looked at the clock there was one minute left and she was still out of arms reach. He decided to trancom her directly, what would he say?

Say anything just get a hold of that woman and get her out of there. "Kedar are you listening? I have you on direct view if you can hear me just nod or scratch your head, something inconspicuous."

He waited for a response, nothing, she just kept on defending herself with the intolerable man that was screaming at her. If this was her boss or one of the people that she works with Tophet thought that he could find her a better job.

He glanced down at the timer there was 40 seconds till particle stream ignition. Still no sign from Kedar. What would happen if she didn't come with him to the South? Would this put his mission in jeopardy? He began thinking about how vital she was to Isaiah's whole plans. 30 seconds till liftoff.

Finally, there it was a nod, "Kedar you can hear me, so I need to you go to the nearest PASTway and come to our directview room now. If you can hear me say something to me or get out your Scroll there isn't much time to spare."

Still she did nothing, she didn't speak and she didn't walk to a PASTway or anything. She just continued to talk. Just before he put up his Scroll he looked at the timer, ten seconds was on the clock. He then prepared himself for the walk to the South. Pretty soon a particle stream would be ignited and there would be colors flashing before him that were said to be red.

Tophet noticed that Kedar was not going to be able to join him so he transcommed over to Isaiah to enlighten his psyche on something that he was wondering about. "Isaiah, I have a red stream over here and now I am waiting on the green one. How important is it that Kedar come with me to visit with you?"

Isaiah was pleased with anticipation, "Tophet, she is of vital importance to this mission. Is there a problem?"

He picked up a piece of trash and threw it through the red stream. Tophet then replied, "I have done everything that I could and I don't think that she is going to be able to make it today." There was a shakiness to his voice.

Isaiah responded, "Just come on through and we'll see if we can figure something out."

After the trash disappeared into the red stream it subsided and folded then starting at the top of the PASTway a silver line across the breadth of the doorway and shimmered down in a flowing and fluid manner followed by the ambiance of green particles. The green layer was transparent with sparkling features and had a darker green set of letters in Greek that were fluttering and spinning around a center axis from the top down to the silver lining at the base of the doorway.

With a Scroll in his hand, Tophet stepped through the stream seeing up close with his eyes the light that is emitted from the particles, all of which were glowing and lighting up his chiseled face. The next thing that he saw with his eyes was that of a nanosecond of brilliant light that ended up with him viewing the presence of Isaiah sitting at an intellichair at the end of a long worn OLED table.

As soon as Isaiah saw Tophet coming in from the PAST-way he moved his thin framed weight about the intellichair that made it boost him up to a walking motion. He then proceeded on to make his way around the table to greet this friend, a sight for sore eyes.

They immediately began conversing as Isaiah started the chat, "Tophet, I pray that the Lord has been good to you."

The receptor of the comment was all smiles as he noticed that his friends countenance was happy and congenial and somewhat troubled beneath the surface. He responded with an enthusiastic, "Yes, good friend, God is always good." They shook hands, interlocked eyes, had paralleled smiles and sighs, then Isaiah motioned over for him to have a seat at the table.

After the two men both sat, Ezekiel Epsilon joined them and exchanged pleasantries and Tophet asked them, "Can we say a prayer for Kedar? She could be in trouble there were complications with her work and I am not sure if I got through to her." Isaiah and Ezekiel both nodded and Isaiah began the prayer, "Lord Jesus, you have instructed me to carry out your plan and I am acting in your will so whatever Kedar is going through I ask in your name that you watch over her and bring peace to her situation."

As soon as Isaiah said the word "peace" Kedar walked through the PAST-way with a frantic look on her face as she turned her head to peer her ruffled and squinting eyes behind her as if she was running from something. Isaiah immediately stopped his prayer, said a faint, "Glory be to God," and then leaped out of his chair and rushed over to help her up off the floor. Arising to a standing position the other two men went to her aid and put their arms around her shoulders and helped her over to an awaiting intellichair.

She was out of breath as if she had been competing in a long distance race in the Olympics. Her blouse had a tear in the shoulder as the seams were frayed and broken into a split. Beneath the split was bare skin that had an open wound that oozed out onto the micro-fiber of her shirt.

When Tophet saw this a wrinkle formed between his two brows as then drew in closer to the point of his nose. He then compassionately said, "Honey what happened? Who has done this to you?"

Attempting to catch her breath enough to get out a word she turned her chin up to see his face and engage in eye contact she intermittently said, "I...Have ... been interrogated by ... someone ... they asked about General Omega." She then took in a deep breath as tears began to fall from closed eyes.

Isaiah let out a, "In the name of all creation!"

Isaiah was thinking that they just might have found out about their plans before Kedar ever got a chance to hear them. "Who was this person Kedar?"

She had stopped crying, "I don't know who he was. He said something about you and that is all. He let me go and I ran to you here. What is going on?"

This was a relief to Isaiah, "There is nothing wrong as long as he said nothing about Sharon Alpha. He didn't did he?"

She consciencely said, "No." Isaiah then understood what had happened.

Isaiah spoke again, "This must be someone who found out about me being trapped in one of their buildings. He is in their Army nothing to worry about."

She was still shook up by the whole deal, "Why did you want me here?"

Finally they were able to get to business so Isaiah began telling her about what God had told him about her. "God has great plans for your life and you have an opportunity to be a part of something to bring peace to this planet. If you are willing to accept God's calling on your life. Are you?"

Kedar was always ready to accept what God wanted to do in her life. "I want to be in God's will. What do I have to do?"

Isaiah began telling her about what God had showed him in the direct view and Kedar began to see the picture of how God could work in her life.

She sat there and thought about it for a moment as he was talking then she came to the abrupt realization that, "This means that I have to betray my country. I am not sure if this is something that I am ready to do. There is much risk in this. What if they find out? Even worse what if I fail?"

There was a serious look on Isaiah's face when he began to speak in a soft tone, "Now listen, and I want you to listen close. God has shown me the future and you are already succeeding so there is no fear or worries in what you should be doing. This is God's plan for our planet and he wants us to live in peace and prosperity as one planet and not to be divided. Accept this if you will, I have seen the future and God is the one who has shown it to me."

There was a picture that flashed very fast, in her mind, that was recalled or actually installed by God that was that of her talking to Sharon Alpha. It was very vivid and with the flash and it was almost like recalling a dream where you see what is happening and after it is over you can reflect on the entirety of it. As she was in the process of reflecting she said, "Okay, and if I agree what type of security measures will there be made on my behalf?"

Thinking ahead Isaiah knew that this one was for, "Ezekiel what can we ensure her?"

"I have already done the proper procedures and set the protocols and encryptions to assure you of a safe passage into stealth mode. I have also created a feature that if anything were to happen, you would be continiously watched, you would have access to any PAST-ways that would be near you at the time to be directed to Athenia here at our base. There should be no worries on your part, just be happy listen to God and he will direct your paths."

Chapter 4
Weapons to Come

"Things to Consider."

Have you ever wondered what it would be like to actually see Jesus face to face? Or maybe one of the disciples, that is precisely what happens here in this chapter. John Lambda goes into his Interactive Bible to Ephesians 3:20 and he finds Paul writing the scripture and asks him about it. Someday technology might make this dream of actually talking to the disciples and authors of the bible a reality. Think about what scriptures that you would like to go and visit that happened over 2000 years ago. Imagine what it would be like to witness an event in the bible or to talk to an author that wrote an encouraging scripture.

Chapter 4
Weapons to Come

There were several birdlike creatures pecking at some of the fruit that had fallen to the ground within a close proximity to John Lambda's bench on the back portico of his house. These creatures were called Nivos, and they were all speckled with various bright colors that imbued John's imagination. He noticed how the red speckled ones would nudge over food to the ones that had a sparkling green color to them and he began to think.

These two kinds of birds were from completely different places of Ionious and while they both defended their young against each other, they helped each other in bringing nourishment for the other Nivos. This brought back some memories to John as he was sitting there with his hands clasped taking in some fresh air. These memories were of an earlier time when he was a Private and he recalled a specific occasion where he was in charge of an op that embellished the supply of Nivio for the South.

He was sent by his C.O. to bring back a vast amount of Nivio to the base at Athenia and once he arrived at the North Olympian Refinery through the Southern Base Megaport he noticed an air of arrogance in the hearts of a red striper. John asked the red striper if they were ready and all he heard was a laugh and then someone said, "That will be a million digi's."

Obviously the man was only joking around, however John was

intent on completing his first op with no problems so he said, "I can show you that I am supposed to pick up the container if you want?"

Kicking the material on the ground in front of the docking station the red striper said, "Why is it that you guys from the South always have to come to us? Why can't you make your own refined Nivio? Oh wait I am sorry, you don't even have a mine down there do you!"

John responded passionately with a raised chin, "Maybe we don't have any Nivio mines in the South. I don't have any control over that. However, what I do have control over is picking up this order, so could you please move it to my transport."

One of the guys at the dock that looked like he was in charge responded, "You heard the man. Load him up!" The man standing next to the control board, all it was, was just a station with a Scroll Data Pad, hit some keys like he had never typed out anything intelligent in his life. The container then levitated and moved into John's back compartment of his Transport.

He whispered to himself before he jumped in the vehicle, "Red Stripers!" and shook his head as he was saying it.

The man that was giving him all of the trouble, well the only one to speak up saw him say that and read his lips then said to him very loudly. "Why don't you just stay down South if you don't like us! Discover your own supply of the fruit."

John then shook his head from side to side and waved, "Have a good one. I made it and I'm free!" As he said I'm free he raised his waving hand out the left side of the Transport into a white knuckled fist and pumped it for good measure.

He remembered something that once was altogether too prevalent which was what it was like when the South had to get all of their supplies from the North.

He watched the two species of Nivos working together in harmony and he thought that, "If we were in a time of peace right now it would be the other way around. The Red Stripers would be getting all of their Vionium from us and even more there would be no restrictions on the product. It would be the same pecking order as it was in the past only now it would be in reverse. The green Nivos would be nudging the fruit over to the Red Nivos and they wouldn't think a thing of it."

With a few graceful flaps the green Nivos was airborne, steadying its wings in flight, extending them to full breadth to find a branch in the upper reaches of the giant Chronos tree, about ten yards from John's position. Gathering his Data Pad he closed the morning news and attached it to his side as he arose to go inside. It was getting late in the afternoon and he had just returned home from a long research project a day after the recruiting of Kedar to the Op. He hadn't slept in over a day, and as he entered his house the praises breathed from the music that was playing all over the house.

The song was one of his favorites and he knew it word for word, singing seemed to be a forte of all of the residents of Ionious. Praise was in their DNA and he yearned to worship as much as he longed to be with his beautiful wife. There was this thing that they all did in the South that is called singing in the spirit, this was a normal part of the church service at Jeremiah's Cathedral on any given Sunday.

To fully understand what it is to sing in the spirit you would have to attend a church service. The musicians start to play very softly a very harmonious melodic tune and then a few people start to sing Hallelujah's and praises, Glory to God, and when they are all singing different melodies the presence of the Holy Spirit takes over and they begin to sing words that are directed by the spirit.

The words are all worship and they sometimes tell stories of Gods glory on the cross or of other stories in the bible. All the while the melodies are all different and the songs and stories are all different from each singer. Nonetheless it composition is an orchestra of incredible beauty to be heard while the other people are praying or talking in tongues.

After a while the music gets more dramatic as the stories unfold and the songs get more passionate and louder in the decibel range to an energetic praise anthem. All of the different singers compliment each other in their tunes and the all add to the whole service orchestrated by God and the following of the Holy Spirit. As he was reflecting from this last week's church service he began to sing the lyrics of the song that was still playing in his house. He moved to the kitchen to get something to satiate his hunger that had developed from seeing all of the creatures eating at the fruit on his portico.

In a voice of praise and thanks he began to sing while making some food,

"This life that I follow not lead is all yours oh Lord,
All that I have within me and that is mine is yours,

Give me courage to let you lead with every breath that I take,
I want to be in your will and to know the Glory that you make,
With the sound of your voice I have seen the stars,
The angels that resound in praise that are all yours,
To find a treasure in the field your voice is my strength,
I give all that I have just to hear you lead and speak,
Such direction on my own I could never find,
You give me hope infinite and peace to my mind,
My soul is tranquil in knowing this part of the Universe you create,
This constant battle is solved and dissolved with the equanimity you make,"

The SWORD processing was complete in a few seconds and he began to prepare the place that he was about to eat as he was singing. When the song was over he finished his meal and then went into his bedroom and keyed in a verse that he wanted to explore before he was to go to sleep.

Wondering when his wife Sarah was going to be home he transcommed her, "Honey, I am getting ready to go to sleep, what are you doing?"

She was at work and kind of busy however she could take a few minutes to talk, "Babe, I am finishing up on some programs that need to be out today if we are going to meet the project schedule."

"So when do you think that you are going to be able to make it home?"

John then got under the covers. Sarah hovered to a spot behind her desk and spun about 180 to get a view of the beautiful trees that were outside in her view, "I think in about an hour."

John had found the verse on his Scroll and was ready to enter into it, "Ok I will be long asleep by then so just pray for me. I am going to be doing some serious praying before I get the rest I need. Honey, there has to be a way."

Sarah's face was angelic gleaming from the sunlight through the trees that reached her complexion with that smile, and after she heard what she thought that he was going to be praying about, "There is a way and you know this, God is the answer in all that we do. So just pray and use Matthew 18:18. God responds to that verse you know that."

The edge of his eyebrow raised as he scratched his head as a sudden

55

rush of thoughts sparked in his mind. He thought of Sarah, and as he was reflecting on what she was saying, he could see her lips move in that intelligent and eloquent way. "I love you, Babe."

She heard him and that smile overtook her whole face. "There is an answer to all of this, I love you too."

The verse that he had selected was one that Daniel suggested that he look into so here he was red-eyed and collapsing if he hadn't already been laying down and he was about to explore the roots of his scripture.

He entered in the verse of Ephesians 3:20 and the text said this, "Now unto him by the action of his power that is at work within us, that is able to carry out His purpose and do superabundantly, far over and above all that we ask or think, infinitely beyond our prayers, thoughts, hopes, and dreams."

John got a pretty good thought when this finally hit him about his answer to the prayers that he had been praying over the last few months. The thought was somewhat of a revelation of sorts and this was the key thing that he needed to be praying and looking to right now. So he clicks on the Dreamstream view icon and then he prepared by closing his eyes. The DTR got the message and immediately in real-time sent the packet of information to the receiver part of his brain. Now he was there in complete whiteness and then in green letters the verse in text form was at a distance then it came zooming up until it was put right in front of him like it was on a billboard.

Then the letters of the words in the verse all turned into angels and flew away, as soon as the last angel had flown away the sun shown directly above him and he looked at it to see what this light was and then he was blinded for a few seconds and when the sun spots disappeared and he regained his vision he saw ancient Rome in about 60 A.D.

The Coliseum was still standing in all of its original glory and he was hovering over it as he noticed that the shade curtains were drawn forward, and he could see several ships scaled back floating on water at the base of the floor. He heard a roar from the clouds as gladiators were fighting and hopping ships then in the roar he was then floating over the Pantheon and directly in front of the inscriptions of the front Portico. The Pantheon was a dome structure with an eye or oculus in the center of the dome. He then hovered over the dome and saw in through the oculus the Roman Gods bright and gleaming in the little bit of sun that reached inside.

Next he was floating through the city of Rome over all of the fine architecture there the columns of great grandeur and all of the amazing buildings that Rome had to offer at the time. Finally He flew over a much smaller building that had been there for several centuries that didn't look like any of the other columnized Greek influenced buildings at all. It was made out of simple stones and was only one story tall.

The door to this building was wooden, and there was a cratered stone beside the wooden door that must have served as a door before it crumbled. He then was on his feet again and he walked in through the wooden door that was all beaten out of shape. It was amazing in itself that it still hinged. John found himself in a large hallway that had one main door and several other doors on each side.

He walked past several doors to get to one door that was locked, he walked directly through this to find a beaten and bearded man huddled on the cobble stone floor. The man looked up and you could see his full beard that was down to the mid section of his chest. The inmate hadn't shaved in over a year obviously and he was in need of some food as his ribs shown through his torn clothes, all bruised and such.

On the floor was a papyrus scroll on top of a smooth tablet with a quill next to it. The Scroll had writing on it and it stopped in Aramaic at the word "dreams". The words on the Scroll were written in the language of Aramaic only he could understand them in English through the programming feature of the Interactive Bible.

John then said to the man, "Shalom, I come in peace. I am John Lambda and I want to know who you are." The man that looked like he was in pretty bad shape, due to his environment, was doing good to actually speak, and when he heard the words of John this pleasant smile came over his face.

"I am Paul of Tarsus a disciple of Jesus and I have been in this prison for almost two years. I have been writing in this scroll to the people of Ephesus. Why have you come to see me?" John was amazed that he was actually talking to Paul, who had been imprisoned in Rome, while writing the letter to the Ephesians. This was the book of Ephesians and John was getting to talk to him while he was writing it.

"I want to know what you mean when you say in the verse that you have just written and why did you write it?"

Paul was very hungry and he wanted to answer John's question, "Do you think that you could get me some food? I am almost dying of starvation. I only get food here once a day and it is always full of maggots and other bugs. I eat them because I am so hungry. Every now and then a bird will come to my window here and I will get a chance to dine on it. Sometimes a locust will fly in here also and that is nourishment that I am very pleased with."

John knew that he was in this dream and didn't know how everything worked. He wished that he could get Paul out of there so he could get him a good meal and see some fresh air and sunshine. "Sure I will get you some food, just wait here."

Paul said, "It's not like I am going anywhere," and showed him his chains of bondage.

John found this quite amusing and sad at the same time and then left the room to go and find some food. "You might be in prison though you still have a good sense of humor, I see your spirits are still in good health."

Paul said to John, "The Holy Spirit guides me."

"Ah, yes, he guides me too, and now to the marketplace to get you something good to eat."

John was back after a good while, that didn't matter to Paul though, he was happy to have met John's acquaintance Paul was looking forward to sharing his beliefs in Jesus with this new face and he thought that God Himself must have sent him.

John Lambda spake, "I have some food here that should satiate your hunger at least for a while."

When Paul saw the chicken unwrap from the linen bundle that John had brought for him, he thought that he was already in Heaven that he had already attained it. You could see the aroma and stream rising and the fresh smell of the juices that are common to that of cooking a chicken on a rotisserie fire.

This was not a common sight for Paul and his thanks and appreciation was not common either as it was a thankover. To be thankful is not enough, that is only being full of thanks, Paul's thanks was overflowing, much more than just full, it was resilient and something that he would remember for quite some time.

Paul gently grabbed a leg from the chickens slightly charred body being careful not to drip any of the savored juices. He then said a prayer,

"Heavenly Father, I come to you in the name of your son Jesus, and I ask that you bless this food that I am about to partake in eating. Praise be to you Jehovah Jihrah, you truly are my provider. Your praise shall be continually on my lips and your word shall never leave my heart. Please bless this traveler John, as he is your servant brought to me by you oh God."

He continued, "Dear God, please help me and guide me in my paths to knowing you more and knowing your will in my life so that all may know of the grace and provision that is in a relationship with you. So that all will know your precious son Jesus who died for their sins so they might have life everlasting. I pray all of this in Jesus name. Amen."

He wanted to relish all that this meal had to offer, as he sunk his teeth into a white portion of the the leg, his stomach watered and groaned in expectation of what it was about to experience. The first bite went down and it hit his stomach like a ball sinking safely into the glove of a fielder in the last inning of the World Series, in that there was much joy and jubilation that was to come from the event.

He then hugged John with chicken leg in hand and all, making sure not to drop any of the dangling skin that was hanging from it, or to get any on John's suit. Paul enthusiastically said, "How can I ever repay you for what you have done for me? I hunger no more, and although I have endured hardships and tribulations since I have been here, it is worth it to fellowship here with you today. I know that I will do my best to answer all of your questions about my writings that God has given to me. Thanks be to God in the Heavens. Glory be to his precious name. To the God that was, and is, and is to come. All the praises be to God!"

Paul devoured the entire chicken savoring each bite, like the guards might whisk in, and as if it could be his last. He was so overfilled with excitement he was ambiguously torn between eating fast to increase the speed of his nourishment, or to relish the intense flavor that his dulled mouth and taste buds were not accustomed to, due to the lack of spices in the food that he regularly eats.

After the chicken was in his stomach still hungry he was beyond satisfied and knew that the bird was in the best possible place that it could be in, and that in his selflessness God saw that this bird's destiny was to aid and help him to regain his strength so that he could be in closer communion and fellowship with Him.

The aroma of fresh baked bread also permeated the once dank and damp cell. "Can I see what else you have so graciously brought me to feast upon?" John then completely unwrapped the linen bundle cautiously, to not drop any of its contents on the rancid floor.

He then pulled out a loaf of bread and gave it to Paul. "My flesh hungers for such fulfillment the bread of Jesus I break this in remembrance of you oh Lord."

Steam arose from the innards of the bread as it's spongeish texture intensified the aroma of the wheat. "My soul thirsts for living waters that can only be satiated by the love of my savior Jesus."

John then reached to his hip to holster the skin of water that he had bought for him. "Here is something to drink, the lady at the well was very kind and the price of the water skin was not too steep."

"This is the cleanest water that I have seen since I have been in here. Overthanks to you, you good Samaritian." Trickles of water streamed down from the sides of his mouth as he was concentrating on inhaling it down to the last drop.

"Now, to answer your questions, I believe that you being here has proved a facet of what this scripture means. God is able to do more than we could ever ask, think, or imagine. I never would have imagined that you would come to me and quench my thirst and satiate my hunger. God did this and his power is at work in you, just saw I have written."

John sat on a bench in the dark cell. "Why did you write this?"

"God told me to write this, I was listening to his voice, and in a very soft and faint voice I distinctly heard him say the words to me, as I have with most of my writings. You might not know that the people in Ephesus, the church, the gathered, have vocalized their petitions to me about the power of Jesus and wondered how that God can work in their lives the way that he works in mine and through the disciples."

"These people need to be uplifted in the knowledge of the endless possibilities and the infinite power that God can manifest in their lives. They need the infilling the overfilling of the Holy Spirit and through the power of the trinity God can do miraculous things through them and in their lives."

"Where I come from we are at war, that was brought on mainly from doubt and disbelief. Does this scripture also pertain to attaining peace?"

"God can give you a peace that passeth all understanding, and He can bring it in many forms, as you pray for peace include this in it... Pray that God will make you of the same mind with one another, live in peace and the God of love and the Author and Promoter of peace will be with you. As I have just written God can do abundantly more than you could ever ask think or imagine, beyond all of the prayers that you could ever think of or imagine. Ask this in Jesus name and you shall have it and God will show you the way toward peace. Jesus says that he is the way the truth and the life."

Paul continued, "That means that Jesus is the way and if you call upon him He will show you the way. Remember this there are no wars in Heaven there is only peace so loose what is in Heaven down to your Earth. Have I answered all of your questions?"

"Most definitely so, I cannot thank you enough for your wisdom and knowledge it is such a privilege to be here and actually talk to you. I must be going now, however keep your eyes to the sky in the hope of Jesus' return. No matter what your troubles are press onward toward the goal to which Jesus has called us heavenward."

John Lambda then opened his eyes and was exited about the Dreamstream application. He was thinking that of all of the times that he has used the Interactive Bible it has never seemed so real so there in the actual moment of when he actually wrote that verse.

And what could be a better time to speak with the author than just after they have written it. I also brought the man who wrote half of the new testament bread and water and he was overthanks to me, this program is amazing, and all of what that they have done with it. For all your answers in life you need to go none further than the Interactive Bible they explain everything personally to me and for this I am grateful. Now it was time to pray for God to show me the way that I can help in this war and in this divided land.

"Heavenly Father, in the name of Jesus I am taking hold of the word of God in that I know that you can do superabundantly more than I could ever pray, ask, think, or imagine so I ask that you envelop me in your infinite power and show me a way that I can contribute to ending this war to bringing peace once again to this planet. And I praise you and thank you for it. In Jesus name I pray."

John snuggled into his bed putting his Data pad on the table at the side of his bed, not knowing when he would get a revelation. So resting assured that God would show him something he closed his eyes and went to sleep. His entire dream is now being recorded and transmitted to the DTR and after several hours into his dream God begins to show him things in an answer to his prayers.

John begins to see a laboratory and does not recognize it and he realizes that he has never been there in his life. On a side scroll walling he sees an insignia of Apollo glittering that notifies him that he is on the North's army base. There are several men and women scattered about the room, laden with talent, wearing a protective energy shield coating over their AIIA suits.

These people are scientists that are working on something and it must be pretty important because one of the men watching over them is none other than General Aaron Alpha. One of the scientists is looking at a lit slide inside a clean box that is transparent in color. As he presses a key on his scroll, a wall forms on the scroll walling in front of them. Aaron is watching the process like a hawk with on hand at his chin and the other on his hip.

This huge energy wall that has formed is something like seeing Moses part the Red Sea in techni color on the big screen for the first time. The energy wall that forms on the huge screen in front of them looks not that different than that of a normal energy shield however something peculiar happens when the techie taps out something on his scroll. All of the water in the microscopic container next to it gets violently pulled through it's membrane type barrier and is sucked directly to this energy shield.

"When will it be ready for an actual trial?" Aaron Alpha says, mesmerized by what he has just seen.

"The shield technician has to make some modifications, just scale it up, and other compensations, then you will get to see what this thing is really capable of."

"I like what I am seeing already, this looks very promising. Lethal, lethal in an energy pack of a disrupter. When are the first trials going to be tested?"

"One week from tomorrow sir, on the full scale model it seems to need a reteathering modification so that the victim is within range of the shield circumference."

"Fine fine, they can work all that out I just want to see this thing in action."

The two men then walk around the corner and outside to a field clearing area where some of the tests are being held. "Here is the shield engineer and some of his technicians."

As Aaron Alpha and the lab tech were watching the Shield Engineer got into it with one of his techies. They heard part what they were saying, "Why is it that every time that I bring your name up around my wife she tells me that she loves me and when I am just being me and not mentioning you she never says that she loves me or hugs me or kisses me. Are you having an affair with my wife?"

The Engineer then grabs the disrupter from off the table and begins to point it at his techie. "Sir, I think that you are being very irrational, I am not having an affair with her and I barely even know her so if you could please put down the disrupter."

Aaron heard all of this melee and decided that he needed to put a stop to this before someone gets hurt. He walks over to the fighting men and voices his opinion to bring peace to the situation, "Men, Sarge, just put down the weapon and we can talk about everything in a civilized manner without a weapon in your hand. Someone could get hurt. You might not know that my wife is friends with your wife and she always has good things to say about you."

"Then why cant she say those things to me." The shield engineer now acts as if he is going to give the weapon to the General.

"Just hand it over that's it hand it over."

"Its been months since she has said that she loves me all on her own. I can't..."

Then he turns the disrupter on himself and squeezes the trigger. A red energy burst splatters all over his chest then retracts back a few feet directly in front of him. A Blue shield forms from the tether point all the way to the ground, and extending to a height equal to his. When Aaron saw the shield he took off running in the opposite direction.

The blue tinted shield refracted light and made for a beautiful display of engineering then as the man said, "Just don't take me back to my first wife, God!"

He said his final words as all of his blood molecules were being rearranged, aligned, and magnetized then as the shield released an energy current that was a brilliant display of light towards its victim, Aaron dove under cover behind a bunker. The next sight was very gruesome indeed His body went limp and it looked as if it were an AIIA suit that someone had just taken off that crumbled to the floor.

In another part of John Lambda's dream he is in a house and there is dinner on the table, Aaron Alpha is sitting at the head and his daughter Esther who was wearing her favorite Dreamstream character Rachel Rho.

Esther was very excited and she was talking to her daddy, very fast, an in a high pitched voice, "She is such a good friend, and all she ever talks about is how God has this special anointing on me and that I am going to do great things when I grow up. And she told me all about how Esther in the bible arose from poverty to be one of the most wealthy women in the land. Daddy I want to be wealthy in spirit."

Aaron lovingly says, "Honeybear, you already are, just think of how God has blessed you and our family and with our last battle at hand it looks like we are going to win this war. How is your school project going along?"

"Well, we are all finished and all we have to do is present it to you and then show our findings to the class and we probably will get an A." Why do you have to present it to me?"

Aaron asked as he placed his napkin around his collar. "Daddy, its about you."

"That's lovely Honeybear, that you would write a whole project on me." He said as only a proud dad only could. "Will you tell me what its about or do I have to wait to find out all on my own when you and your friend present it to me."

"Daddy, you'll see when we do the final presentation, okay?"

"Okay, pumpkin, are you getting hungry?"

"Starving like you wouldn't believe. What is Mom making tonight?"

"I think it's enchiladas and tacos, Mexican tonight honeybear. Do you know who the Mexicans are?"

"I think, aren't they the people that sent Christopher Columbus over to America in 1492?"

Her Dad had a bright smile on his face. "Those are the Spanish and that is the language that the Mexicans speak. So you are almost right."

"We haven't gotten that far in Universal history yet Dad. Why don't the Mexicans speak Mexican and just let the Spanish speak Spanish?"

"That is a good question and I am sure that your history books can tell you the answer to that one better than I can. It's kind of like asking the question, "Why do all of the aliens in Star Trek and Stargate speak English? Well they have linguistics officers to translate and most of them do however speak the universal language of English."

"The Zyahth even know English."

"The reason that most Mexicans speak Spanish is because the Conquistadors all spoke Spanish and the settlers in Mexico and South America all converted the Indians there to speak Spanish. Does that answer your question?"

"Yeah, I am starvin Marvin can we eat?"

Sharon heard them from in the kitchen where she was doing some work on the SWORD. "Darlings, it will be ready in a minute."

She rushed in with some Spanish bread and laid it on the table. "Here is something to tie you over until you get the main course."

Then she set a bottle of olive oil on the table next to General Alpha's arm. The two talking busy bodies went quiet and turned their motors of for a second as they dug into the bread dipping it into the olive oil that was laden with garlic and dried onions.

"Dad, did you know that after dinner we are having over a special visitor?"

"No Honeybear, who might that be?" He said all excited.

"She is my project friend that is doing the presentation with me."

"Do I know this young lady?"

"No, she is new her name is Sarah, she's a refugee from the USA."

"That will be great to hear an outsiders opinion on the war, I have to say I am very much looking forward to this presentation of yours."

Finally Sharon brought in the food and they all began eating and mostly the two ladies just listened to Aaron talk about things at work. After they were all through enjoying the fine Mexican cuisine they headed for the living room where Sarah was going to meet with Esther. "Sarah, are you ready to come over?"

She transcommed over to her with an encrypted link. "Yes, I am ready whenever you are."

"Okay then, just come on over."

"Will do good friend."

The doorway from the living room to the dining room lit up as it usually did in a red streaming light full of letters and particles that reflected in the chandelier. Through the stream walked Sariah Delta, Daniel Delta's daughter, what was she doing here thought John. "Sarah how is your camp?"

"Everything is fine where I come from."

"Let me introduce you to my parents, Aaron Alpha, Sharon Alpha and who knows where Luke my brother is. Anyway are you ready for the presentation?"

They began their presentation with all of the gadgets and technologies that were prevalent during the time and did an outstanding job.

It was well thought out and it clearly stated that, "We should put our weapons down and embrace our fellow countrymen from the south or we might not win the war. They have stopped and thwarted all of our previous attacks, its almost as if God doesn't us to even be in this war in the first place. If Aaron Alpha only had the faith of a grain of mustard seed to believe in what was shown him about the destruction of the Zeus Mountains then we wouldn't even be in this war."

"We need to quit thinking with our trigger finger and start thinking with our heart. In the bible it says in Jeremiah 14:13 "Then I said, "Ah, Lord GOD! Behold, the prophets say to them, 'You shall not see the sword, nor shall you have famine, but I will give you assured peace in this place." Peace is assured to you if you will just lay your weapons down, God will find a way."

Esther was so sure of herself as she spoke and now it was time for her friend Sarah to speak as images of war were seen on the screen. "More people have died in the attacks of the North than all of that that had lost their lives in the great war against the Zyahth over 60 years ago."

"These are our own people that we are talking about here not the foul aliens that have attacked us in the past, and there is rumor that they too will be fighting along side the South if this war does not cease and soon. How would you like for your son or daughter to be killed by one of these evil aliens? When will you realize that it is the Zyahth that destroyed your mountains and not the south. There was a period of weeks that the Zyahth had control over our DTR and this is when they made their attacks on your mountain and not Omega when will you realize this?"

There was a furious rage in the eyes and fists of Aaron Alpha he wasn't sure who this American girl was, he did know that she had a major influence over his daughter and it was against all that he believed in. He was sitting on his intelli-couch and he flexed his arm muscles and clinched his fists.

He was thinking, so Sarah I don't know who you are but do you know what this is? This is the funeral home and this ring is the arranger. He looked at his bare white knuckles and had them clinched as he arose to his feet. Holding back his anger with a stiff upper lip he said, "Wasn't that a very nice interpretation of what someone in the South would think."

Sariah thought nothing of his clinched fist or the tone in his voice, she couldn't tell that he was holding anything back at all. Aaron was infuriated that this didn't bother her and said, "You know that I know a girl that looks just like you only her name is Sariah Delta and she is the Shield Engineer's daughter. Do you know a man by the name of Daniel Delta?"

She was obviously getting nervous at what he might do to her. He could kill her right here. Her thoughts were running wild thinking of how she could get out of there before something happened.

Then she saw Aaron talking to someone on his transcom into the air really and she couldn't tell what was going on. So she reached for her Scroll just as Aaron went to the nearest PAST blockading it. Suddenly four men dressed in AIIA suits with red stripes came bursting through with disrupters in hand.

Daniel seeing this from Sariah's Directview knew he had to get through the PAST and into that room. He sprung in through the particle stream and dove in front of Sariah. One man had a modified disrupter and shot it at Daniel hitting him in the chest then it tethered back and formed a shield. Daniel thought it was a kill shot and nothing was happening.

"What is this?" It started to rearrange the molecules in his body and he screamed in fear. "AHHHHH!"

John woke up and it was time for him to go to work so he hurried along his normal routine thinking back on the dream, that maybe, was an answer to prayer. He would have to research it to make sure. As he was in the clean room thoughts of the weapon flashed in front of his eyes. He would have to tell Isaiah about this as soon as he got there and it might be beneficial for the two to view the dream together.

As he entered the living room and picked up his scroll on the way he heard a song that the praise team at church sings and he could hear his daughter singing which brought back the memories of the two girls talking in front of their parents only the other girl looked like Sariah.

Isaiah definitely had to see this, so he kissed his wife goodbye and told her that he loved her. And, "You are the best wife that I could have ever possibly hoped for I know that God had you in mind when he made me."

"Oh thank you sugarlips, I don't want for you to be late for work now."

"I have an answer to prayer that I think could change this awful war that we are in." They exchanged I love you's like a newlywed and he went through the PAST in a flash. He sat at his desk pulling up the dream and then he transcommed Isaiah over to have a look-see at this contraption as his wife would call it.

Isaiah was working on something else and when he got the call and John told him of the possibilities he was there faster than you could say peace. "So what is it, you have something to show me?"

"Yes sir it's in Dreamstream and I have already set it up for the both of us so just let me know."

"Ready Lambda?" The two men closed their eyes and suddenly they were taken back to the dream seeing all of what God had just shown to John. About 15 minutes later after seeing the condensed version and fast-forwarding through to the essential parts they were mesmerized.

"We have to get our hands on that weapon before they wipe us out. If all of their men are carrying the "Blood Magnet Weapon" then we have some research to do. Daniel would know what to do about this I'll get him in here as soon as we're done discussing this latter part of the dream. So Sariah is friends with Aaron's daughter and this is how we get him to stand down. Sounds simple. What about the part at the end we have to stop it."

"I don't know if we can stop it. There has to be another way, does Kedar have a daughter in Sariah's grade? That is a possibility. Only it doesn't happen for four more months, anything could transpire over this time. We could be demolished to rubble by the time that his daughter talks to him, they could already have control of the south by then. I am worried, do you have any idea how vexed and worried I am about this, if anything goes wrong Daniel could die or even worse Sariah."

"Do you forget Lambda that God gave you this dream, there has to be a reason for it. When God gave people visions and dreams in the bible it was all for some greater purpose. This will happen and what we have to do is be patient and let God work. 2 Thessalonians 3:5 "Now may the Lord direct your hearts into the love of God and into the patience of Christ.""

"Now what we have to do is have the patience of Christ, and not worry about a thing. God has given us a revelation here and we need to stand on it in faith. Daniel needs to hear about this. This can be prevented we just have to believe in God, he showed us this so we can stop it from happening."

There was a problem in the lab that Daniel was working on and he was very disheartened about how the progress was going with his STAR project. This is the Shield Topping Argos Reinforcer system that is going to be the future of combat warfare. When the enemy draws near you activate the STAR and it goes to work for you by aligning the molecules in the bloodstream of the enemy to effect their brain that makes them obedient to the will of God completely disarming them.

This also can be used in conjunction with others near you that have the STAR array on them to make them into a super righteous fighting machine equipped with the full armor of God. The shield forms an energy sphere around the user and when several men activate it, it forms an even larger energy sphere and anoints and arms the users with the word of God. As they speak scriptures they transform into angels able to defeat anyone.

"Daniel we need you in John's office as soon as you can get here it is a matter of urgency."

"Sure thing General just let me get cleaned up and I'll be there in a whiff." Daniel walked in smelling very fragrant as if he had just been to the scripture of fragrant oil.

69

"How can I help you men?"

"Have a seat, John received a dream from God in an answer to prayer about a weapon that is very deadly and which we have no match for its capabilities. Also, he dreamed about an event in the future where your daughter Sariah plays a critical role in changing Aaron Alpha's mind about his stance on his attacks against us. Has Sariah came to you about any school projects yet?"

"Yes, as a matter of fact she has, it had to do with some joint venture with a student from the North. She hasn't told me what it is about yet."

"It's about why the North should stand down, and she won't be giving this report for another four months. We will need to work with you on this, agreed?"

"Agreed sir, I won't let you down."

"We have already seen the future on this one thanks to the good lord, one thing we don't know is how this will play out. So when your daughter tells you about her project be as open minded as you can and let her take the reigns. I am sure that it is instilled in her enough from hearing from you all about the evils of war."

Chapter 5
Judah's Eternity's Past

"Things to Consider"

While I was driving in the car with my mom one day last winter 2010, we were talking about my book and she gave me the idea to write about eternity's past which is talked about in the bible. My pastor Mark Bristow has preached sermons on this and discussed it with my mom so she thought it would be nice to write about. So I take two chapters of this book to write about the supernatural being Judah's eternity past. In my book it is another realm that Judah travels to with differing laws of physics and visitations from Jesus. This chapter is about how Judah got married to his wife Shuah. If you like romance and love stories this is a good one.

Chapter 5
Judah's Eternity's Past

There was a subtle way that Judah ruled his own part of Ionious, and with that nature he was set on becoming the best at what God had given him to rule over. He was given great authority and with that authority came great responsibility. Even before the DTR was given time to think he would interject his own thoughts that made for a complete Democratic ruling Republic, if that makes any sense to the layman at all.

Judah was the final say in his district of property on Ionious and he made sure that all perpetrators paid for their actions against the inhabitants of his territory. Judah was a mediator and he found a stopping point where he believed that the duties on this planet were outweighed by the calling that God had on his life back Home in Judea.

His home planet where his parents lived and where his friends were or once were. Recently he had received an invitation of sorts to come home and visit his family that were very eager to see him and hear of all of his trials against the Ionians and Zyahth aliens. They invited him to a trial of the spirits that was a ritual where he would compete against one of his fellow class-men for the right to bear arms over Ionious for another two years.

Back on Judea there was a special woman that he was interested in, and had been since they were born, her name was Shuah and if he won this battle of beliefs he also would sin the right to marry Shuah if her parents would have it.

So Judah then began telling the other 12 immortals that he had to travel back to Eternity's Past. "Benjamin I bid the farewell, may you keep Ionious fair and balanced in your rule over these people."

"Dear brother, I pray that you find your love in Shuah that you have waited for so long and that someday you may be together here in rule over Ionious."

So as they all said goodbye Judah made his way back to Judea. When you are immortal you travel in another dimension and that is at the speed of thought, no matter the distance or amount of galaxies that one would normally have to travel through. He made it to the dock, safe and on time for the festival of lights that was just beginning.

As Judah was immortal he made a grand entrance as the spectators saw a bright and gleaming star approaching from the South that eventually was so bright that it lit up the sky like it was daytime then he appeared from the clouds and the night was brought back again.

There was much music and dancing and many people encamped around the town square waiting for their chance to dance in the moonlight. As Judah rode in on a cloud he was seated at the table next to that of his father Israel which was at the head of the table. When he saw his son return he was overjoyed with excitement and proclaimed that Jesus' return must be at hand because it was Judah in his lineage that Jesus was born.

Israel exclaimed to the crowd of dancers and musicians that, "The best of my lineage has returned to bring joy to us all once again. Rachel please come and sit at the table with your son. Where is Shuah the wife of Judah to be? Can she be found in such a crowd?"

Then through all of the festivities Shuah produced herself unto the table of Israel and sat next to Judah. "I have waited over one hundred years for this occasion and now finally here you are."

"You are more sweet than the honey on my lips and more fragrant than the rose in the desert sun."

"I have saved myself for you knowing you would return."

"And I have waited in Eternity for you to return for me. For now we shall talk of Eternity's Past, of a time where we were once friends growing up together to one day make a life as our own."

"Adullah has his mind set on making me his wife and his father

Allah will give him his inheritance if he marries me by tomorrow's sun."

"Shuah, you have to tell me if this is what you want? Do you want the inheritance of Earthly things or do you require the things of the spirit. This is the realm that I live in and in much peace at that. Although I have not proposed to you or gone to your dad to request his approval I know in my heart and I have always known that you are the only one for me."

Just then as they were talking a man approached Shuah and asked her in a very drunken breath, "Can I have this dance?" Shuah didn't know what to respond or really how Judah would respond if she accepted. Were his words to forthcoming or to brazen with intent?

As she was unwantingly whisked away he would find out if he was too strong in his words. Judah then went over to Shuah's sister Tamar at another table and asked her to dance with him. Tamar was engaged to the towns Mayor Zarah and Judah did not know this and he danced anyway. As he saw Shuah getting close to her partner it only drew Judah even closer to his partner Tamar. If Shuah would dip then Judah would dip Tamar even further, this turned out to be a dual of the dancing kind that made Judah and Shuah want to be together even more.

After a few dances Judah was exhausted and he had to go and sit at the Mayor's table with Tamar in which Shuah came over to visit and see what they were up to. She whispered into Judah's ear, "My house is empty at this time of night and we could make it in a minute if you so desired."

"Shuah, my sweet, just give me a sign and we shall be there in one of my heartbeats, for tonight they all have beaten for you." Ocran the man dancing with Shuah came to sit at the table and began to talk.

"For there will be only a time when the star shines and then it shall shine no more, for why does the lilly face the true sun in the day time then turn her back on him at night. A lilly is so sweet that it should have the attention of the light of the party in both the day and the night and I know you would agree that I am the life of the party no matter what part of day we are in. Shall I go to your father to inquire about your potential?"

Judah spoke in response to Ocran, "I have the ability to shine on many lilies all throughout my day and there is never a night where I cant see a sun where I sit above the heavens. However there is only one lilly that I am interested in among all the other flowers in the fields that are so vast in number that all require my light. I have already chosen my lily here tonight. My dear are the lily's in season?" He said this to find her sign to leave.

And she replied, "As a lily in the valley I am beginning to bloom and this night air has gotten stale so shall you show me towards the fresher air that I might breathe in life once again?"

"I shall." Judah took her hand as she arose from the table. Then in a flash the man Ocran took a drunken swing at Judah and he caught it with his fist and sent him packing into a stumble over a few chairs where he remained. They both walked a short distance to her house where it was in full vacancy due to the festival. At the portico under the fireworks and spectacles of lights in the sky they both renewed their faith in God.

"You are my one desire Shuah. All of out time together growing up there has never been a day that has gone by without a prayer that had to do with you. I know you must hear it from my parents, I, Shuah, am here tonight to tell you how I cannot live without you."

She held his hand and brought it up to her eyes so that she could see the reflections of the lights in his fingernails and also in his eyes as she looked up to him. They sparkled in the yearning for a dance that they didn't get to dance tonight. They could still hear the instruments play in the background which brought a smile and a tightening to her cute face.

"May I have this dance Shuah?" She rose the hand that she was clinching to and put her other hand at his hip. They danced just as if they were little doing square dances together in Mrs. Black's music class in school. Still the light sparkled in her eyes and he grew nervous just as he always did back then. "How is your back. I pray for you everyday you know never knowing if I will get this chance to be here with you tonight. And it has happened these dreams of mine have come to life. Being here with you is more than I could have ever imagined it to be. You are more than enough for me Shuah."

"My back? I can't believe you remembered that was so long ago. I am doing fine now I don't even notice it, I do notice your special touch though and it brings comfort to my soul. I pray for you too, you know. You are my one desire even when I can't dream, even when I can't see in front of me, I envision you standing there to bring me back to us back to what we were and to where we could be. And now here you are and my utmost prayers are that this couldn't ever end."

"Who says that it has to?" They continued to dance on the porch platform doing turns much as they did in class. Judah's smile would brighten as they would get closer and his heart would beat harder. As they spun inner elbow within inner elbow he flashed back to music class in that moment that he treasured most seeing her eyes light up and her face brighten this was a shining moment for him as he remembered it so nervously as he was at the time.

When their arms would part he listened to the song playing intently focusing on the part where they would interlock again. A tear was found on his cheek flowing down to his jaw as she wiped it away with her soft hand.

"In all of my memories you shine the brightest in all of eternity's past and now I can only think of how you can be in all of my futures."

"The future has yet to be written Judah, we are in God's hands now. Love and love alone is what makes your memories shine. If there was love in the beginning it will be there in the end."

"The beginning, do you remember the trip to the mountain?"

"Of course I do."

"Nothing shines brighter than that moment when I first saw you. At that point I knew I wanted you to be in my future more than anything I have ever wanted. And here we are at the summit, the pinnacle."

A star was shooting in a spectacle of light as their held hands moved to an embrace with cheeks touching she said, "They won't be home for an hour if you have ever wanted to see my room. I have pictures of us together."

"What is keeping us?" Hand in hand they went through the front door as she turned on some lights and went to the right side of the house to her room.

Her heart was fluttering as she got out her picture album and they both sat on her plush soft bed. Through the laughs came tears and tears turned into hugs. The hugs turned into an unbreakable embrace and as they found each other face to beautiful face Judah told a story.

"At church after all was over I would watch you leave and every time I could feel my heart leave with you. When I would go home I would reflect on what our pastor would say mixed with what my parents would teach me and I would lay in my bed at night before I would go to sleep and think. As I was thinking I would always say a prayer for you on my own after my Mom would leave. And I got to thinking about how all of these philosophers would have these theories and ways of life and I created my own. Do you know what it was?"

Their faces grew closer. "No what was it?"

"It was the 'And then what theory.' I would use it with anything I did and think what I would do after this and say and then what?"

"And then what, huh? Do you know what I am thinking right now? As we get closer than we ever have. Starring into your eyes. Our lips so close. We've been talking so intimately. And then what?"

He then got the courage to do something that he had always dreamed of doing and pressed his lips to hers.

They kissed a kiss so passionately that they saw their futures laid out before them all set together visions of laughter and togetherness and unity forever. They saw their unborn children playing in the fields as they were hand in hand. After their lips took a breath to recall all they had seen Shuah said, "And then what?"

"I am ready if you are?"

"I don't know."

"Ionious is such a beautiful planet." Judah said looking directly into her eyes and seeing her soul.

"We could live there together, what do you say to an eternity with me?"

Shuah took a deep breath looked down at their pictures and released a, "Yes." With the sweetest smile looking back up at him. "Yes, with all my heart yes. This is all I have ever wanted, you are my world and you always have been." She lifted up the pictures and said, "I live in these memories of us."

Judah then put his arm around her to embrace for a kiss. "You don't have to anymore we can make an eternity of new memories that will live in our hearts forever."

"What if the people on Ionious need you?"

"I can always step down into time and help them and be back to our realm or dimension, if you will, and we will never skip a beat."

"I want you to believe in me and know what I am for. Your happiness is my main goal otherwise there is no use for even getting married. I know that there is much godliness in what makes you happy so in striving to make you happy I will also be pleasing God at the same time and that is what is important to me I hope you agree."

"I will arrange everything, we can get married here and be back to Ionious to our dimension whenever you want. I hope you want children."

"Many, when do we start?"

"As soon as we are married."

"Lets hurry I don't think I can wait any longer you have no idea how beautiful you are."

"Lets go back and tell your parents at the festival."

"Good we can go now, God has given me a song to sing."

They arrived at the dance and her parents were ecstatic they were so happy that their baby girl was getting married. Judah then asked the man at the harp if he could play. He sat and began singing this song of praise.

I will always praise
For how you saved
Me from ultimate death
When I had nothing left
You reached down
Held your hand out
And lifted me up
When I had had enough
Of all of this earth
Who measures your worth
For all that you've done
The war in me you won
I am forever yours
My heart is sure
My mind is pure
Always stayed on your
Grace to me you gave
For you alone can save
With the storms in what I do
My hope is always in you
You're the beacon of light
Toward which I strive

You are the way the truth the life
Your word in me is bright
The truth I know has set me free
So that the whole world can see
The way your glory shines
The evil that waged war is behind
Never to be thought of again
Erased from earth like sin
One ray of light from your silver lining
Can defeat the evil that is now retreating
That evil darkness can't ever withstand
The peace that is seen in light from your plan
Your love unconditional conquers all
That is why you took the fall
To become flesh and bone God among men
Died an excruciating death to free us all from sin
Can we ever say it enough, thank you
For what you've done and all you do
Thank you from my innermost being
Once blind eyes that are now seeing
Poured into your word
All that I don't deserve
Such grace could never be replaced
To be at deaths edge and now I am safe
Not because of what I've done
Its who you are and how you won
The fight over satan and took the keys
Ressurected for me your heart bleeds
And bled on the cross at Calvary
To bring us into all we could ever be
Or become not in us but in you
Your work is never through
Until the last soul is saved anew
I am your redeemed vine
To let the vine dresser shine
As I grow you mold and make me
Into what you want me to be

Shuah is totally amazed that Judah can play the harp so well. "I didn't know you could play like that, you are incredible what latent talents you have that I have never seen. You know that don't you? I have never really seen the creative side in you, I guess I have a lot to be looking forward to."

Jokingly he says, "Aw shucks you shouldn't have. You mean it you really liked the song."

"I have never even heard an angel that could play like that you are the best and you're all mine."

"Not yet, you will have to catch me." Then Judah takes off running around the premises.

Someone yells, "Run, Judah run."

Then he goes darting around the dance floor and the band and over into a close blueberry field and then dives hands first in the fruits. She follows after him chasing him all the way and stumbles over a Cello then gets back up to meet with him and almost grabs him as he is diving into the blueberry patch. She lands right on top of him.

Face to face he says, "You're fast."

"Not nearly as fast as you."

They sit up and have a moment to catch their breath. Then Shuah says, "Will I always be chasing after you, always being just beyond my grasp."

Judah assures her, "Once we get married I am pretty sure that I am all yours and you will never have to chase me very far. I am thinking living room to bedroom, that's about all the energy that I will have to run from you. I am not sure that I want to run too far because of how much I like our embrace after you catch up with me."

"Are you saying that you let me catch up with you?"

"No, not at all, it is more fun though when you do."

"So to the victor go the spoils?"

"And even though we are both victorious, I have a feeling I am going to like spoiling you."

"And I have a feeling you are going to like being victorious."

By this time their noses are almost touching each other then he shadows his lips to her and she says, "So can I just get a taste of what all of this spoiling is going to be like?"

He leans in even closer almost as if to kiss her then she closes her eyes and puckers up her lips for a big one and he says, "Only if you can catch me!" Then gives her the slightest kiss on the lips and takes off running through the blueberry field in and out of all of the instruments and their players, then jumps over a base drum and attempts to land standing up then falls to his fanny then lands as his feet go sliding out from under him doing the splits right in front of her parents table.

He is so embarrassed that he bows and takes off walking towards his family's house. She runs after him and asks, "You are just a little tease, yes?"

"I am sorry if my tomfoolery has embarrassed you and your family, I will be excused. I got so intoxicated with your personality that I over exuded myself."

"Over exuded yourself, how do you think that I looked chasing after you, I tripped on a Cello and I got right back up again."

"You did not land in the splits in front of your future mother and father in laws. They must think I am juvenile and dumb."

"They love you, and they always have, it doesn't matter if you would have landed head first in their cream pie they would still like you. You are a good man and they respect you no matter how silly you can be in love with me. All they see is a man that is madly in love with me."

"And what do you see?"

"I see you the real you the man who one pulled my hair in class to get my attention, who grew up to be one of the rulers over an entire planet, and more importantly I see that you love me and you would do anything for me and that includes spoiling me if you so see the need."

"So I haven't embarrassed you?"

"Embarrassed me? No all you have done is shown me is that you would do anything to show me that you love me, even doing the splits in front of my parents. Some people say that they are head over heels, I could have sworn that when you jumped that I saw your heels go over your head."

"And..."

"And, that is love in my book."

"Some people say that making a first impression is the most important thing when dating, and I say that it is never too late and more important to make a lasting impression. And all of your silliness was just to impress me and I know that my parents see it the same way too."

They were walking towards his parents house and were in a dimly lit place in the walkway and after all of the embarrassment wore off and the adrenaline calmed down, "I wasn't teasing you I was just leading you to something better."

"Oh, yeah, what is that?"

"That is this." He grabbed her very firmly around her back pulled her dramatically close and planted the biggest kiss on her she had ever taken.

She pulled back gasping for air sort of and said, "So is that just a prelude to something better?"

Judah takes her hand and continues walking towards his parents house and says, "I guess you will just have to wait and see now won't you?"

"I have a feeling that you are not only going to not disappoint me but that you are going to be great at surprises and suspense."

Judah said, "Maybe I am, nonetheless I am still faster than you." Shaking off his depressed emotions about his landing, then he takes off running down the walkway and she follows right after him.

He gets to his parents house and stops to catch his breath bending over holding his knees. Shuah catches up to him after a slight jog and puts her hand softly on his back and gently caresses it back and forth. "You okay?"

"I am fine, more than fine actually now that you are going to be in my life again."

Shuah responded, "Is that right? I thought that you might have just had enough of me for one night."

"I don't think that even after a whole eternity in heaven that I could ever get enough of you. In the past when I would run or distance myself from a woman they would never come running after me so I knew that it wasn't meant to be."

"I will run after you no matter how many times that you distance yourself from me."

"That is one reason why I know that we are meant to be together. I have a feeling though, that I will never want to ever distance myself from you."

"You better not, I am a good hunter and I will hunt you down if you ever do."

Judah straightened his back looked up at the stars then looked into her eyes and said, "You know I don't want this night to ever end."

"Who says it has to."

He then gets this terse look on his face and crinkles his mid-brow and says, "I have to go."

She senses something is wrong. Judah walks up to the door of his parents house opens it and stands in the doorway and tells her, "Good night." Puzzled, concerned and upset she runs up the steps and gets closer to him looking up to his tall stature. "What happened, whats wrong, what did I do?"

"I don't want to talk about it."

"What is it Judah? Something happened and you're not acting like yourself. You can talk to me."

"Okay,in the past things like this don't just happen to me and if it ever does there is some kind of catch to it, and it doesn't last. I have never felt so strongly about someone, and I just don't want for all of this to be just another happiness mirage. That's all, you're perfect in every way, and I just couldn't bare the thought of you being too goo to be true."

"Its not too good to be true Judah, we can have this same happiness and share these same feelings for all of eternity although this night will inevitably end our happiness doesn't have to."

He closes the door and takes a step over to where she is standing and gives her a big hug. "Listen there is a reason that you are in my life and I know that God has plans for the both of us. I will chase you every time that you run just don't run away from our wedding and I think you'll be okay."

She then gives him a soft peck on the lips and cutely touches his nose with her index finger and turns her head looks back at him and says, "I'll be seeing you tomorrow."

Then she turns takes a step away from him looks back winks and walks off. He watches her walking away and mentally searches for something to say something witty or something sweet he can't figure it out. She continues walking as he is just standing there speechless at the door step.

Finally he can't take it anymore and he still has just as much of the no idea of what to say as he did before so he goes off chasing her anyway thinking, that he will have something to say by the time that he gets there. He arrives and gets in front of her walking backwards with his hands over his mouth then to his side and finally has something to say.

She continues walking back to the dance. "Babe, it is okay if I call you babe isn't it?"

She looks at him then looks back down at the walkway and the pebbles. "So now you're chasing after me are you? This is nice."

"Babe, I couldn't bare the thought of going to sleep tonight with out telling you that I love you."

She looks back at him and gives a subtle smile. "I know."

"How did you know?" Her eyes go up to the stars in the chilled air.

"Girls just know these things, Judah."

"Oh. Do you know everything that I am thinking?"

"Mostly. I know all of the important things. I don't pay attention to all of that other guy stuff that goes on in your head."

"Oh, yeah there is a lot of that."

He starts walking beside her, "Do you love me? I know just isn't a good enough response for me right now."

"Judah, if I tell you that I love you I want it to be special and I don't want it all making you go crazy for me, I can tell that you are already that, and we have only been together for one night since you have returned. Girls need time."

"Shuah you're killing me here, okay I know that you have feelings for me only you won't say out loud that you love me yet. Okay then, did you love our night together?"

"Yes, very much so."

"Okay, that is good enough for me."

"Don't worry Judah I am pretty much a sure thing. So go to sleep thinking about what its going to be like over Ionious married to me. No worries you knucklehead?"

"None whatsoever, just one more thing."

"Yes I am all ears."

"One more kiss?"

"Of course Judah." He puts his arm around her and she places her hands at his jaws and they kiss.

"You know you really are a knucklehead." She says in the cutest way possible.

Chapter 6
Asher's Eternity's Past

"Things to Consider"

In this eternity's past there is a visitation from Jesus with stories of trial and triumph among the children of Israel. In the book of Jeremiah it says that God knew you before the foundations of the world. Think about what it would be like if you could go back before you were formed in your mother's womb.

Chapter 6
Asher's Eternity's Past

The mansion that Asher and his family call home was that of one that could have been built by Aristotle in ancient Greece. From the outside there were great Ionic columns that reached as far into the heavens just as the columns of the Parthenon and were a sight to see to all of the Ionians that were blessed enough to travel to this dimension.

The columns were seated on a carefully orchestrated magnetic base where they jirated and hovered around it both above and to the structure base below. There were no signs of wear or weather to all of them that were carefully placed to support the weight of the house, or palace if you will.

Rested back from the columns were scroll-wallings that encompassed the entirety of the outer surface that flashed brilliant portraits of the Ionian Sky, as the sun would peek through the clouds and provide eye hiding splendor in that of silver linings. The magnificent and thoughtful programming of the exterior allowed for a porticoed door frame that was snuggled at the center of the front and back entrances of the house.

There were no windows as the scroll-wallings provided inside and out brilliant lights that were equal in wavelengths to the sun of Ionious. The inside of the palace was brilliantly designed by Adon herself and such great scope of the imagination was there to be invoked upon entering the front door. There were two main staircases that curled around to meet at the top of the upper floor.

Adon, Asher's wife, programmed the scroll-wallings to be very warm and inviting and at certain times of day. When their children were in the palace they would switch to suit their interests to spark the most proper and intelligent conversations that would fill their time with their parents.

All of the rooms were spectacular in nature as best arranged to provide a thought provoking environment that would encourage the word of God to be manifest all throughout their day. The offices of Asher were designed by him, and allowed for the most industrious use of space that would best his duties as watcher over the planet.

To aid him in this venture were the wallings that encompassed the room that showed the most important events that were taking place on Ionious in real time according to the ranking of the DTR. He had full command, though to investigate any matters that he deemed necessary on the scroll-wallings. If need be he would invite a visitor to counsel them on the matters at hand.

There were also occasions that required for him to be present in person on the planet so there was a PAST way that he had full access to. Adon and Asher lived in the palace very happily and were madly in love with one another and there was not a place in all of the universe that would suit them more properly than to be living together there in their humble abode. There was a continual communication between him and his dad Israel back on his planet of Eternity's Past, though they rarely got the opportunity to visit.

So one day Israel found himself in need of help, help that only Asher could give. There had been an incident on Israel's planet Torah, that involved his grandson Zohar which was Asher's nephew. The incident occurred while a group of visitors from Odyssey were staying on Torah and Zohar became good friends with one of the men that went on a climbing expedition with him.

The group needed an instructor that knew the land and could guide them up the Mountain of Olives which was very difficult in various places. Israel knew that Zohar was an extremely good climber and would be a perfect match for the tour group. So he instructed Zohar to set up camp at the base of the mountain and then begin climbing the next day, and that is when the incident occurred.

Israel sent a word over to Asher concerning the problem and spared the details, "Asher, my son, we are in great need of your assistance, and only you can help in this matter, so please get here as soon as you can."

"Dad, I will be there later on today after I finish some work here."

"Sounds good see you then."

Immediately Asher went to go tell his wife Adon about the news and asked her, "Honeycakes, my dad has called us to resolve a problem that has occurred on Torah. I am leaving in a few hours I will need you to be with me on this one if you can."

When she heard him say that she came rushing through the PAST to make sure, "Babaliciousness, what has happened with Israel? Is everything okay."

"I am not sure, there must be some distress for him to call me out like this so I have to go so when can you be there?"

"Tomorrow, at the earliest, I have a conference that I am speaking at in Athenia they need me too. I hope that is okay with you, if you really need me then I will come immediately."

"I will make due until you can get there. I love you and may God be with you and bless and anoint your words to the women of Athenia."

"I will be praying for you Asher. Send my love to your Dad."

Hours later Asher took the trip, traveling in the realm that Asher was in didn't require the use of a Quest Starship all he had to do was to make a request to God and he was instantaneously transported to Torah. When he arrived the family was all huddled around a bed and were all praying vigorously. The house of Israel was very much like that of Asher's house. He saw Israel and rushed over to go talk. "Dad, I am here what is it that you require of me?"

"Asher it is so good to see your face once again, Zohar is in danger of losing his life to a fall that happened yesterday on the Mount of Olives. Right now I need you to pray that God will spare his life. Plead the blood of Jesus, Asher."

Asher and Israel began to pray, "In Jesus name we come before you here today and dear Lord only you know the circumstances, I do not. All I know is that your word says that whatsoever is loosed in Heaven shall be loosed on Earth. Lord there is healing in heaven and I pray that you loose that healing power the same power that raised Jesus from the dead that now dwells in me, loose that power upon my nephew Zohar in Jesus name I pray."

Asher was laying his hands on Zohar, and when he said the blood of Jesus his eyes began to open he was immediately loosed from the coma state that he was in. He began looking around the room and saw Israel and Leah and all of his other family beside him he attempted to talk and he couldn't he was only murmuring.

After the pain in his body had died down his eyes began to spark life into his being. The gash on his head miraculously began to seal and he started to speak. "Dad are you here?" He called out to Simeon and he came beside his resting place and held his hand.

"Thank the Lord Jehovah that you are alive and that he has not taken you from us. Son do you remember what happened yesterday?"

Zohar was still not talking to his normal articulate self. "Yes, I was anchoring the support for Zuri and then I remember someone jumping on his back and I was vaulted in the air and I hit the wall, that is the last memory that I have. What happened to me dad am I going to be okay?"

Simeon was so glad that Zohar had at least partial memory of the incident that he squeezed his hand and kissed it. "Son, after you hit the side of the rock on the mountain you fell to the base over 100 feet and your ropes cushioned you before they broke and you landed on your back. Can you move your legs?"

"Yes I can move them they are moving now." His legs didn't move.

"Zohar," Israel said, "You might be paralyzed."

"God can heal me I know he can, when I was in heaven I heard you praying for me and God told me to go back to Torah because he was not done with me yet and it wasn't my time. If he can bring me back from the dead he surely can heal my legs."

"I believe it too so we must pray." Israel said as he bowed his head and closed his eyes.

"Father in the name of Jesus, humbly we come before you and are asking you for a miracle we know that all things are possible to those that believe, and Lord we believe that you can do anything beyond all that we could ever ask, think, or imagine. So we ask in Jesus name that you heal him of this paralysis."

Israel lifted his head and looked to see if his legs were moving and there was nothing not a single movement and there was no trace of the healing yet. "We know that the healing will come all we have to do is wait on God because it is in his timing for his glory to be revealed."

Israel went into another room in the house, which was his office, and pulled Asher aside to talk with him about the situation. "I haven't had the opportunity to tell you all about his fall. He was helping, at my request, a group of climbers from Odyssey that were camped out by the base of the Mount of Olives."

He continued, "Zohar was at the base securing the people that were climbing when a few of the men went up ahead of the group on the rock surface the man that Zohar was holding the rope for was about half way up the embankment and then one of the others, a portly man, started clowning around. The man jumped on his back and held on and would not let go. Then the man lost his grip and plummeted downward."

"The grip took hold of Zohar and he went flying into the air towards the hook grip that he was tethered to. Once he went all the way up to the hook point he hit his head on the rock surface and that is when he got the gash in his forehead. Then he plummeted down from over 100 feet in the air and fell to the rock base landing on his feet. At this point he was unconscious and he hasn't moved since you got here and prayed for him. It is a miracle that he is alive and that we haven't lost him."

"Is Leah still in there praying for him?"

"Yes, this is all that we can do now it is beyond our medical knowledge. There is no cure for paralysis if he does not recover and if God does not intervene and heal him there are some procedures that we could take. However we are not sure as to how much mobility that he will have."

"Have you talked to the Odyssian that made this happen?"

"Yes, he is very sorry and has been sent back on a Quest Starship to Odyssey. He will be punished, there is no way that he can atone for the evil that he has caused us here."

"Let him know that he is forgiven by our family and that everything will be fine after God heals Zohar."

Just then the two men Israel and Asher heard Leah yelling from the other room, "Israel get in here quick you have to be here for this."

They jogged into the other room on the other side of the house and found a scene that they thought they would never see. Jesus was standing next to the bed with his arm around Zohar and they were talking out loud to each other.

"Can you stretch out your legs and bend them?"

Zohar in perfect speech said, "Yes dear Lord. Thank you for healing me."

"Your faith and the prayers of your family has made you whole."

"Oh, Lord Jesus I give you all my praise I cannot thank you enough."

"I must go now to my Father who is in Heaven, go in peace and tell others of what the power of God has done for you today."

With the brightest smile in the room Zohar responded, "I will dear Jesus I will."

Jesus ascended to hover over the people in the vaulted room and said, "Asher, there will be a time where I will reveal myself to your people the people of Ionious so be prepared for my return. As we speak I am at work with some of the people on your planet and I am doing a great work in them and in their hearts. Go in peace and seek it for your people with all of your heart and I will soon give you the desires of your heart."

With a mighty sound of trumpets and a resplendent burst of glory Jesus ascended into heaven. Israel's family was left there in awe and they immediately started worshiping Jesus for what he had done in their life today. In tears Israel and Leah went over and gave Zohar a huge hug as they all were worshiping. Tears also were flowing down the cheeks of Zohar as he lifted his hands and began to praise and sing.

"I was lame and now I am healed,
Jesus glory has been revealed,
He has made himself real,
And my legs I can now feel,
I will praise the greatness of your power,
I will sing healed and revel in this wonder,
You can do all things now I know,
Jesus let your power flow,
Manifest yourself in my life,
Make my testimony a beacon of light,
That all may come to know your glory,
In the wonders of your power in my story,

You are great and mighty to be praised,
I stand in awe and will always be amazed,
In your works and in all of your promises,
Your glory resounds in all of my praises,
You alone are God,
I will stand in awe,
Forgiven by grace,
I have seen his face,
I will never be the same,
For when his glory came,
I will sing of his love forever,
Of his power and mighty splendor,
I will worship you with an open heart,
Ready to receive all that your grace imparts,
This freedom that I now know,
I will live for you and let it show.

"What glory and grace you exhibit oh, Lord. We cannot thank you enough." The others in the room were all singing their own songs as Zohar was singing his. Leah sang a beautiful hymn and her voice was angelic and her melodies were that of a choir from heaven.

Israel loved to hear her sing and would always give her a standing ovation after every performance that she gave. He would tell her of how proud he was to have her as a wife. Asher could hit some notes too he was more of a Bass singer and would fill the melodies of the others as they all melded into unison.

As all worship should be they sensed the presence of Jesus even after he had left the room. The thought of the essence of Jesus was on their hearts as they praised his holy name. As Asher sang out he could still see the face of Jesus in his mind just as he had revealed himself to him just moments earlier. His mind traced back his words and his actions and the way he moved then elevated above them. The most striking image that he thought of as he sang was the brilliant light that was left in his departing wake.

Asher's heart leapt wildly as he concentrated on this picture beating so much that he took his right hand and placed it over the left side of his broad chest on top of his clothing. His hand detected a rapid beating he could even see through his shirt as the threads bounced with the throbbing pulse behind his ear and on his neck.

With all of the pulses sent throughout his body it all stemmed back to a pure relief and thankfulness of the miracle that they all had just witnessed. He had never seen Jesus face to face before and imagined his face to be somewhat different in structure however, the feeling, of seeing him after his entire life of serving him, was something that he never wanted to forget.

During the singing and worshiping the Holy Ghost fell upon all of them and poured out his spirit as some of them found themselves speaking in tongues. This was the language of Gas they were able to communicate the feelings of their heart knowing that God alone saw their praise.

All alone in the south corner of the room there was a young man with his arms held firmly around his knees weeping. He was not speaking in tongues nor was he singing yet his tears flowed like the Acheron River streaming up mount Olympus. During such times of worship it is normal for the Israelites to be moved by the power of God so much that they find themselves in tears. For a moment Leah opened her eyes and saw Hezron son of Reuben there in a puddle of tears and instantly she thought that was a normal sight. God told her to go over to him and pray for him in a small quiet voice from above.

"Is there something that I can pray with you about Hezron?"

"I just don't have it." He bowed his head again and wept some more.

"Have what my grandson?"

"I cannot speak."

"You can tell me anything and I won't think any worse of you. What is it?"

"I can't speak in tongues in the spirit, I cry and I pray but nothing do I say."

"Have you ever prayed for the infilling of the Holy Spirit?"

"I am Baptist."

"Since when did you identify yourself as being a Baptist?"

"We don't believe in the upper room or in the speaking of tongues."

By this time he had raised his head and spoke enough to stop the tears from flowing so much however, his spirit hadn't changed. "It doesn't matter what denomination you are in the Bible it says that the disciples had the Holy Spirit and so can you."

"I will pray with you if you want me to. Do you?" "Please."

She said a prayer and he repeated it after her and then she began to tell him about how he was supposed to let the Spirit work with him. "Okay, listen to the other people in the room and just use your own language to speak and it will happen."

He stopped crying again and he listened very carefully to the voice of Israel every word sounded like nonsense, he listened anyway. Then he heard something that sounded like Aramaic and then a Hebrew word came out of Israel's mouth. "Its not about how it sounds its about whats in your heart that is what God hears Hezron." Leah told him. With that extra amount of inspiration he was speaking in the spirit immediately.

After the outpouring they all gathered around the dinner table and the women were in the kitchen preparing the food for the celebration. Reuben and Hezron were talking in another room of the house and his son was telling him all about what had just happened and he was again almost driven to tears.

Glowing he started to mention, "There is a friend of mine at school who is very popular and has many friends except he has told me that he is very empty inside. He has all of the technologies that anyone could want and all the friends however, he knows there is something missing in his life. He knows he wants to get married someday after graduation and that is about all that he has to look forward to long term. Really he has nothing to live for and his status at school just doesn't fill the void in his life."

"Have you told him about Jesus?"

"Yes, on many occasions."

"Is he willing to listen to what you have to say, did he accept him into his life?"

"No, he just said that it all could be explained and there was nothing to the supernatural. He says I have never seen a miracle."

"Was he around his friends at school when he said that?"

"Yeah, dad I never thought about that. Do you think he would act or respond differently around me if I got him alone?"

"I almost know that he would accept Jesus if he were alone and not under the influence of his friends."

"At first I wasn't even sure if I could talk to you about this."

Hezron hugged his dad and said, "I am glad I did." They moved it into the main dining room and were sitting down when Israel wanted to know why Hezron was crying again.

"Reuben are you beating him again?" He said sarcastically.

It got a laugh out of Reuben. "You gotta put a whip to the boy every now and then, you know how it is Dad."

Reuben then showed the table the lashes on his back. "Don't even. You got that from fighting with Simeon in the fields and you know it. I never laid a hand on you boy and don't forget it."

This brought a huge roar of laughter out of the men at the table. "No, dad, really, Hezron was just sharing with me about how he had just received the Holy Spirit. Even though he is Baptist."

"Is that true Hezron?"

"How did that happen are the Baptists going door to door now or what?"

Hezron chuckled. "Grandad you know what really happened? I had a friend that was telling me about John the Baptist and I just got to researching it and the whole denomination and I became a Baptist."

"Since you're the only Baptist in the family then you can Baptize my new son?"

"Your wife is pregnant? Congratulations dear son."

They walked towards the nearest sink not being used right past the table of the righteous and Adon was holding the base of her shirt up in a pouch. She had gotten food all over herself.

As they walked by they heard Shammua say to Israel, "So she went to Samaria."

"What did she finally get tired of putting up with your trumpet blowing in the house. Or was it the noise that comes out of your mouth when you talk. Either one can be equally harmful to the ears."

Most of the gathered men giggled out a few laughs. "Israel are you ever serious? She went to visit a friend."

Israel saw Adon walking by and said to the men, "At least your wife knows that food is to be eaten not worn. Adon love the new outfit, is it Italian or American. You know that would be a great investment edible clothing. We have clothing that can play any video, you just can eat it though. If you could eat your clothing now that would be something to look into."

Reuben spoke up while downing a cup of cold ice water, "Then no one at work would have to ask you what you were having for dinner that night and they could sample it on your shirt to see if it was something that they wanted to cook too."

Hezron laughed as he said, "Yeah you wouldn't even have to go to the SWORD for a snack break. You could just eat it off your shirt." Israel piped in giving props,

"Now that is some good thinking. You could have your wife wear your favorite dessert to bed."

Simeon chuckled, "Just pay the maid double to clean up the mess in the bed."

Israel found some more humor, "The maid? In the morning I'd just tell my wife its not my morning to do the dishes. So get to it woman."

Hezron thought, "Good one grandad."

The men at the table joked as if the women in the kitchen couldn't hear them so then one of the women stepped in through the swinging door and said, "If it weren't for a woman cooking in the kitchen you wouldn't even be having this degrading conversation."

"Cooking? Could you really call doing what the SWORD does cooking? I can call up any meal that I want on that thing, and it doesn't take any work. All you ladies like to do is rag on us here men so just step back in the kitchen and get back to pretending that you are cooking. You've been doing it since you were little girls so it shouldn't be too hard."

Then Leah heard what was going on out there and she had to get a word in for her own. "Israel it's all fun and games until you hurt someones feelings now I want whoever said that to say that they are sorry."

The men were all pointing fingers so she didn't know who had said it. "When we get in there all of you better be on your best behavior. Got it?"

Israel spoke up, "Honey, we didn't mean to be rude or anything just hurry up and bring in the food."

"It'll be a few minutes till everything is ready."

Leah had an idea and gathered the ladies around, "Okay ladies I know how we can get them back, here's what we do..." She went on telling them her plan as they heard it the men heard a roar from the kitchen.

"Oh that's good Leah I can't wait to see their faces." One of the ladies said as she sampled some of the fine cuisine from a plate on the dining table in the kitchen.

Leah went over to the SWORD and pulled out her Scroll she found the icon that said SWORD restaurants on it. Next she scrolled through and typed in hot Tex-Mex. Up came a plethora of choices.

Fermin's Mexican Food

Pasaditas Tex-Mex

Habenero's Mexican Food

Taco Bell

She clicked on a definition of Habenero then it quickly popped up: Habenero Pepper: A cultivator of the tropical pepper *Capsicum Chinese* having small, round, extremely hot green to red fruit. Causes burning of the mouth and eyes and induces vomiting.

Leah proclaimed over to the girls, "I think I found the restaurant, take a look at this."

The ladies huddled around Leah and her Scroll as they saw her searching the menu for something inconspicuously hot that had one of those peppers in it. There it was the mother load of practical jokes: Habenero Cream stuffed Biscuit: Our hottest meanest item on the menu. So hot it will make you cry.

"Perfect, we will just give them a taste of their own medicine." Leah hit enter and in seconds there were about 24 biscuits steaming in the SWORD.

The ladies heard Israel cry out from the other room, "Honey, I am starving in here could you at least bring us an appetizer or something."

Under her breath and to the ladies she said, "Can we ever!"

"Sure thing honeydew."

She picked up the plate from the SWORD and it was being brought. She went into the dining room with beads of water forming on her face from the steam that was billowing in front of her. She sat the heaped full plate on the table right in the center where they all could get to it.

With a cute smile she was almost to pleased to be bringing them the food she said, "Enjoy men I know your just something awful hungry." Then she sat down a box of tissues on the end of the table and made a run for it.

In no time she was chuckling in the kitchen with the girls as they waited for a response from the men. Leah asked, "Is it good honey?"

Israel responded, "They're just biscuits, they're okay I guess."

To the girls she said, "Oh, you just wait till they hit that pepper cream in the center, then we'll see if they think that it's just another biscuit."

The men dug in all of them grabbed a few biscuits and began eating as much and as fast as they could. They bit into the cream and didn't know what it was, as the heat of the pepper takes a few minutes to take into full effect.

Hezron spoke up through a couple of bites, "What is this cream in the center it sure does taste funny?"

"Mine is the same way." Another man said.

Israel got to wondering, "Honey this cream filling sure is good."

"I hope you like it honeydew. I made it just for you." She said with a crooked smile of course.

Shammua had on a clean shirt by this time and she, just like the rest of the ladies were waiting on the results from the pepper biscuits. "Any minute now they should be feeling it."

Leah said, "Give it time ladies they will be running for the nearest sink any second now."

One of the men started tearing up, "You okay?"

"Yeah I am just hungry that's all."

Then Hezron started choking and coughing, "Grandad aggghhhh." He couldn't finish the sentence.

Then it hit all of the men they started screaming, "Honey, we need water or lemonade, something, we're dying in here."

"Look there are some tissues throw me the box Asher." Asher took out some for himself and then tossed the box across the table. Unfortunately Reuben's eyes were too teared up to see it coming and the corner hit him right dead in the forehead. He let out a gasp.

Leah and the women in the kitchen had the entire scene playing on the scroll-walling in the kitchen and they were bent over laughing so hard that they were in tears.

"Honey, I think that we are going to need that box of tissues in here."

"Sorry we already used them all."

"That whole box? What is going on in there?" Knowing what the men were going through and laughing all the way to the SWORD to cook up some tissues. In a second there were a few boxes of the stuff in the SWORD and she took them out and handed them to the ladies. She then took a box into the dining room and sat it on the table again.

"If its that good that all of you are crying then I will just make some more."

"No No. Please don't. No more biscuits." Reuben heard laughs from the kitchen and held out his hand shaking it in protest.

By that time everyone at the table was either crying or running to a sink to get the burn out of their eyes. "Honey, just rub your eyes with your hands you really don't need tissues."

There was habenero cream all over their hands as some of them began to wipe away their tears and really dig in with their cream soaked hands. Naturally this only made the men cry even more.

Israel did this and in no time he too was running to the bathroom. Hezron had his whole face submerged in the sink in water. "Move out of the way." Israel said. Hezron didn't budge. He went to another sink and stood there face to the stream soaking in and washing off his hands and eyes with soap.

About ten minutes later they had all calmed down and were back at the table speechless and dumbfounded. Hezron asked, "What was in those biscuits?" Israel thought for a second, "Let's ask Leah."

The ladies were still laughing their aprons off as they had replayed the scene on the walling and were watching it over again.

"Honey could you come in here for a minute." Israel tearingly said.

"Sure thing honeydew." The always perfect Leah responded.

She got there and, "What is it? It looks like those biscuits didn't agree with your stomach's."

"No, they didn't and that's what I want to talk to you about. Can you tell me what was in those biscuits? And where did you get them from."

Leah responded, "Just a recipe that I found on the SWORD that's all. Listen I would love to answer all of your questions, I have to get food on the table though so y'all just hang on."

"Hold on there honey, why did you give us those awful hot biscuits?"

"Okay, it was just to teach you men a lesson. You shouldn't go around hurting people's feelings."

"So that's what all of this is about?"

"Now, what I think all of you should do is go and tell your wives and mothers that you are sorry."

Reluctantly Israel stood up and went into the kitchen as the other men did the same. "Okay we'll say we're sorry."

All of them men began hugging their wives, "I am sorry babalicious, do you forgive me?"

"I guess, from now on you have to be nicer and more sensitive to a woman you got it?"

"Got it."

He then leaned in to kiss her and, "No, no! Those hot lips? You better soak those in tomato juice before you kiss me with those habenero things again. I don't want to get burned."

Israel heard the conversation and spoke up, "Habenero peppers? Is that what you put in those biscuits?"

"No, I didn't put the habeneros in there it came like that I just ordered it. That's all."

"Okay I get it we men are all sorry for saying that you girls aren't good cooks. Forgiven?"

Leah piped in, "Not until you sample out latest creations." Israel grabbed his stomach, "I don't think I am hungry anymore."

Reuben said, "Yeah me either."

All of the food that the ladies of the house of Israel had been preparing were now being placed on the table and the women were starved and ready to enjoy the fruits of their labor. The setting was established in all congruence with an air of honor to the holy and magnificent God that they all served as they began to close their eyes and pray.

Israel began the prayer, "Father in the name of Jesus we come to you with thankful hearts open to your Holy Spirit that He may guide and bless us as we gather on this day that you have given us. Let us partake in this blessed food in the memory of the life of your son Jesus and may we grow to be more like him in body, mind, and spirit. We thank you for all that you have done in our lives and for all that you continue to do for us in the name of Jesus, Amen."

Dan was back from the restroom and had finished wiping his eyes of the effects that the intense heat of the habenero peppers bring. He took his seat after the prayer was over.

Simeon said to Dan, "How has Hushim been doing in school? Last that I had heard he was joining the choir."

"Yeah, you should hear this. He is doing amazingly well. He started out in the basic Choir and couldn't hit a note if it was played for him. After a few weeks he became friends with some real note ringers. He began practicing with them and the rest is history."

"His teacher is really down to Earth, has a real knack for bringing out the best in his students, and he can do it and make them laugh like the best of comedians. So he has been working with him and found a range that he can sing in and hear in so he made him a tenor. Hushim worked everyday after school was out and he developed a Luciano Pavarotti flair for the classics. His teacher selected him in a duet for competition and they struggled through the first song."

The story went on, "However, the other competitors made some mistakes and they advanced to regionals. Before regionals we prayed that God would bring all things to his remembrance and that God would anoint his voice. He sang and it turned out to be his best performance and the duet went to the Global contest."

Israel was pleased and said, "That is really something so how did he do at the Globals?"

"At first it didn't look good at all because his partner Beth Haran got laryngitis two days before they were to go on stage. Then the doctors said that she couldn't sing or even talk for another month, their instructor prayed for her and God miraculously healed her. They went on stage and Hushim said that his eyes got very blurry right before they qued them to start. This was a song that they gave him a few hours earlier to work on and when he had his vision he envisioned how he would sing it. He said a prayer being totally deprived of his vision and closed his eyes and sang the entire song from God."

"Does he have a photographic memory?"

"Not at all, he said that when his eyes were closed God showed him the notes a few seconds before he was supposed to sing them and he hit every note perfectly."

"We want to know how did they do?"

Dan looked down in between a bite from the spoon. "He did his best and as you all know sometimes that there are just other people that are out there that are more talented than you are and he had only been in Choir three months so..."

"That is so sad he made it that far and they didn't win. How did he take it?"

"How did he take it?"

Dan whipped out his Scroll and then on the Scroll-walling all around them there was a picture of him holding a holographic note that said something at the base that was not discernible with the picture quality.

"At least they gave him a trophy for his efforts, I bet they didn't even know that he couldn't see the notes."

"Actually the judge told their instructor that there was something that was resonating from Hushim's voice that sounded like an angel that had visited him, and he could just hear the anointing in his voice. So they gave him a perfect score and Hushim and Beth won Globals."

Israel reflected, "That is truly a testament to what God can do when you believe and call on his name, and ask for his blessings."

Leah agreed, "That is so amazing after three months of singing and he won Globals. God is at work in his life I think that he has a calling to be a worship leader."

Dan smiled, "His instructor has moved him to his elite class called Choir worship and praise, where they learn to write and perform praise and worship songs all to glorify Jesus."

Leah saw Hezron there not eating a thing talking to no one, "Hezron would you like to tell us about how you are doing in school or about how you became a Baptist. I am sure you are very excited about that."

"Sure, I am very excited about Jesus and all that he has done, I am not so sure if you could confine my beliefs to being just a Baptist I just researched it and found it to be completely amazing. I am like the rest of you not being constrained to a denomination I am just stricken with the love of Jesus and what God did for us."

"Have you gotten a chance to witness at school?"

"Not yet, I will though and I am praying that God gives me the words to say."

Simeon was in between potatoes and a bite from a burger. "I know that when I was in school I was very timid about witnessing and Israel gave me some encouraging words that really helped."

Hezron's eyes perked up like a dogs ears that heard his masters voice, "You were a witness in school? Did you lead anyone to the Lord?"

Simeon began his story, "I remember the first person that I got a chance to talk about Jesus to it was definitely earth shaking. I was sweating and I had no idea what to say and God just gave me the words. The person that I was talking to was somewhat popular and after she received Jesus she told her friends and then one day they all came to me and started debating theology and other cultural norms."

"One of the girls said that in the 17thcentury on Earth there was a man named Rene Descartes that said, "I think therefore I am.""

"What do you think about this statement Hezron?"

Hezron seemed puzzled, "I don't just think I am saved by the blood of Jesus I know."

Simeon picked it up there, "I am infers identity and our identity cannot be based merely on what we think because we think many things that prove to be right and wrong. I think that the truest statement should be said, "I believe therefore I am." It matters not to our true identity what we think but what we believe. I told them what we believe is what defines us. And then I asked them what do they believe in. They said that they really didn't believe in God."

Hezron was at the edge of his seat, "So did you lead them all to the Lord?"

"No, I didn't." Simeon said taking a sip of water.

"Well then what happened?" Hezron had to know.

Simeon continued, "Not at first, what I told them all, as they were standing around me, was that if they wanted to go to Heaven that there was only one way to get there, and that is through Jesus. The bell rang and they scattered. A few days passed and one of the girls that was there that day came to me during lunch and asked why there were so many religions? I told her that in all of the religions around the Universe there is only one that can actually save you from going to hell and that is through Jesus."

Simeon had a quick bite then got back to talking, "Jesus said that, 'I am the way, the truth, and the life and no one comes to the Father accept through me.' Then I told her about the life death and resurrection and that no man accept for Jesus was God's son and that no other man in history has ever actually been resurrected by God to live forever. This was God's gift to mankind that they might be forgiven of their sins and receive everlasting life in Heaven. The girl then said that she wanted to go to Heaven and I lead her in prayer and she accepted Jesus. After several weeks had passed the entire group of girls had received Jesus and they all went to my church. The girl that I talked to at lunch that day became my wife."

Leah saw that Hezron was very inspired, "You never know, Hezron, maybe one of these girls that you minister to at school could someday become your wife just like Simeon."

A voice from the other side of the table came forth, "Just make sure she is good looking and that she likes to cook."

Israel had to get his two cents in, "That doesn't mean for you not to minister to the ones that aren't pretty because God wants all to be saved and to know the grace of Jesus. When you witness don't be a respecter of persons, God isn't."

Asher needed to explain himself, "All I was saying was that when you get married and you pick out the girl just make sure she has a nice face that you won't grow easily tired of seeing because you will have to see her for all of eternity."

"Asher, I have good tastes in women don't worry about me I look at the heart more than I look at the exterior."

Leah was happy to hear that, "You have great wisdom Hezron you will make an excellent husband and Dad I just know it. When God chooses his people to represent his Kingdom he looks at their heart."

Israel was busy talking to Dan and he asked him, "Do you think that you could get Hushim to sing for us sometime?"

"Sure, I don't see why not. I don't think he is doing anything right now I'll get him for you and he can sing after dinner. How does that sound?"

"That would be wonderful."

With his Scroll in his hand he selected the option to talk to his son, they talked, and in minutes he was there in the room giving hugs to everyone.

"Your Dad told us about your new found singing ability that God has given you. Congratulations on winning Globals."

"Thank you so much, I am sure you know it wasn't my ability it was all God and to him be all the glory."

They were all finishing up on their food and most were already standing around talking. "So what do you want for me to sing? I can sing a song that I wrote in class if you want."

Hezron spoke up, "Have you written any about witnessing to the lost?"

Hushim had to think of all of the ones that he had written, "Yes, I have its called..."

Israel then said proudly, "Well we are all ears." Hushim began singing:

Thinking of the life she wanted her baby to have she was rocking,

Gently and searching for answers as her husband was leaving,

He said that he was going to church and that there was an answer,

As he returned he spoke of the love that Jesus has even for the sinner,

I was once a sinner and I am here to tell you of the wonders of his love,

Accept him in your heart and you will find the fruition in God's word,

The pastor said that he is the only way to Heaven all you have to do is believe,

Say this prayer with me and he will give you all that you could ever need,

She repeated after him and the tears began to flow forgiven and free,

I am alive with Jesus living in me making the best that I can be,

Now I live with purpose to serve and worship as the Holy Spirit moves me,

The darkness parts in the wake of this freedom and love I can now see,

This light burning within leading me to the truth that is the word,

Forever I will praise Jesus the savior of my soul the Lord of
Lords,
    Jesus alone is the answer,
    No longer a sinner,
    I am free to believe,
    Jesus alone lives in me,
    Through the gates of Heaven is my destiny,
    And Jesus alone is the key,
    I am saved and no longer bound,
    So let his grace and love resound.

Chapter 7
The Weapon

"Things to Consider"

In being part of a family there are many things that you would only do around them. In this chapter there is a dance that Ahaz does that I only did for my family. They always thought it was so funny so I thought that I would use it in the book.

There are weapons for peace and also war. Both are seen in this chapter as the Bozo's find out about a new weapon of peace that the south has created. The weapon for peace that I have invented is quite amazing and could be used to neutralize an enemy's attack. Think of times when you have been attacked personally and what you could have said to neutralize the threat though the Bible. 2 Corinthians 10:4 is a good scripture to do just this.

Chapter 7
The Weapon

The face of the General was perplexed with tension as he was consumed by the daunting task at hand. His pulse was fluctuating between borderline arrhythmia and normality, as his train of thought was derailed by each blockade of his strategies that seemed to grant success for a moment, then were suddenly overcome by the brain of the software.

He was interfaced with Eye 2 Eye in a battle creation simulation that he was conducting to seek out the possible solutions to his next move. This General was Aaron Alpha and his goal was to generate a battle plan that would surely bring victory to the North and once and for all crush the feeble attempts of the South to defend their porous territory.

Deep in thought, his stream of conscienceness looked like the terminal of Grand Central Station constantly being re-routed to avoid traps that the software extrapolates with one main goal, always with the final destination in mind. With Eye 2 Eye your eyes are the control and your mind does the work all projected on a Scroll walling in his war room of an office.

When you are sunk into the intellichair and you're gripped by the interaction that your eyes have with the walling, the outside world is just drowned out. You are zoned in like a tiger eying its next meal and if you're like Aaron you have the next several moves locked in before you see it on the screen.

The parameters are all set before the interaction occurs and basically what happens is you determine the locations of where the battles will take place and set a specific date in the future and the DTR extrapolates the rest. The DTR was giving feedback on the effects that the newly developed Blood Magnet weapon will have on point blank combat.

In the simulation Aaron was finding that this new weapon would not be matched by anything that the South would have by then. However when he selected future battles there was an outcome that always found Aaron on the losing end.

Aaron was furious, he could not accept the fact that he did not have the right strategies to overcome this force that was dominating this simulation. So he researched it and there were security codes that were needed to access the reason why he was being defeated. The South was up to something and it was up to Aaron to find out what.

So he began praying, "Father in the name of Jesus I ask you to guide my paths and show me the reasons that I cannot find victory on the battlefield. Lord, either give me the codes to access this weapon or strategy that is overtaking my Army, or show me yourself what it is that is making my Army to be defeated."

Aaron opened his eyes, got out his Scroll, and started hacking the South clearance personnel. After several attempts he was getting nowhere, "Encrypted, invalid entry, its the same thing every time!"

He couldn't get past anything so he decided to call it quits and as he was putting up his Scroll some pictures started to surface on the walling. "Thank God. Maybe this is what I have been praying for."

A scene started to unfold before his eyes, he was seeing some kind of lab. He saw people working then it panned over to a dome, it was someones Direct-view. It was a dome of polarized energy fields swirling around like the colors that glimmer in sunlight on a soap bubble. A worker was doing some sort of tests on the dome and one of the tests included the engineer throwing a rock at the dome.

During the first throw the dome was covered in an array of colors and the result was that the rock sliced right through the shield. Next an engineer commanded a near by energy terminal to emit a current to the shield and then the colors turned green. Now the worker threw the same rock at the dome and it bounced off like it had hit a wall.

Aaron scooted back in his chair as it adjusted to his movement, he was unsure what this shield was for and knew though somehow, that it was some sort of weapon. He could easily see that it could be used in defense, what he couldn't see was the big picture. He had to have a better look at this new contraption that they were working on so he called on some soldiers that were trained in reconnaissance.

If he had this in the hands of his scientists then he could use it against the South and they would be crippled if it was an offensive weapon.

At the base Aaron gathered the men and instructed them to, "Go through the main megaport and proceed to this lab. Once you are there take out any resistance spare nothing to obtain the item. Take the shuffle cruiser. Uzziah will do the navigating, Ahaz will do the disconnections, when it is secure load it up with all of the equipment and return it here. AIIA suits ready, and take the Blood Magnet cartridges you might need them to get into the lab. Once you are in the lab they should be unarmed, if they fire at you blast them. More than conquerors!"

They all shouted, "More than conquerors!" The soldiers jumped in single file picking up the red striped cartridges from the table loading them in their packs clipped at their hip.

In the locker room they were suiting up and Ahaz had his on and he started stretching and doing some quick jumps to get the wrinkles out. Uzziah sounded out, "Alright there twinkle toes, are you ready for the dance competition?"

"The only dancing that I am going to be doing is shuffling in and out of there with a new weapon."

Amos was doing something on his Scroll and Ahaz reached out his arms above him when the men started laughing.

"Now that's hilarious." Said Uzziah as he pointed to Ahaz's suit.

Amos jutted in, "Break it down now."

The guys erupted and Shaphan said, "Go Mickey Go! Dance for us Ahaz."

Ahaz started laughing to blend in with the guys, oblivious to what was going on. Then he looked down at his suit where there was some kind of video playing. He couldn't see so he went to the mirror.

It was a mirror that went from the ceiling to the tiles and then Ahaz saw his suit. "Real funny guys. Who did this?" It was a video of Mickey Mouse and Goofy freak dancing shaking their booty like they were in a club. Then Minnie walked over and did the robot all playing on his suit.

Shaphan had to know, "Where did you get that from Amos?"

"I got it from one of the new American recruits."

Uzziah said, "Bring back memories of Space Mountain Ahaz?"

Then looking down at his suit and shaking his head in a real pouty way Ahaz mumbles, "Disneyworld is fun guys."

Uzziah went over to him and put his hand on his shoulder and said, "We know Ahaz, do you think that you could break out a couple moves of your own for us."

"No way you'll just laugh."

"Come on man, just do the robot."

"I can't dance guys."

"That's not what your wife told my wife when we were over there at your house last month. She went on about how you can shake it."

"I only dance for my wife guys."

"Alright, we wont laugh."

"Really?"

"Yeah, we promise. Turn up some music. We'll dance with you."

The music was playing a song with a good beat. Some of them were doing the robot and another was club dancing churning the cream. Once he saw them he decided he would since they promised not to laugh at him.

"Okay, here goes." He started bouncing and shaking his hands to the right and left.

"Now that's it, doing good, now break it down." So then he began shaking it side to side.

He wasn't that bad of a dancer the men thought although it was still modest so Amos said, "Now freaky deaky." Ahaz then bent his knees and put his hands on his knees and was backing it up.

Then he started doing something really funny that he only does for his wife. As he was moving to the side as he was shaking it, he shuffled and moved while really getting into it so much that he was acting like his booty had a mind of its own and it was getting away from him and said, "Uh oh, its getting away, its getting away."

He was scooting away booty first till he hit the wall. Then slapping his moneymaker and scooting the other way acting like he got control of it again he said, "Bring it back now, bring it back." Then the men just burst out laughing.

As he was saying bring it back and slapping his booty Aaron Alpha walked in. All of the other guys saw him and stopped dancing accept for Ahaz. He was still grooving it up as Aaron got this puzzled look on his face. "What is he doing?"

Ahaz didn't recognize the voice and as he was really shaking it said, "Oh, Oh, there it goes its getting away." He shuffled and shaked it all the way over to Aaron and then bumped into the General. Ahaz looked up and saw the stiff chiseled face of Aaron and he could have died right there being completely embarrassed. The music abruptly was cut off with a screech. The men did everything they could do not to laugh.

Aaron gave him a stern stare as Ahaz removed his behind into attention mode with a salute. Aaron was shaking his head and Ahaz thought that he was going to get reprimanded he said, "Now that is hilarious. Where did you learn to dance like that?"

"You mean you're not taking me away from the operation for goofing around?"

"No, actually back in my day I could really lay it down."

In respect Uzziah said, "I am sure you could Sir."

Never imagining the General out dancing. "The reason why I am here is to tell you guys to keep up the good work that you have done in the past."

Uzziah went to at ease position and wiped his forehead. "Yes Sir, we will do our best."

Aaron turned to leave and said, "As you were, nice music by the way."

After he had left the locker room Amos said, "Whew! I thought you were surely a goner Ahaz. How in the world did you get out of that one. You backed up your booty and hit the General are you crazy?"

"I never saw him I was just busy breaking it down."

"If he didn't have a sense of humor you would have been toast."

"Load up the Cruiser men we have an op to do." Uzziah shouted out.

They all had on their suits by this time and they were getting their gear together. They then moved it over to the Cruiser Bay and started packing ammo and unloading equipment from the compartment that they would put the weapon into on the Cruiser. They were now all inside with some goof balls hanging out a window and ready to make it a go for the megaport. "Alright now back that thing up." Ahaz said confidently as the Shuffle Cruiser began to hover and go into reverse.

With Uzziah at the helm he said, "Brace yourselves men and strap in, into the west we go!"

Ahaz had an idea, "Can we go to Disneyworld instead I want to go on a roller coaster?"

Uzziah chuckled and said, "Maybe when we get back big guy."

Amos had one, "Don't worry Ahaz, with his driving you will think you are on a roller coaster. So enjoy the ride." There were a few new recruits walking around the training field that were in their path to get to the megaport.

"No casualties this time these are our guys, if you are going to hit someone wait till we get to the site." There were large rubber materials that encased the perimeter of the Cruiser so if they did hit anyone they would just bounce off.

Shaphan was taking out one of the striped cartridges and said, "I heard these things are brutal. Has anyone seen these things in action?"

"They have only been used once and I heard it was on some guy that shot himself with one."

"I heard that they liquify your bones and then it pulls all of the liquids out of your body or whoever you shoot them at."

"Yeah so don't load them until we get there, we don't want anyone of us getting hurt." Shaphan said as he holstered his disrupter and slid the cartridge cubes back into place.

Uzziah heard the guys in the back saying, "What if we run out of ammo, I hear that they have thousands of soldiers guarding their weapons lab."

"You're right, there aren't very many of us and how does Aaron expect us to just go in there and annihilate all of them or what?"

"I wonder how many shots you can discharge with these Blood Magnets?"

"No clue, I can tell you that between all of us we don't have enough to take out a thousand men."

Very seriously Uzziah lowered his head while looking up over the base of the windshield then turns his head to the guys in the back and said, "Listen up, if we run out of ammo and we get ambushed then we have a secret weapon that I haven't told you about. We should only use this if we are in trouble."

Ahaz got very wide eyed, "What is it boss?"

"I'll tell you, if we get cornered by too many of them I want you to do something for us Ahaz."

"Sure thing boss what is it, do I get to hold the weapon?"

"Even better you are the weapon Ahaz, I want everyone to line up and get behind him."

"Then what?"

"I want for you to do your "it's getting away" dance and bust them with that booty shake of yours."

"I can't dance without any music."

"Alright then Shaphan will turn up the music for you."

"How is my dancing going to do any good if they are going to shoot us?"

"They will see you dance and then they'll die of laughter."

Shaphan had a tear leak out in his whooping. "Oh stop, you maka my side hurt so bad. Stop it you maka me raph." In his best Japanese accent.

"No, really though, from what the General has said to me about this op is that we should have no trouble just going in there and taking the thing. There are not going to be a thousand soldiers to meet us there, just a few guards at points around the perimeter. Nothing to worry about."

They had passed the recruits that were out on the field and now they were nearing the megaport. "Hold on to your Mickey Mouse ear hats men we are about to jump." Amos had a red flag that he was waving out the window with his lips about to beat him to death since they were going about 70 mph. Shaphan saw the moron and grabbed his head, that was about to hit one of the side posts of the megaport, and pulled him in right before he got decapitated.

Amos looked like he was kind of weeping, "That was a close one, I was going to get back in. What about my flag that I left it back there."

Uzziah dramatically lets out a, "We're not in Olympia anymore Bozo's."

In the back it got them talking where Uzziah could faintly hear them. "Like I haven't heard that one before, thanks for the enlightenment Captain Obvious, really, I thought we were in Kansas. That southern grass looks like a wheat field." Shaphan said sarcastically.

"Nice grass by the way I wonder if they mulch?"

Uzziah was entering the target zone and he just couldn't take it anymore, "Enough you knuckleheads! Can't you see just over that next hill is the secret base."

Then Shaphan says, "Some secret looks like we found it."

Uzziah pulled himself up with the bar in front of him to get a better look at what was ahead of him. "Ladies I am parking this kitty right here and then we go on foot. Got it?"

"Yeah, yeah we got it boss." Shaphan said reluctantly shaking his head.

"Unload all ammo we don't need to resort to our secret weapon now do we ladies?"

"He's right, if he could get the General laughing then he could make anyone laugh."

"Pretty dumb if you ask me, seriously laugh so hard you die? Really, he's funny just not that freaking funny."

As the men were getting out of the Cruiser and packing up Shaphan said to Ahaz, "Why does he always have to call us ladies, that hurts my feelings. I am a man with a full grown beard and if he can't tell me apart from a lady then he must have known some pretty ugly ladies in his day."

"He does it to inspire us, Jerky. You should know that, you Bozo."

"No, really though one time I was at this circus and there were all of these performers and one of them was this tall lanky bearded lady. Hair all over her face, if she was your wife at least you wouldn't have to shave your mustache."

"What are you talking about? Shave your mustache?"

"Yeah some women don't like to kiss a man that has a mustache, it tickles their nose."

"No way, I wonder why that is."

"No idea, I wonder if the disciple's wives made them shave their mustaches? Or did they even have wives?"

Shaphan shrugged. "Why doesn't the bible talk about women that much?"

"I guess it was just their male dominated culture a long time ago."

"If you go into the interactive bible you can see women everywhere its just that all or most, I should say, of the books in the bible are written by men and not women."

"I wonder if they talked very much back then? My wife sure can talk her head off. She talks about everything. She can talk up a storm." Proverbs 29:20 says, "Do you see a man who speaks in haste? There is more hope for a fool than for him."

"I'll tell that one to my wife when she really gets long winded."

"Yeah, you just do that and get slapped."

"It's in the bible."

"So what, she'll still slap the heck out of you even if you're holding a bible in your hand. Bad idea."

Uzziah noticed that they were all packed up and decided to make it a go. "Lets move out!"

Trailing in the back was Ahaz and Shaphan, and Ahaz said mockingly, almost under his breath so that Uzziah couldn't hear him, "Here we go. A Hippiety hip, and I'll have a Hoe. He is always so serious what's his problem?"

"Really want to know?" They were all walking towards the base staying close to the tree line.

"Yeah."

"I heard that his first wife left him for another woman."

"What? That doesn't even happen here on Ionious."

"I know, see, she was vacationing in Europe and she got caught up in this thing called Scientology and she got to be friends with this lady that was you know."

"Okay, Okay, I get it, so his wife left him so what, that doesn't explain why he is so serious when we go on these ops."

"He found out that she was going to stay in Europe with this Scientology lady and traveled to Earth to go get her back. When he found her she was in this pool swimming with this lady so he jumped in to get her out of there and then the Scientology lady jumped off the diving board and Uzziah got a face full of European lady underarm hair. And he has never been the same since. They said that he had something called post traumatic stress syndrome after that."

While they had the target building in sight and there seemed to be no resistance to obtaining the object, a transcom then was sent to Uzziah from General Alpha. "Uzziah I hope that I find you in good standing with your objectives."

"Yes, sir we have the target in sight and we are about to approach."

The General responded, "Good, then you should be back here in no time. After the object is secured, drive the Shuffle Cruiser to the pickup point and start loading. I will contact you later so get it done. I have one of my best doing some more research on it, over."

"Yes sir, will do."

"That was the General, our orders are the same so proceed with caution."

"Caution? This place looks like a Ghost Town. There is nobody around, and if this thing is that vital to their defense, then why aren't they protecting it?"

Uzziah thought that he had the answer, "Perhaps, the thing is underground and there is more security at the descent point. We will have to check this one out for ourselves. You never know what they could be up to. Let us proceed to the target area."

The men gingerly made it to the building and met no resistance they secured the perimeter and Uzziah decided to go in first. It was a large double door that had a body scanner for access. A laser light enveloped his head and then Shaphan saw the origin point of the laser scanner, it was mounted about two feet above the door. He whipped out his side arm disrupter and blasted the thing then the light that was now at Uzziah's chest fizzled out. "Don't think it would have let us in even if we would have said please."

"Good move, now lets get in and get out. Set your disrupters to level 3. There could be dozens of soldiers just waiting for us behind these doors."

The men all simultaneously reached for the gun like object at their hip and adjusted the setting. Uzziah blasted the door and it must have been at a greater level because it vaporized a hole right through the center of the metal alloy.

The door was then easily opened and they all proceeded through it to find that there was no one there. "This was just too easy, where are all of their engineers? Something must be going on here."

"Sir, there the thing is lets just take it. It looks the same as it did in the photos."

"It could be a trap sir, you never know."

"I don't see any reason that this thing is some kind of booby trap."

Uzziah motioned over to the instrument, "Ahaz do your thing." Then he jutted his arm out to the side pointing at the door.

"And Shaphan stay outside in case anyone tries to get in. Amos get the Shuffle Cruiser and bring it back here. Don't let anyone see you."

Ahaz looked like a real pro, despite his demeanor, he was moving around like a robot. He was detaching cables left and right, jacking up the base for a hover plate, and before you knew it the whole thing was floating out of there right through the battered door.

The Cruiser was there right on time and they all pitched in and moved the weapon into the compartment. It was kind of bulky, they made it work though. After it was loaded Uzziah motioned for the men to gather around, "I am getting a transcom from the General. So keep it quiet."

"We found out what this thing does and you might have noticed that there is no one around you. That's because they are doing testing on it at another location."

"What does it do sir?"

General Alpha said, "I don't have any time to tell you about it now you will have to see it for yourselves. Take the Cruiser to this location that I am sending to your Scroll. Let me know when you reach the destination. I will be watching you so keep up the good work."

Reaching for his Scroll Uzziah pointed to the Cruiser for them to load up and get in. With the Scroll in hand he hopped in the front seat and gave the directions a thorough going over and plotted their route with the info on the screen matching it to his surroundings. They had a course and they were off and moving.

The terrain was easy going for the first 100 yards they were going through a grassy knoll that must have been their training ground or clearing for testing new equipment. It was smooth sailing until they reached a hill and then they found themselves plummeting down a steep embankment.

The Shuffle Cruiser was capable of handling any kind of terrain however this plunge was moving them through jagged rocks that were taking it's toll on the outer hard casing of the vehicle. They were rumbling bumbling and stumbling, each hit after another. This took the crash course training of Uzziah's skills to a whole nother level. He hadn't had to go across anything like this in the past and he would find out precisely what this Cruiser could take.

Ahaz seemed to think that this was somewhat fun and after the outer casing was punctured and it disrupted flow from one of the jets underneath the Cruiser, Uzziah thought otherwise. On his screen red text and diagrams were alarming the Captian of the destruction to the vehicle. He was typing 100 miles a minute attempting to fix the problem or reroute the jet boosts to other flow dispersers. "If I could divide the output of engine 3 and reroute its path I think we might have a chance."

"Do what you gotta do boss, you know more about this thing than any of us." Ahaz said seeing the concern in Uzziah's face.

Finally they were past the rugged obstacles and were on a much more tranquil landscape that of tall grass. Now we would find out if his corrections would prove to work. The Cruiser took a sharp turn to the left and was heading towards some large redwoods in a plush forest directly in front of them. Uzziah frantically beat in some commands doing something different this time that might fix the problem.

Nothing changed and they were closing in on a redwood at about 70 miles per hour. The tree looked to be about the size of the lab building that they had just heisted. He kept on chugging and found another engine that could be used.

"We might be toast so brace yourselves." Uzziah warned the guys.

"Captain we're going to hit that tree. I am outta here." Shaphan opened the top hatch and climbed atop the outer roof then bailed for the grass and went tumbling to a safe location.

Just as the tree was growing a mere 50 yards away his life was flashing before his eyes. He thought of many things at a rapid pace even the tree that he had seen in a California brochure that was of an enormous redwood that had a huge hole at the base that you could drive a car through.

He wished that this tree of fate had one of these drive through options, however it looked like he was now running out of options to take. The impact no matter how well secured they were in the vehicle, would certainly trash them all. So he prayed and...

As soon as he said, "in Jesus name," they took a hard right and barely dodged it and then all of the engines came to a halt as Uzziah had instructed. They were on the edge of the tree line and in waist tall grass. Amos noticed that Shaphan was up and moving around and motioning with big waves of his arms for them to go over and get him.

Uzziah saw him on the screen and decided to circle back and go pick him up. When they got to him he was panting for breath and needed a drink. He got in and Ahaz saw that from his waist down Shaphan was covered in grass. Ahaz said, "Nice pants or should I say nice grass."

"Listen to me you lazy bones, I saved my life back there, while you were holding your hands in your lap waiting to run into a redwood."

Uzziah noticed the tone in his voice and said, "I had your back knucklehead we dodged it over there and everyone is doing alright. So you didn't have to go jumping out and making a crazy mess out of your AIIA suit."

"Now, I know that, and I thank God that we all are alive. So where to next boss?"

"I think that we are going to get a taste of what this weapon can do by what Aaron had to say. We just have to stay inside the trees for cover and proceed to the destination point. Let's all stay connected in case the General calls upon us."

The wild grass and rye mixture made for a swirling crop circle in the making as they hovered parting the top greens into wake of the dead yellow underneath. The cruiser did just that it cruised and the Captain was sure to meet his deadline that was delineated in the orders from the eagerly expecting General that they will find this weapon in an actual testing location.

The course plotted was designed for them to breeze across this grassland for another mile or so and then to dodge the tree path until they arrived upon the scene. Aaron's specific orders were to stay in the covering of the trees until help arrived.

What he meant by help, Uzziah was unsure of, however he did trust that the General would provide for them if they did follow his orders. Judging the outlay of the land was his only duty right now and he saw that the screen was telling him to duck into the trees. Now the fun begins, he could either Cruise on auto pilot mode and let the computer do all of the maneuvering for him, or he could take this thing manually and see how his hand eye coordination would handle something like this dense terrain. His decision was to do some tree dodging on his own.

If he was to actually hit a tree they would just bounce off it and look like a pinball until they resumed their course. The brain of the Cruiser was set to avert any collisions and correct his path before they hit any objects.

Ryan Miles was blasting as Shaphan was singing along, "Every crazy mess we get ourselves in was paid on the cross forgiveness for our sins."

Ahaz was head nodding to the music and when Shaphan asked him what he thought about the tunes he said, "Miles is rad!"

"I know Rhino rocks."

Then he picked up the singing again. Ahaz was in the back with the weapon waving a Scroll around and typing in something. Amos asked, "What are you doing?"

He smiled and simply said, "Just doing my dream job that's all."

"Really?"

"Yeah after basic I did weapons specialist training."

"So you know what you're doing?"

"All this is from memory. My instructor would be proud, I can still see the sign in that classroom. The free that are called wait and harken unto the word of the Lord."

"Did Aaron give you clearance to mess with the weapon."

"Yeah, he would go magma if I didn't have authorization for this. He was cool about it. No hair pulling or anything."

"Can you even grow a beard?"

"Yeah, I took the pill, look no shaving necessary. I want to grow it out when I get back. Here's a picture of me with a beard."

"Nice, who is the beautiful woman next to you?"

"Oh, that's my wife, we were dating back then. It took an act of God to get her to say yes."

"You remember your dates too?"

"All of them, I even remember talking to her on the transcom." A bright stream was being emitted by his Scroll to the weapon.

Uzziah was steering and veering through the maze of trees finding a pathway to the destination. "How did you learn how to control this thing?" Amos said.

"Think of it like this, imagine cornering around the trees right before you get to one and its kind of like religion, you need to know the manual before you can cruise through life on autopilot. You have to have your wits about you to do this one. You have to be in the game and on the ball to beat this tree bomb obstacle course."

"Uzziah have you made it there yet?" Aaron said.

"Almost, we're a few miles away."

General Alpha piped in on the transcom, "General John Lambda is doing tests which you will see as soon as you figure out what's going on, call me when you get there. Follow my orders and remember its just like what you have done a million times in the Eye 2 Eye theater simulations."

His right hand clinched the throttle making slight adjustments with each white knuckle turn with his left. On the last turn he glanced away from the impending target of obstruction to the next one, and the Cruiser barely grazed a good chunk of wood or bark really out of the tree. Fragments went breezing by, sucked into the vortex behind them.

The body of the vehicle was insignificantly swept a few yards off course with the back of the Shuffler being whipped a bit. Committed to the completion of this op, he kept going on to the next one with out flinching.

On his screen he locked eyes with the target distance that was rapidly changing .9 miles it said as he looked up to judge the distance for himself. Just a few more gargantuans to swift around and they would be ready to get to work or whatever the General had planned for them. The distance between the target location and the actual position grew closer until they were blinking on the flex screen.

"Ladies, we made it and with no scratches bumps or bruises, pretty spiffy driving I might say. If you turn up with any Cruiser related injuries please send your petitions and requests to sue Air Uzziah to: flight: bite me, City: friendly fire, State: didn't know the safety wasn't on, Zip Code: OOPS Sorry, Extension: that's gonna hurt. Now let me see what Aaron wants us to do before we get shot."

"General we are here."

"Alright now to the good part. About 1 hour ago I sent an ACT 3 to intercept one of the South's ACT 1's that is fitted with the new weapon that they are doing tests on. If you will all look in the air to your right you will see the large vehicle that is the South's ACT 1. No bid deal right we have ones just like it, if you will look closer you will see that on the runners there is the emitter weapon, the same one that you have in the back of your Cruiser."

General Alpha continued, "Stick around until our ACT 3 gets there and you might get a chance to see what it does. Stay in the cover of the trees if they see you then you will be their next dinner."

"So what's the plan? I mean how are we going to get a hold of there ACT 1 without becoming a member of the torched club?"

"The ACT 3 will do all the work we just need you there just in case they need you in the acquisition. However after the acquisition I want for you to fly the ACT 1 back. I have read your records Uzziah and I know that you have flown these birds in the past so this should be of no trouble to you. Have Amos drive the Shuffle Cruiser back through the megaport."

The South's Argos Combat Transport edition 1 was making rounds over a wide open field that had several soldiers patrolling the area that were all scattered about. "Give me those things I gotta see whats going on over there." Uzziah yanked the ops specs from Ahaz while they were still attached to his neck. The cord broke and it snapped around and hit him in the eye.

"You're killing me over here Bozo you're killing me smalls. Give me a break."

With the ops specs in hand and glued to his peepers Uzziah said, "You want a break you gotta break."

Then he made this screeching noise like the sound of the Cruiser coming to a halt. "URRRREEECH! There's your break Bozo."

Shaphan was now in his seat and was facing the right window checking out the action. "Hey boss that's pretty good, a turtle named Bozo, if I ever get a turtle I think that I am going to name him bozo. I'll paint his snout red. I'll paint his whole head red, that would be hilarious."

Amos piped in, "Yeah and give him some huge shoes make them red too." They all chuckled for a bit.

While they were waiting to see the thing in action they got to talking about Billy Graham, Ahaz pitched in one, "You know that my granddad went to see him preach in one of his crusades while he was in Chicago for a Golf Tournament, he told me all about it, he said that he hit 3 under par and on hole 9 he was on the green in two on a par five and on his second shot from over 200 yards away he hit the pin right below the flag. Later on that day some of his friends invited him to go and see Billy preach. He said that he remembered it like it was yesterday."

Shaphan now was looking through the ops specs and he said, "Doesn't Billy have a lot of sons that are now preachers, and isn't Jentzen Franklin one of them?"

Amos said, "Yeah, I have heard Jentzen Franklin preach, and he is pretty good."

They were all looking out at all of the soldiers that were in the field and Ahaz said, "You know that I heard Jentzen preach a sermon about one of Jesus' parables about the kingdom of Heaven being like a treasure in a field."

"Are you sure that is Billy's son?"

"He has another son named Franklin Graham."

"Yeah Franklin Jentzen's last name isn't even Graham so he can't be Billy's son"

Uzziah thought that his was particularly funny listening to them talk all about him being Billy's son and they didn't even have the same last name. "Unless he took his wife's last name there is no way that he could be his son."

Shaphan quickly interjected, "I know, I know I was thinking of Franklin Graham."

"You bonehead." Ahaz said to Shaphan.

Shaphan had a response, "You're one to talk Mr. Faffles."

The ACT 1 that was doing some flybys touched down to gather troops. Ahaz thought he made a discovery, "Guys, its landing."

"Thank you Captain obvious." Shaphan said sarcastically.

Uzziah was watching the scene unfold and he had an idea, "If we Cruised over there we could take out those guys and capture the entire vehicle. The General would be really proud of us then."

"Yeah right, what about the General's orders to stay here."

Uzziah made an elixir, "If anything happened I would take the blame, okay."

"Okay, I am for it as long as we don't get hurt doing it."

"I promise we won't, we have enough Blood Magnet cartridges to zap all of those guys over there."

"Let's do it!" Ahaz said obliviously confident.

"Here's the plan." Uzziah told them the plan and they seemed to have no reservations about it so they called it a go. Uzziah asked them all, "More than conquerors?"

Enthusiastically they responded, "More than conquerors!"

Now the plan began with Uzziah at the helm and with Shaphan manning the top hatch armed with a disrupter plasma rifle. Ahaz and Amos stuck their heads out of the side windows with Blood Magnets in stock. The path was plotted and then Uzziah put the thing into auto pilot. They were one mile away from destiny and were accelerating until they hit 70 mph at about 3 seconds flat. On the way the field started to fly by and a few of the soldiers shot at them but nothing hit it only bounced off the exterior.

There was one idiot however, that decided that he could stop them from proceeding and he stood directly in front of their path to the super weapon. Shaphan had him on target and just before he fired he set it to stun. The guy tumbled to the ground and was safe in a landing on the grass. Now nothing stood in their way and on Uzziah's screen it said .4 mi and closing. As they approached the Cruiser put on the breaks to stop in time so they wouldn't just barge into the thing and decapitate Shaphan. It was slowing and when they came to a stop Shaphan pulled himself up on the roof and made a dive for the passenger compartment that was left wide open.

The ACT 1 was about the size of half of a football field and there was one main opening to where the soldiers could enter on both sides, and then there was a larger opening in the back that had a ramp that was hydraulically moved. The pilots were encased in a plastic canopy at the front of the vehicle and there were four turrets on the top at the bow stern and left and right sides. Thank God there were no men manning them right now, they needed as little resistance as possible for them to pull this crazy and insane brained idea of Uzziah's to work.

Shaphan was there in the entrance doorway and waved to the guys to get out and get in. All of them got out except for Uzziah he was still doing some typing to get the Cruiser on auto pilot to go back to the megaport. Ahaz was stepping up on the ladder that lead up to the entrance-way and the ACT 1 started to ascend vertically and take off. After it got about 10 feet off the grounds Ahaz was shaken and fell into a grass convergence to his safety.

Shaphan was trying to save him and he got stuck out on the railing of the ladder and he was hanging on with one hand clinched but slipping. His knuckles were glistening with sweat as it ran down the inside of his suit. His heart was pounding as his grip was giving way. He knew that he had to do something so he looked down and they were still ascending into the clouds, they were gaining altitude. This wasn't good at all and to make matters worse the door to the entrance-way just slid shut. He was stuck in a rut and was on the verge of plummeting to his death unless God did something and soon. He said a quick prayer, "God save me." With all of his might he gave a last hard grip to the railing and pulled his other arm up so that he could have a two hand grip. Finally he was getting somewhere.

With the left hand now secured he slid his right hand over to a non-sweaty part of the pipe. He then, while exhaling, pulled himself up the ladder and clung tightly. He was now standing on the railing and had his fingertips clutched to the opening in the doorway trying to pry it open. Then he noticed an external panel so with his left hand he typed all of the access codes that he knew by his pounding heart. He had just one more to go then he looked down.

Uzziah was getting fired upon and then as he was peering up at the ship he noticed the super weapon was being divulged from the shell compartments on both sides at the front of the vehicle. Amos was back in the vehicle and they were circling around to go and get Ahaz from the grass pile and then they saw the weapon shoot one blast at Ahaz.

Uzziah floored the throttle and they went breezing towards him. Just as they got there to pick him up with Amos reaching out his hand to grab him the energy blast hit Ahaz. They both thought he was a goner then suddenly they hit a brick wall or something very sturdy that was encircling Ahaz. The Cruiser bounced off of it and it redirected their path sending them straight for a set of trees.

Quickly Uzziah corrected their path just before they were annihilated. They drove back over to Ahaz and they realized that there was no saving Ahaz, he was in a force field cage, and that was what they just bounced off of. Amos shot an energy burst at it as they approached and it too just bounced off. The ACT 1 was making a turnaround and was heading in their direction and they didn't want to be sitting ducks like Ahaz. Uzziah gave it a full throttle and punched it for the tree covering.

They made it up to about 200 skidding across the swaying grass in the wind. Just when it looked like they were going to make it into the trees their vehicle came to a cataclysmic halt. They slammed into a tree, Uzziah thought, as he was sailing towards the windshield. Thoughts of death and near death experiences surrounded his cloud of a brain now.

He had always heard of people saying that their life flashes before your eyes right before you die all he saw was chaos, he knew however that if he did die that he would be spending eternity in Heaven. He instinctively prayed for the best though whatever that might be if he were to live. He didn't want to be in a wheelchair or to be paralyzed without hope.

Luckily the Shuffler had air bags, quick dry foam was injected into the interior of the Cruz. In the air they were immediately frozen in their tracks safe and suspended. As Uzziah broke free from the foam he could already hear what the General would be saying to him and it wouldn't be very nice.

Amos said, "Dang it, some of this nasty foam got in my mouth. Passsttthhooey." He spit it out as he struggled to break apart large chunks by shifting his arms.

"Don't complain, at least we'll live to see another day. Be thankful you're alive." Uzziah said as he was spitting out some too.

"I am just glad that you're ugly mug isn't the last thing that I saw here on Ionious."

"That's just great, do you have any idea, can you possibly fathom how much trouble we're going to be in if we get back? Who knows after this we could get captured now that they know we're here. Think about that Mr. Faffles."

Somehow they made it out of the vehicle unharmed to find that they too were in a caged force field. That must have been what they ran into the inside of this shield dome. Amos looking above them, noticed how it glistened in the sun making lots of swirling colors refracting the light. "We've got company." There were a wave of Southern Soldiers running right at them and nearing quickly.

"Yeah, we could be faffles after all."

"Unless God does something so start praying you moron." They both closed their eyes and prayed silently.

Daniel Delta was with the soldiers holding something in his hands that was sort of bulky, more so than a Scroll. One of the soldiers was very proud of their new weapon. "Look what we got here men. It seems that they thought that they could get away."

"Yeah, we had other plans though." Now the soldiers were circled around the semi-sphere and Daniel was hitting keys on the electronic bulky thingy. Nothing was happening.

"Isn't it supposed to dissolve the sphere, Daniel?"

"Yeah, I am working on it haven't got that part down yet. You know this whole thing is still a prototype?"

"No."

"Lay off it then and give me some time."

"Uzziah you there?" The General said begrudgingly.

"I am here sir."

"I saw what you ignorant crazys did out there. What in the world were you thinking?"

"I don't know sir."

"Next time learn to follow an order. I have good news there is an ACT 3 inbound heading your way in about one minute."

"We don't have much time they are about to dissolve the cage and capture us as prisoners."

"I see whats going on don't worry they will be there. Get in the vehicle and get your weapons at least make it a fight if they don't get there in time. There is hope just pray."

They scuttled into the vehicle and took arms loaded them and readied their aim if it were to dissolve. "You think God can get us out of this one?" Amos said with hands and disrupter shaking.

"God can do anything lets just hope that our lives are in his will, and that he still has a plan for us." With the ops specs Uzziah was looking over the green field at Ahaz's dome. There were several soldiers over there too and one of them had the same device that Daniel had, and for all he could see Ahaz was faffles.

He zoomed in to see the look on Ahaz's face, he was terrified with disrupter in hand, aiming at the man with the contraption. His dome dissolved and things looked grim for poor ole Ahaz as they took him into their possession and started a march back to their base.

Meanwhile up in the air there was a battle of epic proportions going on with Shaphan. He had made it past the sliding door and was now working his way inside the cockpit of the vehicle to find the pilots. He had two disrupters that were both set to stun. He didn't want to harm anyone unless he had to. Shaphan thought to himself that if he could gain control of the cockpit then he could seal off the back compartments where all of the other Southern soldiers were. This was his plan as he rehearsed every move while strafing towards the front.

With his back to the wall he slid over to the only door to the cockpit and then noticed an entry screen that would need to be used to to open it. He then holstered the weapon in his right hand and began to hack away...

DTRSouthOmega3pass.

A clicking noise came from the left mid section of the door, followed by an air vacuum breach that sucked the air from the corridor partition that he was in. The door was opening and he saw on the right side one pilot and lifted his disrupter that was set for stun and fired it at the only visible part of his body, his head. Conked out in his chair, the pilot would wake up in a few minutes so he had to hurry.

There were many screens that were placed in front of the windshield that were at a proper working angle and he noticed that all were touch controls. He began typing and gained control over the aircraft and immediately sealed off all compartments in the back of the ship where the passengers were.

He sat down in the seat on the left and thought that it was very odd to not have a co-pilot on board. He continued to work to turn the vehicle around to go and save his crew. He heard another air vacuum breach and immediately felt a sharp stinging pain in the back of his head. Dizzy and losing consciousness he went to the floor to retrieve his weapon that he had dropped earlier. The co-pilot must be back from his potty break.

With gun in hand he hit a screen on the handle and then touched the base of the disrupter to his chest it revived him and he immediately gained full alertness and awareness and the gun was kicked from his hand. Shaphan stood to his feet and punched the co-pilot square in the nose making him backpedal, so that he hit the back of his head on an overhead locker.

The copilot didn't know what had happened and it felt like someone had poured hot water over his head as blood began gushing from his skull. When he crumbled to the floor he went unconscious. Now it was time to go and rescue the men.

This is almost identical to driving the Cruiser, he thought, as he changed the course of direction to whip it back around to return to the open field. He needed to see what was going on down there so he changed the windshield to a screen and enhanced its zoom to target Ahaz and the Cruiser.

There was a firefight at the cruiser so he fired the new weapon and not knowing how to use it with all of its features it let out a burst of energy in many directions all at once.

In a nanosecond there were dome shields over all of the personnel from both North and South including over the guys at the Shuffler. "Now I have to figure out how to land this thing." Shaphan said aloud searching the screened panels for answers. "Ahh there it is."

The ACT 1 then approached the dome over the cruiser and descended to a soft controlled landing within yards of the firefight. The main pilot was now waking, so Shaphan picked up his head and knocked it against the panel. Thinking, that should keep him down until he goes and gets Uzziah and Amos outta there. Grabbing a remote control he then breezed through the ship and out the same sliding door that he had climbed into. Jumping down the steps he hit the screen and the dome dissolved and Shaphan stunned the last standing soldier which was Daniel.

Uzziah and Amos were still inside the Cruiser, "You guys alright in there?" Uzziah's heart was about to explode,

"Thank God, see Amos I told you God answers prayers. Yeah, we are fine, one hit to the shoulder and neck area, only a stun though, nothing serious."

Just like the eyes of Texas the General was still watching, "Uzziah I need for Amos to drive the Cruiser back through the megaport and you take control of the ACT 1 keep those sections sealed we'll take them as prisoners. Shaphan you really saved our hide out there we all owe you one. I need for you to go with Uzziah and bring that kitty back to poppa the ACT 3 will lead the way. Oh yeah, and don't forget to go and get Ahaz. That's all from me, see you soldiers soon."

The men found themselves making their way back to the North's base leaving only a trail of utter elation and jubilation in their wake of blown air and dust either from the newly acquired ACT 1 or from the much beloved Shuffle Cruiser. You have to admit that it was all out and complete thievery however, they had a good reason for it, and to them their cause was just and they had collateral, actual prisoners from the south.

This was enough to make the ecstatic General Aaron Alpha filled with glee. The sky was orange and pink and very fittingly so because they were coming up and the men at the base better get this party started and Aaron would be the first to pour the bubbly.

They were all Christians of course however they looked at it like this, Jesus' first miracle was to turn water into wine so they thought imbibing a little bubbly in moderation was only appropriate for this kind of situation. One of great celebration and the extension of which would all be decided when the time came. When the ACT 1 landed on North soil there was naturally a welcoming party that imbued the air with a buzz of excitement, Aaron and Sharon were the first to do the greeting of the much heralded Captain.

Aaron's smile permeated the emotions of the stair descending Captain Uzziah and then Aaron threw his arms up in the air saying, "We did it!" with all the exhilaration that his heart was capable of containing.

The crowd that was gathered cheered as Aaron hugged Uzziah and Shaphan and a minute later the men got the hugs that they had been waiting for. The new Mrs. Upsilon was there with tears, wiped, then a smile as her head dropped in relief he was okay, then the embrace just seemed to seal it all.

Today was different for the men that were catching a new glimpse of a side of the General that they hadn't usually seen. Some would say that the General even gave himself orders to have this or that emotion and unless it was an order from the top he wouldn't even think of that emotion. It could be said among the ranks that Aaron was a tough and hard man, the men that really knew him saw that he was just as capable of honor and love as the rest of us, perhaps even more so than the norm as the occasion was justified for it.

Ahaz and Amos were quick to follow in the greeting as they arrived in the Cruiser to a warm welcome. After Ahaz got past the greeting of Aaron and Sharon, he ran to the loving arms of his wife, and in the hug he lifted her up off the floor and she bent her knees in the summer dress and they did a twirl swishing in the cool breeze God had sent just for them.

The General couldn't have been happier with his men out there on the field today. Now they were all gathered around the tables that were set up for them closer to the base. Aaron saw everyone out there, celebrating like they were, and he decided to make a toast. "Everyone listen up the General wants to make a toast." Shaphan shouted out above the crowd.

"I would like to make a toast to all who serve under the North Army and all North Forces. Today four men went out there and made history for us and I want to personally thank them for all that they contribute to this planet. In the simulations that I have undergone it seems with the acquisition of this new technology we will win this war, as of now it is only a matter of time before we destroy the South and gain complete control of the element Vionium. So to winning the war!"

All that were paying attention and that could hear the General said in unison, "To winning the war!"

Chapter 8
The Receiving End

"Things to Consider"

I have a friend Tregg Passmore that I grew up with in school and he has to be one of my funniest friends. In school we would always joke around about being picked up by aliens and talk about the movie Fire in the Sky which is a great alien movie. Tregg is now a pilot and I thought that it would just be great to have him fly one of my ACT Argos Combat Transports which is a large aircraft in the book. Eddie is another one of my friends that is hilarious too and he is now a great musician and we always used to joke about anything so together here in the book I have Captain and Co-pilot Eddie and Tregg two of the funniest guys I know. Think about what some of your friends from high school are doing these day and maybe you might want to give them a call.

Chapter 8
The Receiving End

Athenia had just suffered a cataclysmic string of events that would leave them crippled and unable to defend their territory. All of those who were at the scene were now back at the base and telling the other soldiers about what had just occurred. Daniel had the task of telling General Omega of the horrible news. Walking straight into the General's office where he found Isaiah already talking to John Lambda. "Sir we have been attacked."

"Spare me the news I already know, what do you think I do all day long play tiddlywinks, I saw the whole thing on my Scroll."

"Sorry sir I didn't know."

"Let me ask you something Daniel, do you know what the word of God has to say about this?"

"What sir?"

"It says that in the beginning there was the word the word was with God and the word was God."

"I am not sure I follow."

"In the beginning God gave me the idea that we could bring this whole mess that we're in to a stand still with one weapon. And that weapon is the Shield Cage, it is a peaceful means of disarming an entire battlefield. The Shield Cage is not some Blood Magnet, a horrible brutal weapon, it is a weapon of peace and not violence. The North are out for blood and revenge we are out to seek peace and resolution."

"I have sent out a message to any one that thinks that they can just take things from us. Daniel did you know that stealing is a sin? Did you know that you can go to hell for stealing? The inventions that God gives me are like the sheep of Jesus in John 10:27, I give them eternal life, and they shall never perish; no one can take them from my hand, My Father has given them to me and no one can take them out of my Fathers hand."

Isaiah points to his Scroll and says, "Look here on this screen if you don't mind."

The co-pilot was doing the main navigation and plotting a course while the Captain was programming the projected target points that they would hit once they were there. "I have a lock on their position."

"Are we in range?"

"Negative we are closing in 10 miles to go before we get visual."

"Copy that, notify one of the Big fourteen that we are taking back what is ours. There will be no casualties if we can help it. Proceed with the current course."

"Copy that Captain." The co-pilot then started talking out loud to one of the Big Twelve explaining the situation and Simeon seemed to think that the act would eventually lead to peace. Simeon was also being heard by the Pilot and he heard him say something to the extent that he approved our actions and to proceed.

The condition was that there would be no casualties and the co-pilot agreed that they would sustain this measure. Now they were closing in on three miles to visual, the pilot was watching a simulation of his latest adjustments to his program for the Shield Cages as he wiped his mouth and a bead of sweat trickled down from his brooding forehead through his eyebrow into his right eye blurring his vision.

He grimaced with disgust partly for what had just happened and partly for the sting. He took the sleeve of his arm and got the sweat out of his eye and his vision returned in full, after a few blinks he continued to view what was about to happen down there in the simulation.

"We have visual." Through the tree line they could see their ACT 1 that had some unusual flair around the left side as the nose was facing them. Near the same proximity there was the Shuffle Cruiser that was parked and just begging to be taken by our soldiers. It too had this type of carpet around it that led to a sidewalk.

The co-pilot could see a crowd of people gathered around tables,

"This should be fun." He thought as he envisioned what their new weapon would do once it was fired.

"Copy that commencing dispersal." He had the program set to automatically engage in the mass dispersal of the energy stream once the ACT 1 sensed the visual point. Like a flock of geese the other aircraft formed a V flying in formation that lagged behind the leader all ready to pounce. Only the frontrunner had the Shield Cage fitted to its vast array of weapons, this meant it had to work with no glitches. One shot, one energy, one chance to end this war once and for all.

The outer shell of the ACT 1 leader was that of beauty, as the pearlized coat glimmered in the mid-day sun and refracted a spectrum of amazing colors off of the nose and midsection. Good thing these aircrafts were engineered to spec because the celebrating enemy had no clue to what was about to happen.

At the party at hand that was oblivious to what was about to take place Aaron Alpha said to the gathered people that were all chowing down on the SWORD replicated delicacies, "What a marvelous day, we captured their new weapon, what do you say Uzziah could you go and teach me how to fly the thing?"

"Is doom unavoidable to the South. Sure, I'll teach you."

"Great I am about brimmed so lets go take it for a ride, maybe test this thing out on a small Southern Army base. Whaddayasay?"

"Do clouds make rain? Well lets make haste." The two shouldered each other as they set out a course through the dining soldiers for their new treasure.

The scene was now forming and Aaron got a sinking feeling in his brimmed stomach as he looked up to the sky over his left shoulder and saw a fleet of aircraft all with pearlized green stripes approaching. The frontrunner had two weapons poised in the front underneath section that were identical to that of their new acquisition. One huge energy charge was streaming from the front right weapon and it looked like rays of sunlight peering through the clouds. The many streamed tentacles all went in a flash to their selected targets.

On the carpet Aaron and Uzziah were trapped and they had no application on their scroll that could get them out of this. The General looked through the color refraction dome and saw that his entire Army was now caged by this weapon that they were just hoping to use. They were all frantic and clawing at the shield trying to find a way out, there was no hope, they were trapped.

General Alpha got an idea he thought that if he could transcom some of his soldiers that were in the base that weren't already caged then maybe they would have a fighting chance to get out of this one. He talked, "This is General Alpha speaking, we need help this is an S.O.S. to any soldier that is in the base. We are outside and we have been compromised." Uzziah and the General just looked at one another expecting to hear something anything back, time went by and nothing.

"This shield must be a barrier to all frequency communication." General Alpha said uninthusiastically.

"Sir, I think we're trapped." Uzziah threw his Scroll at the shield and it just bounced off as pieces of the keyboard went flying to the grass.

A collective sigh of relief was let out by the pilots that were on the first wave. "Thank God, and we shall capture our enemies for the sake of bringing peace to this land."

The ACT 1 positioned itself for a landing as the blowers all whirred and scorched the grass as it swirled under each jet of air. They sat down right next to their stolen aircraft and the others in the V followed in formation. The doors began opening from all entrances and exits on the ACT 1.

Isaiah, not playing tiddlywinks, watched them land let out a decree to all soldiers that were aboard the aircrafts, "Alright men, its time to take back what is ours, round them up set the Cages to motion and lets get the heck out of Dodge."

The men looked like they were armed for a modern day Beowulf, clad in their AIIA suits, green stripe of course, and a vast arrays of disrupters and rifles all piling out of every port on the vehicles. If you were in a cage all you saw were weapons floating jostling side to side in the air as their hood was over their faces. The majority of the men deployed their move from the back of the ACT 1 and all set their Scrolls to engage a motion parameter to the cages for extraction of their new prisoners.

Each soldier was assigned one Shield Cage and as they approached their designated dome they hit their scroll and they all methodically moved towards the back entrance ramp of each of the parked ACT

1's. Some Cages had just one person it didn't matter though as they all would be accounted for once they got back to the main base in Athenia. Some of the new prisoners still had their drinks and food in hand and were eating while their departure was happening.

As the dome of Aaron and Uzziah moved toward the ramp Aaron shouted out damnation and plots of revenge for their act against his Army, no one could hear him though only Uzziah who also was pretty disgusted with their capture.

"One minute we have the whole war won and the next we are the prisoners. What can you do?"

"Sir, you just have to think there is a way out of all of this it isn't over for us we just have to pray to God and ask for his guidance."

"You know you are right, in the bible the Israelites were surrounded and what they did was send out their trumpets and worshipers and their enemies fled. In time we shall make our enemy flee."

That never say die mentality was the only thing keeping the General from giving up hope. Nevertheless they all were being rounded up just as General Omega had ordered. About fifteen minutes later the North crew was all aboard and the birds were set to fly. A platoon of Northern soldiers were marching out of the entrance near the tables and a firefight broke out between the last Southern soldiers that were in the process of closing the ramp.

A Blood Magnet flew past a green stripe almost hitting him and hit a Cage Shield the energy burst just slid down the dome to the floor of the aircraft and fizzled out in bright colors like a sparkler at the end of the stick.

Aaron saw a energy burst from a disrupter hit the ceiling directly above him as the back entrance door went shut. The burst fell in a clump and rested glowing on the top of his shield cage. Eventually it slid down the side of the dome letting out small bursts of glowing plasma that shot sparks in several directions. The colors were mostly red and orange like looking into a stick welders bead. As it was fizzling out on the floor Aaron felt his stomach sink as the bird took off in flight in a direct vertical ascent much like that of a helicopter or Harrier jet.

The Co-Pilot, Eddie, was plotting the path that was to be set before them in their return to Athenia. "This should be a quick flight home. I will notify you when we get to 10,000 ft. captain." Eddie said in a very businesslike manner to Tregg the Pilot.

Tregg nodded and continued searching the screen for security issues. "All good on my end just do your thing Bern. This time we land try to steer clear of the lake." "

Come on man, it wasn't even on the map how could I have known?"

"Knuckleheads of little knowledge never cease to amaze me."

"Are you calling me dumb?"

"No not at all Bern you always enlighten us of your own ignorance there is nothing wrong with your speaking ability. Quite eloquent ignorance I might add. Come on now you have to admit that it was pretty funny once we landed in the lake that you hit the eject button and went swimming with the birds."

"Okay, okay, lets just rag on Eddie today. Open the transcom lines to all take a shot. You know I have the controls over here to hit your eject button anytime that I want. At 10,000 ft. that would be pretty funny, I know how much you just love parachuting. Maybe I could do it over the ocean leave you to the sharks."

"Lets not get carried away now, you wouldn't do that to a friend like me would you?"

"Now that's funny, you think we're friends? As much as you rag on me how could we possibly be friends?"

"Fine then, Rhino breath just get us home."

"Hey, I use minty fresh Sonic foam and I take pills, I'd be surprised if you even know what Sonic foam is..."

"Captain we have a problem arising back here you need to take a look at this." A soldier bellowed out beneath sounds of a melee in the background.

"What seems to be the problem Private?" Tregg replied scanning the screens in front of him for a visual of what was going on.

The soldier could not be found only heard. "I am in the main deploy bay and something went wrong with one of the shields."

Tregg tapped out a couple of commands then he found the scene. "Okay, I have visual, what do you want me to do about it?"

"Sir let me explain what happened."

"Go on."

"Jeter was showing me the new tech about the shields on his Scroll and he hit something that sent out a pulse to the Shield that Shaphan was in. The new colors started swirling and then he said watch this and he stuck his hand inside the dome. That's when the crazy thing happened his hand sliced through the dome and Shaphan grabbed it and pulled him in."

"I put in a command to return the shield to normal casing." Private Jay shrugged into the camera that Tregg was watching through. "And then all hell broke loose."

Tregg interjected. "Yes."

"And now you want to know how to get Jeter out and keep Shaphan in there?"

"Yes sir can you help?"

"Private Jeter got himself into this..." His voice ascended leaving a cliffhanger end yet to be spoken.

"Yes sir." Jay respectfully said to his superior.

"Let me ask my brilliant Co-Pilot what he thinks you should do. You know his ignorance is omniscient?"

Eddie put his index finger on his chin and looked to the clouds with his eyes, then gazed over at Tregg with a revelation. "I say you charge the guys to see the fight."

"There you go, Einstein couldn't have thought up a better plan."

Tregg smirked and the Private spoke up taking the offer seriously. "They're both pretty bloody, I guess I could collect money from the other guys."

Eddie was just laughing at how seriously he took it. "You idiot, really, now what you should do is fizzle out the shield and spray some bio-cuffs on Shaphan and then re-shield the moron."

"Ignorance shines." Tregg said sarcastically, giving Eddie a hard time.

"You got any better ideas Captain Genius?"

Eddie watched Jeter give a hard uppercut to Shaphan blood was slinging across the dome then Tregg had seen enough. "I was going to say that, moron."

Eddie got him back. "Sure you were knucklehead."

"No, do what he says Private."

"Yes sir Captain."

Private Jay then did as Eddie had instructed, dissolving the shield with bio baton in hand and readied. Good thing that upper cut that Jeter landed rocked Shaphan into next week. He was out cold on the cold hard metal floor.

Jay rolled over the sleeping Shaphan positioned his hands together on his back and sprayed away. "Thanks Jay, one more hit I would have been faffles."

"No Problema muchacho. I got your back. You know it." Jay said energetically, then pressed in some commands that wirelessly routed the energy required from the weapon to his scroll and sent out a burst aimed directly at Shaphan's head.

The dome magically appeared and Jay got this I have just jacked a homer smile on, and said, "Bad to the burger, burger bone! I love this thing. I am going to have to thank Daniel and Titus for inventing this thing, it rocks! And most of all..."

Jay pointed over to Jeter expecting him to finish the sentence and they both said, "God rocks! Ahh yeah he's tha bomb. You know it!" Jay said again energetically with his personal air of personality signature to it.

Tregg watched the whole thing on his screen and got a good feeling in his stomach that reminded him of a good friend of his when Jay said, "Bad to the burger bone and you know it."

Tregg eased up on Eddie for a moment taken over by his memories of his friend and said, "Sure is a good thing he's on our team. You just don't find guys like that everyday."

Eddie was watching Jay's signature energy spark on the screen too. "One of a kind that Jay is."

"What's our position Eddie?"

"We're on schedule for a safe landing. ETA 1600 bearing South by Southeast steady at 10,000. Any bets? I say one round for you Jay and Jeter on me."

Tregg's eyebrows raised that perked up a smile, "I'll take you up on that one good buddy and I'll give you a tolerance of three minutes."

"I was going to buy you guys a round anyway when we get back."

Colonel Grant Eta was notified of the General's capture and he was outside watching the last ACT 1 disappear over the treetops as his head began shaking his head in disgust. Then when the feeling of helplessness had completely taken over his countenance his eyes got fixed on the only thing that the South didn't take. It was the ACT 3 and it was staring him right in the face. If he wanted to see his soldiers again he had to act and fast they were getting away.

The Holy Spirit prompted him in a still small voice, "Go and go now Grant, I will show you how to control the aircraft."

Grant turned his head and saw a few soldiers that were still watching the South take their friends. "Come and go with me, have any of you ever flown one?"

A tall and lanky Private nodded and then they all ran over to the aircraft and another next to it. In the cockpit everything, the controls, the screens, the lights, all looked foreign to Grant and his towering co-pilot. They took their respectable seats and the Holy Spirit instructed Grant to lift-off, in minutes they were off the ground and flying, however they were far behind the ACT 1's and they could not see them in the distance. The other two soldiers were in the air by now in the other ACT 3 that the North had and they were following Grant's lead.

Grant was a formidable 6'1" with a buff frame however, his new co-pilot was thin and so tall that he had to duck his head just to get in his seat. Grant was receiving flashes of knowledge transmitted to his brain by the Holy Spirit this helped immeasurably as he would have been a clueless chump only able to give the complex controls a college try at best.

"What's your name private?" Grant said over to his newfound hope in this fly by the seat of your AIIA suit rescue attempt. A deep voice came forth, "Casey sir, glad to be flying with you. I had no idea..."

"You're an American? That's great we need more of you guys to join us, tell me when you get a visual Casey."

"For the life of me I have never flown anything before much less this house with blowers."

"Ask the Holy Spirit he will guide you, before I got the word I was as clueless as you are."

Casey said a simple prayer and in no time he had a lock on their co-ordinates. "At this speed we will never get a visual, however if we accelerate to Mach 3 I am pretty sure we will intercept them in two minutes."

"You prayed, good work soldier. God is always there for you, always know that no matter how far away you are, He is there."

"Yes sir, I am beginning to find that out for myself living here on Ionious."

"Make it so." Grant said respecting his abilities.

Private Casey tapped out some code and then they both were in the backs of their seats being taken over by the sheer force of gravity. They had to sail low just above the treetops in order not to be detected. "I have visual on the last leg."

Colonel Grant Eta said, "Increase acceleration until we reach interception point. Take them out with our toroblasts then commence with with a string of ener-g-siles."

Casey was hacking away at the transparent keypad with his right hand, viewed the simulation, then summarized the results. "We can take out one in two minutes time of intense blasting, we are going to have to count on the other guys to take out the rest of them."

"Is there anything else we can do?"

"I have ran several weapons variable simulations none of them show us taking them all out we need reinforcements."

"Do what you can and lets just pray."

Eddie had a juicy hamburger in his hands that one of the guys in the back had just cooked up for him in a mid-kitchen SWORD. The Holy Spirit began speaking to Eddie as he was utterly pigging out on lunch or now linner. "Eddie scan for UFO's there is someone following you."

Eddie was wiping a red onion from his face and said to Tregg, "Gotta do a pull up there gizer-man."

"What on Ionious are you doing you moron? I will override that command."

"Too late I am doing this one in manual mode."

"What was in that burger?"

"The best red onions that I have ever ate, that's what."

Just as Tregg was taking the helm from his co-pilot the Holy Spirit said to him quietly, "Tregg you are being followed trust in God and you will defeat your enemies."

He then brought his hands back to himself and eyed the half eaten cheese burger sitting on the mid-screen. While he was picking it up, "To the victor go the spoils." Eddie was now conduction a ten mile area scan of the air.

"Thats fine with me take it, it sure is good isn't it."

"MMMMmmmm. It sure is."

"See that french fry mixed in with the burger right there around that red onion?"

"Yeah, makes it even better. Did you order it like that?"

"Ever heard of backgurge?"

"What is that?" Tregg said with a mouth full of pattie cheese and onion.

"Its like backwash on a cheeseburger."

At the thought of Eddie regurgitating some of the burger back on the burger revolted Tregg as bits and pieces of burger went flying in the air only to hit the windshield in front of him. The rest of the backgurged burger hit the cold metal floor. Yeah he spit it up, pretty gross, at least Eddie thought so as he fixed his concentration on the results of the scan.

Looking over his right shoulder Eddie shouted, "We've got company."

Tregg was thinking very sarcastically with no panic to be detected. "Great maybe they can cook me up an uneaten cheeseburger."

Eyes peering up at Eddie just below his slanted eyebrows. "Without backgurge, you knucklehead."

"Tregg, this is serious our last leg of the formation is being attacked. And you're talking about backgurge. Get in contact with the pilot tell them to pull up. We will do the rest."

"We gotta get in position to hit them with the Shield Cage."

"What are you crazy? Like that would work, that ACT 3 is the size of Prime Minister Jacob's house."

"It will work I am telling you. Get Daniel on the transcom he'll tell us how to do it."

"Roger that."

Daniel was watching the whole thing go down with the General and he was already on top of the situation. Daniel heard Eddie say that and he answered back, "Listen those Shield Cage emitters are not designed to create a shield the size of an ACT 3 its just too big."

Eddie had other ideas though. "What if... call me crazy... if we mess up it will be all on me... hear me out. Here's my hypothesis, what if we used all four of them and made a focal point into one energy stream and then directed the superstream right at the ACT 3? Would it work?"

Daniel seemed puzzled looking at the General then back to the screen with index finger on his chin then to his ear. "In theory it would work accept I am not on board and I am the only one who can hard wire a collaboration of the emitters"

"Daniel there is this soldier that has worked on shields before and he is in the back should I get him to talk to you?"

"Who is it?"

"His name is Jay Private Jay I don't know his last name."

"I remember a Jay that was in one of my classes, yes get him to go to the first emitter and have him contact me. I'll walk him through it."

"I'm on it."

Jay and Daniel were talking Hebrew or Aramaic some kind of Shield code that Jeter couldn't recognize. Jay was on his knees with about a million tools at his disposal and using all of them. Still talking to Daniel he went to another part of the aircraft the Den an area Daniel was all too familiar with. Before you knew it they were all aligned in perfect collaboration. Sweat pouring from his face Jay shook his head like a cat getting out of water. "Eddie man, I got it."

"Good work Jay we needed you on this one, I can't thank you enough."

"That's great I just can't wait to see it work."

"Soon enough, good buddy."

Eddie did a sweep back far above the North's ACT 3, maneuvered into position, and pressed the screenpad. Electricity crawled in a glow all over each emitter as they charged up to collaborate. Simultaneously they all four blasted out a plasma stream that banded together and formed one single stream a mega-stream, if you will, that landed right on the nose of Grant and the North's ACT 3. Nothing happened.

"Great we got a dud. Fire it up again."

Jay notified Eddie, "Can't do it sir I guess that ACT 1 is faffles, it will take at least three minutes. Can they sustain the fire?"

"I am not sure they've been hit pretty bad."

This was Tregg's part to rag on his co-pilot, "Isn't something supposed to happen like a big shield or something? Way to go Eddie it was you're idea, way to go man. Why don't we listen to my idea first next time you idiot. Okay, I say that we all turn back and go in an all out brawl, our firepower against theirs, we will pummel them."

Tregg was completely ragging on Eddie. Eddie shook his head in defeat. Eddie sadly said, "I already told Simeon that there would be no casualties. My idea can work we just need more..."

Suddenly tentacles started shooting out from where the burst hit the nose it looked like the Terminator was being brought back to the past with all of the lightning and fireworks consuming the aircraft. In no time an enormous shield was formed over the entire aircraft that looked like a spherical ellipse clad in green crawling electricity. The ACT 3 fired on the target and their torobursts only slid down the ellisphere as they immediately lost atmosphere and dropped altitude and crashed on the forest floor.

Jay was watching over Eddie's shoulder and said, "Bad to the burger burger bone. We did it. God did it."

"Its not over yet buddy we still have one more to go."

"Well then get on it, buddy."

"Three minutes you said, if they attack the leg I don't think that we will make it through the firefight."

Captain obvious Tregg that is thought he had a eureka moment, "Man, we gotta do something."

"Really, were you trained in these situations to always say the most obvious thing that could possibly be said."

"Yeah, it was rigorous the first week they called it hell week. We just sat around saying how hot it was. Special ops training isn't for everyone."

Eddie definitely had a good response coming on this one, "For the rest of us who aren't in the negative when it comes to brain functioning, yeah we gotta do something. Omegabird follow my lead we're breaking formation and we're going to fight off the last ACT 3 until the emitters charge up."

"Got it Bern, on the double."

While the aircraft was getting into position to fire an all out melee on these pesky North morons that just don't quit, "You know a people should know when they are defeated."

"I completely agree with you on that one buddy."

"I am just glad that there is only one left."

Jay enthusiastically spoke out, "You know it."

Eddie was pecking away at his keypad looking at the screen as his fingers were breezing at a cool pace. The program was set to send out starbursts to intercept all fire from the ACT 3 until the emitters were charged. Sffttt! Ssffft! The starbursts went sailing to their targets as all of the torobursts were averted.

Jay checked his screen on his Scroll and said, "one minute – nineteen seconds."

Eddie replied, "Roger that."

Before you knew it the time was up and it was time to take that bird outta the sky. "Charged and ready to go. Punch it."

Eddie thought he would give the canny phrase that Jay used so well, "You got it." All with the same enthusiastic inflections and everything. They were cruising over trees and coming up on a hill top and that is precisely where the newly Caged ACT 3 would crash land. They were pretty sure that it would be just about midway up a pretty steep hill. Notice no grass was harmed during the writing of this book.

Jay piped in, "Ouch that has to hurt."

Eddie had a comeback and said, "I most definitely wouldn't hug a tree and call it mommy however I do respect the environment and the grass that was pummeled in the crash will certainly grow back, that I am most certain of."

So Green-peace don't come calling my cellphone when you read this.

"Yeah, don't worry about the grass just worry about the suit, did you see that guy go through the windshield, its not the suit on the man but the man in the suit because when the suit is off all you got is a man. Last time I checked I don't think that a suit is capable of making babies."

"You gotta admit that the suit could help you in getting that far though, I have heard women talk about a man in a suit just does something for them."

Tregg just laughed this was a pretty interesting conversation. Tregg had nothing to worry about though he was married and had a few little ones of his own. Jay though was the single bachelor that knew the dating scene in America and on Ionious.

Jay had something to say, "Naw, its the personality of the man that makes the man, homer, for instance look at Homer Simpson he is fat and bald and he got Marge, she might be a cartoon but in this case buddies it was the personality that got the woman. Homer is hilarious."

"You got it backwards Mr. Faffles, Homer didn't get fat and bald until after they were married."

"Still though it was his personality that won over Marge's heart. When you got a comic routine like Homer you could land any bombshell."

Tregg got an idea, "Speaking of landing how far off are we?"

"20 miles to go sir." Eddie spit out glancing at his screen.

Jay continued, "Anyway let me tell you just how hilarious Homer is, one time on the show Homer got taken away by these one eyed aliens and they were going to kill him. Do you know what Homer said?"

"I bet you're going to tell us though."

"Being the loving selfless Dad that he is he said, "No you can't take me I have a wife and children."

"How patriotic."

"Let me finish here then he said, "Take them. Pretty funny huh? Just when you think that he's is thinking of his family he offers them up as a sacrifice."

Jeter was in the cockpit by this time and he heard Jay talking, "Who is this Homer that you speak of, is he one of the great comedians like Frank Sinatra, or Frank Caliendo or maybe Jackie Chan or Chris Tucker. What about Bruce Lee?"

"Jeter, you're American you should know who Homer Simpson is."

"You will have to show me when we get back to base."

Tregg wondered, "So yeah that was funny and all, but where is the moral value in it?"

Jay thought about it for a minute and then he had a revelation. If he ever needed to have a moral to the story he could always count on thinking about the bible and he found one, "Think about when Jesus said take this cup from me. In Mark 14:36 when he was contemplating in the garden of Gethsemane on how horrible it would be for his fleshly body to perish. He said not my will but your will be done."

"See he knew that for his mission on Earth to be accomplished he would have to physically perish for the sake of all humanity to be saved and have eternal life. So Homer said that in jest to get a laugh from the audience however if you were to choose between you dying and your family I am sure that you would take the fall so that your family would live. And if the creators of the Simpsons were to have an episode where they show how much Homer loved his family he would take the fall for them and sacrifice himself."

Jay had more to say, "We don't always get the opportunity to show our wives or our children how much we love them in a way that is that dramatic however we can show them through doing little things to let them know how much they mean to us. Eddie, when is the last time that you got your wife roses? Jeter when is the last time that you spent your last dime on buying your daughter a snow cone? Tregg, when is the last time that you bought your wife chocolate when it was the last money that you had in your wallet or in your bank account. I have never been married though I know how to show a woman that she is loved. She might not need to know that it was the last dollar that you had, God sees that though and God will provide if you honor his commandments and live in His love."

The atmosphere of a Shield Cage is not one that anyone would want to be stuck in for any long period of time. This was something that Colonel Grant and his new compadre Casey were finding out the hard way. It had been several minutes and they were still in the cockpit of the ACT one that was just demobilized and oxygen was a valuable element. They weren't sure if the Cage allowed oxygen from the outer atmosphere in through the energy dome or not, they didn't want to find out that it was the latter no matter what the condition might be.

Back at the base several of the soldiers and pilots that had heard about the retaliation effort were suiting up·for backup. In the aircraft the pilot was Commander Pashhur Psi and he had been trained in all areas pertaining to Ionious defense aircraft. He graduated from Athenia University with a Masters in shield programming before being recruited into the Air Naval Forces of Ionious. Everything was routine he had made a couple thousand flights like this one in the past only against a different enemy.

During their procedure list the co-pilot Magor did a sweep of the area and targeted the fallen aircraft. After a check with the Big 14, AI computers they notified him that the people in the ACT 3 were none other than Colonel Grant Eta and Private Casey Gibson. "Sir, I have a lock on their position."

"I'm seeing what you're seeing too Magor. I'll check their vitals to see if they're okay."

He tapped out some commands on the screen and poof, "Just a few bumps and bruises nothing major."

"We will have to forgo the retaliation."

"No, we won't someone else can go save them. We are going straight to Athenia."

Magor interjects, "Think about it, they are probably all locked up in the hangars by now what are we going to do with one bird in the sky? Sir, I plead that we rescue the Colonel. I am altering our course."

"No, we will stay on course for Athenia."

"Sorry I can't do that and just leave them there."

"I will issue an order for another ACT 3 to do all of the rescuing. That is all I want to hear from you plot the course for their base immediately."

"No, sir I can't do that."

"Do you realize that I outrank you and you must obey my orders. I am the pilot and commander you are the Ensign you will follow my orders at once or I will find another moron to take you place what will it be?"

"Fine, if they die for some reason I will not forget to include this conversation in my report."

"Go ahead include it in your report if it does go all the way to the top it won't matter anyway, Aaron Alpha is a prisoner and Colonel Grant will be dead."

Typing in the course Magor hit the keys only with his index finger and very deliberately so that Pashhur would see that this is not what they should be doing. As they were in the air and approaching the site where the Colonel was Magor did another vital check to see how they were doing.

"Sir, you're going to need to see this, both of them are passed out cold unconscious and they are rapidly depleting their supply of oxygen in their bloodstream."

Passhur said forcefully, "They are probably just sleeping."

"Sir, they are dying. There is no oxygen left in the cockpit, they might not make it unless we do something and now."

"Let me see that." Pashhur tapped his screen and all of their vitals popped up.

"Okay, we need to get down there, change your heading."

"Yes sir plotting a safe landing in the field next to where they are. Sir have you ever dealt with a shield like this?"

"I am not sure, I'll bring up the specs on it." He did something and then a complete diagram showed up on his screen. "I haven't Magor, I think we are going to need some help with this one. I'm gonna start praying and you just land this thing."

So Pashhur started praying, "Dear Lord I ask that you guide me in my ways so that I might rescue Grant and Casey safely."

They were on the edge of the field and jogging towards the Shield when the Holy Spirit began speaking to Passhur. "You are going to have to use your Scroll on this one and send a burst containing a packet of negatively charged particles that will be sent to the source that reverses field polarity and neutralizes the Shield."

Magor was running out of breath panting he said, "Can you do it?"

"I think so. If we save them this will be all God because no one else has my knowledge of shield technology on this base that wasn't already taken by the South. And the Holy Spirit just showed me how to neutralize the Shield."

Still jogging as fast as they could Magor let out a, "Yeah, I would say that's all God."

Finally they were to the Shield and now was the time for Pashhur to see if it worked. Sweat dripping in all directions from his head he flipped out his Scroll and began to program a pulse packet. Magor had his hands on his knees and was gasping for breath as he hit something on his Scroll that turned on the self cooling option on his AIIA suit. His body temperature was now getting back to normal. Magor said, "Thank God for these suits."

Now with his hands on his head and catching his breath Magor wondered, "Well, do you have it yet?"

"There, that should do it. Now all I have to do is hit this key and..." An energy packet hit the shield that was directly in front of them and then it went swirling around the ellisphere to the nose where the hit was sustained.

The entire shield suddenly evaporated in thin air. "Now to save the Colonel."

They went barreling up the stairs and through a few hallways into the corridor to the cockpit. Pashhur hit in the entry code and the door opened. Their heads were limp on the backs of the seats. "Are they dead?"

"I am not sure, just get the oxygen masks from the compartment."

"You got it."

Magor hurried as fast as he could fumbling around all of the equipment to find the masks. "Here, you take this one, I got Casey."

Both of them put the masks up to their face and it began to pump oxygen back into their lungs. "Any response?"

"Nothing, keep them there." Magor was starting to get this sinking feeling as he let fear creep up inside his mind and take over his thoughts. He imagined what would happen if he couldn't save them. This was the next in line to the General and if he were to die on his hands. Magor couldn't bare the thought of it.

"What if all of this is our fault and they die because of us."

"They are not going to die Magor, keep it there, they will start breathing I know it."

"I dont know Pashhur they aren't breathing or anything."

"The body can go for long periods of time without oxygen being breathed in, you know that there are massive loads of oxygen stored up in your blood cells? Just pray."

Magor started praying, "Dear Lord, in the name of Jesus, heal these soldiers, in Jesus name."

Casey was the first to start breathing, it was more like a wheez then a cough, which lead to a huge gulp. Then he sat up stiffly in his seat gasping for new breath. He was very dazed by the whole ordeal and was extremely disoriented. "Did they get away?"

"Yeah they got away."

"Goodness." He just shook his head side to side.

"There was nothing more that you could have done."

"What about Grant? Is he dead?" He grabbed his arm and bicep and squeezed.

"Wake up, sir you have to wake up." Grant regained consciousness and came to, of course with the gasping and all. Needless to say Grant and Casey were thankful to God to be alive.

And thankful they were for all that they were able to come back to when it seemed for a moment that they might not make it. Now there were more pressing issues that were at hand. "What about the others did they make it to the base?"

"Sorry Colonel, they were gunned down."

"What are we doing? We have to save them before they run out of oxygen."

"Lets go, do you think that you can make it?"

They were off in a flash and ready to save the fallen comrades that had just sustained a major crash into the side of a hill. The Colonel needed extra help in getting back to the ACT 3 and as they limped arm in arm the crew lay disabled. The Colonel Grant wheezed as he gimped all the way to the aircraft and through the field.

Just while they were running they were receiving a message from the Holy Spirit, "Though you run through troubles I am with you always, I am with you always." This brought strength to the crew as they picked up the pace and carried onward towards their aircraft. When they arrived they placed the injured Grant and Casey in the compartment just behind the cockpit that was developed for deploying soldiers.

Swiftly they flew through the air scurrying to the place that their people were. Pashhur asked, "Notify me when we are in range." It wasn't 30 miles before they came upon the crash and Magor reported, "I have visual and I am landing."

Magor and Pashhur departed from the craft and ran down the steps not knowing what would happen next. Pashhur typed in the codes to disarm the shield as Magor checked their vitals. "They are fading fast we have to get in there." Magor blurted out with much disdain.

Pashhur was doing exactly what he did before but nothing was working. "They have changed the codes I don't know if I can do this."

Then the Holy Spirit spoke to him, "Remember your training, you must emit a pulse equal to that of the opposing force."

Pashhur then was enlightened by what he had heard and typed in a new code that worked this time. The beautiful shield then disappeared in a bolt of electricity all folding back upon the entry and consumption point.

Magor had their vitals pulled up on his Scroll Datapad and then they realized that it might be too late to save them. "Sir we have to hurry I don't know how much longer that they can go." They rushed up the steps and swiftly they impetuously scampered towards the inlet that held the path to where the fallen were.

Once they got to the door Magor imputed the code, "Open says a me." And it did, as a rush of air flew in to them and both of the soldiers were completely conked out, limp as Texas toast in a puddle, upon the backs of their chairs.

"Get the oxygen Pashhur we're going to need it." Pashhur was already ahead of him and had already dug them out of the cabinet.

"Two masks, as required." He handed one of them and administered the other as the recipients recovered with deep gasps of air.

Magor shouted out, "God is so good."

Pashhur resembled the remark, "You know it."

The pilots recovered and they were back to the rescue ship as Magor recounted their actions, "We're completely covered in God's mercy as far as I see it Pashhur."

"They all could have died and if it weren't for your persistence we could still be chasing the squadron and all of our pilots would have died."

"Its grace."

Chapter 9
Another Way Out

"Things to Consider"

As Christians we know that all of our problems can be solved by going in pray and asking in the name of Jesus for an answer. No matter what you are going through there is always an answer and that answer is Jesus. If you don't know Jesus I would like for you to get to know Him as your personal savior. As a testimony Jesus has saved me from a life of pain and brought me into the fruition of a great life knowing Him. He is always there for me when no one else is and I know that I can always count on His answer to my prayers. He is a God of forgiveness and grace and never condemn you if you live by His word and by the Holy Spirit. You can do all things through Jesus who strengthens you. When you are weak He is strong and the positive motivator to allow you to accomplish all of your dreams that pertain to life and Godliness. Jesus loved you so much that He died for you to forgive you of your sins so that you may have everlasting life in Heaven with Him.

Chapter 9
Another Way Out

There was a great tension in the base as the new prisoners were being taken to their new living quarters. All of them were now sprayed with bio-cuffs and marching in succession to their fate. Many tried to make an escape, it was all in vain though as the South far outnumbered the few Northern captives. Arms were flailing and a knife couldn't cut the astriction that was being experienced in the Generals office.

Some were praising the coming soldiers as they walked by, and still Isaiah was displeased with the outcome. "You're trying to tell me that you got everyone in the place?"

"Yes sir, that was all that were captured." Tregg pleaded with the General as he watched on his screen as they marched inward to the restraining tanks.

"This isn't even a fraction of the soldiers on the base."

"Yes sir, this was all that was in attendance, we couldn't get anymore."

"Don't give me that. I saw at least a thousand out there and all that we are laying claim to is 340 what happened? Tell me what happened out there?"

Tregg paced as if he had an answer and nothing surfaced so he spoke, "Sir I beg, I pressed the ignition as you demanded at the appointed time and this was all that was out there at the time."

"Well then look at me soldier, and look at me good, because this just isn't good enough. At one point out there we had the possibility of ending this terrible war and now all we did was stir up the hornets nest. They will be back for their fallen and they will be back in droves. All I have to account to is God and as it stands I didn't do my part. And why is that? It's because of you and your negligence."

Tregg felt like he was dead meat and there was no hope when Eddie sounded in attesting for Tregg's actions.

"Sir, I am sorry that there was nothing more that we could do, and as much as you don't like it it was our best, and as I recall isn't that what you require of us is to do our best as what God blesses us with. So now let us be thankful for what God has given to us and although we have not ended the war, let us rejoice in the measures that were taken to eliminate the future threat of what could have been. Because I assure you that they had much worse planned out for our demise. Think of it like this Sir, we now have their General Aaron Alpha and many of their high ranking authorities and without them they are like a chicken with their head cut off not knowing what to do."

"Don't think that for one minute that I am not thankful for what God has done for our side of this whole thing. However, something that you are overlooking is that orders still stand and as long as the DTR is giving out orders we will be in danger of being overtaken. Nothing has changed Captain, nothing has changed."

Now the entire captured forces were restrained and being accounted for in their respective quarters ready for interrogating. This would be the next phase in their processing and the South were trained in this art and would not fail in getting the information that they required. It was only a matter of time before they would divulge their secrets to the South and with this the General was pleased.

Sorrow ran down the cheeks of Ahaz as he entered his tank and for once there was a moment when the whole crew was stricken by a loss for words, and even worse hope. The ones that tried to get away were now on restrictor slabs that hovered to their destination as the interrogations would soon begin.

Ahaz saw one of his men on one of these floating slabs all strapped down and his disparity silently screamed as the absence of hope was filled with eye proof that imbued a greater space of empty emotions that his heart couldn't feel. The void was real and so was the flowing sorrow that could be wiped away at will however, the pains of capture remained and lingered, and were impossible to just wipe away. Maybe the worst part of the whole thing that Ahaz was feeling was the separation from the Holy Spirit, yeah how would you feel if the positive voice in your head just took a vacation and now the only thing that fills your head is silence and thoughts of the flesh.

It was like being unplugged from the constant flowing word of God that delivered without ceasing, and the rock that you always stood on is now rubble, and the tree that you leaned on just toppled over. There was nothing left accept for the memories of what had been there always, and they were only mere phantoms as they struggled to recall verses and even worse the empty extrapolation of what the Holy Spirit would say during the situation.

They could imagine all they wanted, and they could fill the words of the soft quiet voice that always prompted them to righteousness, however their best extrapolations couldn't even sustain that of a twig compared to the great pillars and columns that were their strength in knowing God's will.

The DTR was just that the Trinity and it was their lifeline and now they were deprived of their source for righteous living in the perfect knowledge of God, and now their knowledge stopped mid-page in an unfinished book and left them to mere imaginations of what was to happen next.

They could thank Ezekiel Epsilon for this, he was the one that did the unplugging so to speak, simple really a few keystrokes and they were disconnected. To access the DTR he used his digital abacus codebreaker and in minutes the entire North captives were cut off.

There was one who had a strong foundation in the word of God and who knew its promises and this was the unshaken Aaron Alpha. Hands glued to his back, he sits in the interrochair as its tentacles wrap around him and secure him for what is to come. He recites scriptures and plots a way to escape even though all looks grim. He knows that with God all things are possible and as the Israelites were once in bondage he envisions the promised land, no matter the time of wandering that could be required by him being captive. There is a way out of this and Aaron knows that he just has to believe that God will be his redeemer to free him from this mess.

Asaph's joy could not be contained as he prepared his line of questioning he was about to administer to Aaron. A smile in hand and a gleam in his eye he asks, "For the record, what is your name?"

Aaron smirks, "They will come for me, you know that don't you, its just a matter of time before I am restored."

Asaph looks to the Scroll Walling which is all mirrors now and slightly shakes his head saying, "Aaron Alpha, do you admit to stealing our new technologies?"

"You'll have to talk to Uzziah about that one I was back at the base sipping some Oranos."

"Don't get smart with me pilgrim. You gave the order did you not?"

"Orders? You want to talk to me about orders. I would like to get your General in here and ask him about the orders that he gave to destroy our mountain."

"Frankly, it doesn't matter if you gave the order or not your attempt was unsuccessful as you know so lets move on to some more pressing matters."

"Shoot. God knows if you give me a disrupter I will." Aaron mocks Asaph like he will give answers to anything.

"We need your passwords to all of your accounts, Directview, Dreamstream, and uplink to the DTR. Place your hand on the screen then look directly into the eyelet."

Asaph held out his Datapad. "I'll give you my passwords I am not touching that screen or looking into any of that."

"I've got all day until you do, so you can just sit here and play tiddlywinks all you want, but we're going to get your GDA. You can change your passwords and I am sure that you do that everyday. We need your genetic digital abacus your GDA and we can't get that unless you do as I say."

"I believe George Bush said it best, "Not gonna do it, wouldn't be prudent." Or was that Dana Carvey? Doesn't matter pilgrim its just not going to happen. If I do that I forfeit the war. Sorry do you take me for a moron? You should know that's not going to happen."

"All I have to do is inject you with this, and I can get half of the GDA its that simple, however you must be conscious in order for me to get it all so what's it gonna be?"

Aaron held out his arm for the injection when Asaph hit a key on the datapad that popped out a small device. Asaph then used the device to press it into his arm. Aaron said, "Here goes." as he lost consciousness and went limp in the interrochair.

Asaph picked up his noodle of a hand and placed it on the screen with one quick beep it was done. One quarter of the process was complete. Now was the time to get the other quarter, he lifted his eyelid with his index finger and hit a key, and a beep later it was done.

Now was the time when Asaph had to report to the General about his progress. Disheartened his joy could not be taken it was his strength, the Lord was his strength, from which his strength arose. One PAST from the report Asaph was in the office and there was some commotion going on so he thought that it might better to come back later.

Ezekiel Epsilon was in the room and the General was flaired, "We have everything installed is that correct?"

"Yes sir, this was short notice we were able to get them in all of the officers rooms."

"Is it connected to our servers?" General Omega wanted to know.

"No sir, I am still working on it."

"Well don't just stand there and thumb wrestle with yourself get to it soldier."

"Yes sir, it could be a few days until everything is interfaced with the DTR."

"I don't want it on the DTR Zeke, I want it on our servers so they can't access it, got it?"

"Yes sir, will do."

"Am I going to have to babysit you and walk you through all of this?"

"No sir, I know what needs to be done, uhh, consider it done sir."

"That's more like it." Ezekiel exited the room and now it was Asaph's turn to get railed he knew he was in for it. He had trained in persuasion and force techniques and they didn't work or he didn't use them right, and now he had to face the fiddler.

"Sir, do you have a minute?"

"Of course I do for you Asaph, so how did it go? Get everything that I requested?"

"Not really."

"What? That is unacceptable soldier the only reason that I sent you in there is because you were the best, or were supposed to be the best, and now you don't follow through. What did you get?"

"I got half."

"Outstanding, wonderful work."

"What? I thought you were going to rail me sir. I didn't get it done. I was one yard short."

"Did you hear Zeke and I talking?"

"Yes sir."

"Well what do you think that we were talking about soldier?"

"I am not sure."

"Half is all we need Zeke has done the rest, really quite genius actually, he set up the eyelet in the Scroll walling of all of the rooms, and that is where we get the other half, they're conscious and they look at the mirror on the Scroll Walling and boom we got the other half of the GDA. Now we won't have it for a few days until he gets everything set up. I am proud of you though, good work soldier, I knew I could count on you when I needed you."

"Thank God, and thank you too, sir."

"That's right thank God for all of his blessings he has given you talents that are blessing me so, you're right on about thanking God there soldier. Now is there anything else that I should know about."

"I have to go pee pee."

"Goodness gracious I didn't need to know that now get outta here, the bathroom's on the left."

Druel and slobber were seeping down Aaron's cheek as he was coming to in his room, all laid out on his bed. Uzziah was glad to see his commander in chief doing so well, well at least consciousness is better than being conked out, he thought sitting at the edge of his bed. Aaron would completely come to in a few minutes and the words that would come out of his mouth surprised Uzziah who was now on his back counting tiles on the ceiling.

"Uzziah, I have seen the future."

"That's great, were we all in Heaven?"

"No dipstick, we were in our base in Olympia, I couldn't see that far in the future, what do you think I am a prophet?"

"You're always so together, I didn't know sir."

"Listen, in my dream we get out of this place and it is Colonel Eta and some guy named Casey that gets us all out of here."

"So you didn't see the future you just had a dream. Well that really helps us now doesn't it."

They were both sitting heads forward at the edge of their beds facing one another. "I saw the future in my dream, numbskull. Anyway we get out of here."

"How?"

"You'll see, when they get here just follow me okay."

The next day all of the interrogations of the North's officers were pretty much over and they were all back locked in their rooms. What most were plotting was that they could escape, the others were so distraught that they could only sleep in their depression. Ezekiel was going in between their rooms and getting everything connected to the South's servers however progress was slow and it wouldn't be operational until tomorrow.

Methodically Ezekiel worked onward through all of the passageways, and constantly on his Scroll. It was about noon and he decided to go to the mess hall for a bite to eat as he ran into Eddie and Tregg who had just finished eating and were on their way out.

Ekzekiel said, "Tregg, that was incredible what you guys did up there yesterday, God has really blessed you."

"Thanks, actually Jay did all the work he should receive all the praise not me, I have heard about your new project, that's really great what you're doing."

"Thanks, I appreciate that we'll be done by tomorrow Lord willing."

"So I guess after you're done, even if they escape, we will have all of their GDA's and we will know exactly what they're doing before they do it. That definitely has its upside. Well hey, go in peace, and to God be the glory."

"Shalom." Ezekiel said hungrily, in his customary greeting words.

Tregg smiled and nodded as they both walked down the hall towards the exit. "New orders, there could be a potential retaliation threat so we need for you to patrol our border zones and notify us of anything unusual." The DTR spoke to Tregg and Eddie simultaneously as they took a decent jog towards the hangar. They could have easily gone through the PAST, they like the exercise though, and they had plenty of time so they could afford to take some anerobics for themselves.

In minutes they were up in the air getting oriented to their surroundings. It had been months since they had flown into the borderzone area that they were instructed to go to. Eddie was checking out and tapping on some key locations on their instruments. Tregg was doing the same and like the good little monkey that he was, he was curious,

"Whatcha got cookin' Faffles?"

"Blue clear skies, round eye, what ya got over there?"

"Lots of laughs, all clear."

"Let's hope it stays that way."

"Hey monkeyman, I just got an order to go East."

"East it is." And into the East they went just on their side of the border, staying good enough into their own territory so that the attack drones didn't bother them.

Both borderlines were set up with them and that's kind of how you knew where the borders were if you were in a shuffle cruiser. There were plenty of times that a Cruiser got tagged by a drone for wandering over the line. On Eddie's screen there was video of the ground below them and he saw one of the turret station launchers. He began to be thankful to God for making him a pilot and not on the infantry, man those guys had it tough.

Although the air does have its battles too and they can get pretty hairy, its just better to be able to hit a key and then you're at mach 3 and 100 miles away from the fight. Now if you're in the infantry you have to run away from the fight, and if there are ACT 3's above you it wouldn't matter how fast you could run you can't outrun a toroblast zeroed in right for your head.

You would be dead upon impact this was something that Eddie didn't like to think about so he would settle for being safe up in the sky, the blue clear skies of Ionious. Tregg looked over at Eddie and noticed a displeased demeanor and started laughing, "You look like you just got cast in a role with Aaron Alpha in a play, what's going on with you man?"

"Nothing, just thinking." They were now at least 100 miles away from their base and Eddie decided to do a scan.

"Whatcha thinking about knucklehead, Quantum Physics?"

"No just deep in thought about how good we have it up here that's all, I'll leave the Quantum Physics up to Ezekiel and his crew." Tregg was doing a scan at the same time as Eddie.

"Bogey spotted 6 o'clock, on course for Athenia."

Eddie started freaking out, "Another bogey same heading."

"Now 6, no 8. Oh my Lord in Heaven there is a whole fleet of them."

"Somebody let the barn doors open. Now to intercept, whats our ETA?"

"According to my calculations." Eddie was taking his time to make sure he was right.

"On with it Faffles."

"At Mach 7 we got interception at 20 minutes."

"That should put us there right before they get there."

"There's nothing we can do. There is only one of us and a herd of them, too many cows not enough cowboys."

"Well lets make it an even fight, round up some of our cowboys and lets just see what happens."

"Smileycat we have a fleet of North bogeys heading your way, do a scan for their location. They should be hitting you in about 20 minutes."

"Roger that Eddie I'll be on the lookout and we'll bring out the guns and armor. Strength for the journey."

Smileycat was the air traffic controller back at the base and just as soon as he got the word the soldiers were notified and taking the closest PAST to their birds. They all crawled into their fighters known as the ONOA or Oranos Nivos Omega Aircraft. These were built for combat and for taking out ACT 3's, they were small quick and agile armed with torobursts and nebusiles. With several hits to key locations to an ACT 3 they could take one out with persistence if they were a skilled fighter.

The coming of the fleet of ACT 3's had just stirred up an angry hornets nest and the birds were in the sky poised to attack and defend their base and city. The pilots who were flying the one man ONOA's were lining up into formation and were talking to one another. "Dirty Sock, got your ears on?"

"Sure thing Madcat whats your ETI?" Madcat was leading the pack and had a hankering for some sweet revenge for what they had just done. He didn't like those Northy's one bit and he was sure to make his presence felt.

"I am right behind you and we will be blasting those punks in approx 3 minutes you ready?"

"Yeah, I am just programming the formation after we make first blood, then we will break up into firefights and take these suckers out."

"Sounds like a plan."

"You ready for this?"

"Been waiting on the word to blast one of these dilly dunks since I was in school."

"That's right you're a newby. Well good luck and lets make it a good night sha nah nah nah hey hey goodbye for them. Whata ya say?"

"Man, I am on this like white on rice, what you talking about? Its time to set the record straight and like Omega said 'Thou shalt not steal.'"

"I am with you on that one knucklehead, one minute and counting keep those trigger fingers pissed."

"Hey, I hear Eddie and Tregg are on an intercept course to head these guys off."

"Yeah, dirty-sock, they should be here any minute. Do they have the Shield Cage?"

"Afraid not. I guess were just going to have to fight with archaic weapons."

"I'm itching to spit some death sunshine their way."

"Torobursts then nebusiles for the cou de tah men. Just remember God is with you. If you need any help just ask the Holy Spirit. Got it?" Madcat was talking to all of the guys in the formation.

They responded with a, "You got it!"

"Ten seconds, I can see them now. Get ready."

"Holy Cow I have never seen so many of them in one pack before this is crazy." One of the pilots sounded out over the airwaves.

"You can do this men, you have been trained, and remember God is on our side. Now lets get those suckas."

Their formation was a V and when the first shots fired they all broke off into a man to man formation. The front ACT 3 took out one of the guys, "I am hit man down." as he ejected to safety.

Madcat's ONOA administered some first class can of whoop em up, "On engine down one to go, dang it he pulled up. Looks like I am gonna have to go and get him."

"Gotta love those nebusiles!" Madcat hit the other engine which sent the ACT 3 to the grassy knoll. Some were now firefighting over the base and the building was taking some inadvertent hits, nothing too serious though.

Eddie and Tregg were now in the radar and were coming up on the scene, "Madcat we're here and we will do what we can."

"Thanks for making it to the party guys, I thought you might never get here. Just do your thing" Eddie was trained in fighting and with the smaller size to that of an ACT 3 the ACT 1. It had a slight advantage over the other guys that were now giving an all out assault on his midsection trying to take out his engine to no avail though.

Tregg was doing the maneuvering and Eddie was firing toroburst after toroburst right into the cockpit getting it prepped for a nebusile that would surely cripple them men in there and could possibly take them down. "And now for the nebusile."

Tregg then piped in, "The cou de tah."

They hit the windshield of the cockpit of an ACT 3 and it soon went barreling into the grass below, "Up in smoke." Eddie rifled out.

As soon as that North ACT 3 hit the ground Eddie and Tregg would be in for the fight of their life, as a Northbird came in and shot a nebusile directly at their aft engine. Running on one engine they could not do such high stakes maneuvering anymore.

Eddie screamed for help, "Madcat, we have a problem."

"No problema muchachos Madcat to the rescue." The ACT3 that was hot on their tail that had done the damage was now being trailed by Madcat himself.

Madcat fired a few torobursts into the fuel tank of the ACT 3 which caused liquid Nivio to come pouring out of a hole the size of a grapefruit. Madcat saw the leak and had an idea. He barreled into the wound and aimed his targets right at the hole. The Act 3 was oblivious to the hit, and was firing off some shots that clipped party of the left rudder of the ACT 1 that Eddie was controlling.

Madcat let out a yell and fired a starburst into the hole, "You guys say you needed some assistance." The ACT 3 went up in a blaze of glory and exploded from the midsection out."

"Thanks, Madcat we couldn't have made it without you. You da bomb."

"I ain't no rookie, guys I got your back, this ain't no thing for the best in the business."

With all of Madcat's skill he did have some cock in his step when he was in the air doing his thing. Meanwhile at the base an ACT 3 had broken through and destroyed a few ONOA's in the process and just launched a nebusile directly into a part of the roof of the base. There was a wide gaping hole and there were now men climbing out.

The South was short handed and all of the ONOA's were tied up and very busy with their own problems with a big herd of ACT 3's still firefighting it out a mile away. At the base the ACT 3 that had broken through the defenses was now hovering over the hole that they had just made. Their back door was now open and some life rings were being thrown out and were being picked up by the North prisoners that were being lifted up by the hovering life-rings.

Soldier after soldier were being taken up into the back of the aircraft. There were some North soldiers that were on the back end of the aircraft that were looking down to see what progress they were making, as inside the smoking hole there was a gunfight between the South's guards and the North prisoners.

So with the next life-ring that hovered down a red-stripe soldier threw in a blood-magnet disruptor with it that floated inside the middle of the red and black round thing. Aaron Alpha grabbed it and shot it at one of the guards as it sucked the life right out of the poor guy. Aaron climbed up into the life-ring and hovered to safety aboard the ACT3. Freedom, yes freedom was now his, and he knew it was coming he just didn't know when, and now that it had arrived he knew that he had heard from God.

Aaron Alpha sighed, "It's good to be back."

"Yes sir, its good to have you back sir, I didn't know if I would ever see you again. Colonel Eta was in charge of mounting a comeback to get all of you guys out of here."

"This comeback isn't over yet we still have more guys down there, so keep it going."

"Yes sir." One of the red striped soldiers said, as he lifted one of the captives out of the life-ring. The life-rings kept on flowing, as the people kept on coming up the hovering road to freedom.

Aaron was now all the way up to the cockpit and he asked the pilot, "Do you think we can make it out of here alive."

"Hard to tell sir it seems that we are winning the firefight in the air, however we don't know if we can sustain this little victory much longer. Their ONOA's are so fast they could take us out with one nebusile, so its going to be a rough ride back. That is if we can make it through the barrage of fights."

"Well, let's just hope that we can bust through the attack."

The newly freed General said as he clinched his fist while he was talking, willing the men to hurry up so that they could get out of there without a scratch. At least that was the objective, not to get hit by anything as they were about to take the scenic route around all of the airfights. Finally the last man was pulled up and hovered into the back door as it swiftly closed shut.

The pilot could tell that the General was a little on the edge not knowing if they would make it out of there, and he was willing the aircraft to safety, as they pulled up to an altitude far above the melee that was going on below them.

Now they were all safe and were skying high above the airfights and were on a complete different path than they had taken to get there. The pilot and Aaron knew that all they had to do was to just make it to the border and their drones would do the rest to fight off any attacks. Climbing in altitude they ascended methodically into the air above them and the passengers were all taken back in their seats as they broke away.

Uzziah was the last of the men to be taken upward and now he made his presence felt inside the somewhat claustrophobic cockpit. They were all in there like sardines as Aaron's back was against the wall, and Uzziah was scrunched in between a wall and Aarons left side. Uzziah picked up an oxygen mask from the floor and put it to his face to breathe in new air that would revive his lungs from the destruction that was inflicted upon him by the billowing smoke made by the nebusile.

Nonetheless all were now aboard, and were as happy as they could be looking out the windows recognizing the ant-like drones that protected their land from the South. One of the drones lit up a flair and launched it to their altitude and it was red and white striped which notified all of the passengers that they were on their way home, God willing.

The presence of God could be felt throughout the ship as they were very solemn and quiet hoping that they would not be followed. And with God's mighty hand their fears subsided in congruence with the marking on the ground, and the scan that the co-pilot ran showing that

168

there were no one chasing after them, so pretty much they were in the home stretch of the race to get back to the base.

"What a beautiful wight it will be once we make it home." General Alpha said, as his dark brown eyes scanned the screens for any signs of bogeys headed their way.

"What's our ETA?"

The co-pilot responded, "We've got about 10 minutes before we make it there sir and I plan on doing just that and making it there to safety."

"Good work soldier, you have done an excellent job in rescuing all of us, and don't forget to remind me to thank the Colonel for all of this. Most of all I thank God for what he has now blessed us with. You know that living where we live we could easily take for granted that we are always safe."

Aaron continued, "You got here in the nick of time they were about to make me undergo more interrogations just before you guys got here. And that is something that I was not looking forward to."

"The way that I see it is that you would have done the same for us, if we were taken prisoner. Am I right about that sir?"

"Leave no one behind is my motto, and you bet, I would have done everything that I could to get you guys out of there if that was the situation."

"ETA three minutes and drawing in." Now they could see the base and the trees that lined their entrance.

"I wonder how the rest of our guys are doing back there, it looked pretty brutal being so high above them and all."

"I am sure that they will make it okay sir, don't you worry about them, lets just concentrate on what we are going to do when we get back." The pilot said to Aaron as they neared in on the base.

Chapter 10
The Future of Christianity

"Things to Consider"

Technology has allowed people to connect in so many ways and as it continues to do so it will only serve to strengthen your relationship with God. The technology of this book the Digital Trinity Republic allows you to audibly hear from God and know that, yes, you are really hearing from Him. He sees all that you see and knows all that you know and knows all of your thoughts. With this He is able to lead you and guide you into a closer relationship with Him. God talks to you through His word the Bible and Jesus leads you through his words spoken while He was on this Earth. What I want for you to think about is how would your life and relationship with God be different if you could audibly hear from him through technology.

Chapter 10
The Future of Christianity

There was a great and unsurmounting deal of commotion in orbit on the IU Athenia. The Athenia was the jewel of the whole fleet and the latest in a soon to be long line of AI controlled QUEST Starships. Once they were explorers in the Galaxy and in the Universe, for that matter, all in a QUEST for peace to do nothing more than help any alien beings on any planet that they stumbled upon. Traditionally the captain was the one who called the shots and it went through the ranks of the ship until the order was executed.

What really went on there in the Ancient QUEST Starships is now sealed in a vault for no one but the Generals and Ezekiel Epsilon to see. You see the onboard computers on the ship could not be inhabited by the AI consciensness of the trinity, so everything was vocal. Some say that without hearing God's direct voice to issue the orders and commands that they were closer to God. Well at least that is what they said back then, however after they installed the first copy of the DTR in the IU Athenia traveling entertained a whole new slate of faith for those on board.

You were no longer living on blind faith it was real and undeniable. There is something about hearing from God and knowing that what he is telling you is his will. It leaves out all of the if's and maybe's that arise in a blind faith expedition. Could you imagine being blind and only seeing darkness your whole life and then in an instant you can now see in color the entire world around you. The word of God is always there for you only we as humans have both a fleshly body that includes part of the fleshly mind, and then it also has a spiritual mind and glory bound body.

In the bible it says that faith comes by hearing and hearing the word of God. So you're probably wondering what are the benefits of knowing that you are hearing from God? Its easy you will gravitate toward the spiritual side of your mind and away from the fleshly side to become a better Christian and a mighty warrior for God in whatever realm that He has called you to operate in.

With the primitive technology that Earth has in the year 2033 they are not capable of knowing that they are hearing from God in every aspect that they so desire in their everyday lives, like the Ionians have, as they can all upon God and ask for His guidance at anytime, and it is there for them if they need it. The Americans have faith just not to the level that the Ionians have. The Ionians have great faith because they hear from God all the time and they hear the word of God which as we know is how faith is formed.

They still have free will to make their own decisions that they want, only if they want they can, at anytime, hear what the unchanging word of God says about whatever it is that they are facing. And this technology that the Ionians have converts, all who are willing to take the leap of faith and take the pill. One pill part transmission builder and one part receiver builder and this is how the Ionians live in such great foundation of the word of God.

Think about it for a minute if you knew that you were hearing from God audibly in your inner ear then you would know without a doubt that you were in God's perfect will. This would dramatically change your life you would seek God in all that you do and do only as He instructs you to do.

Now in America we know that God is omniscient and omnipresent however there is no feedback on how we are doing from God Himself. In the year 2033 on Ionious Jacob the Prime Minister, of Ionious, has Tech Talks with the President and Vice President of the US, in order to inform them of what they have developed over a few mellinnia that could be beneficial to their citizens.

As you already should know the Civil Refuge of the Americans has seen a great success in the new adaptation of their technologies that Ionious has to offer. All of the Americans that sought refuge were already Christians and now their faith has been magnified by the power of God through the DTR and the Trinity pill.

Jacob has offered the Trinity pill accompanied with a DTR AI computer that will give orders from God to their soldiers that are now fighting at home and abroad to spread Christianity to the far reaches of the globe. Johnathan Houston, the president, is now considering signing a bill that, if passed, would allow all citizens of the planet Earth to hear from God the way that the Ionians do.

Right now in Washington D.C. everything looks like it will get passed, accept for the fact that it still needs the approval of the American public that is now on Ionious to vote on this issue. Once the vote is passed it will bring new levels of faith to them as outlined above and should give them new insights on how to defeat the Army of Islam that has taken over most of Europe and all of the Middle East.

President Johnathan Houston and Vice-President Ed Young are now in the process of praying for God's will to be done, and it seems that all systems are a go from God on their part, and it is now just a matter of getting the new inhabitants of Ionious to vote yes for the bill. The tandem knows what this will mean to their current state of affairs in Washington D.C. and they are willing to take the leap of faith and go ahead with this new kind of government and way of living.

When Johnathan saw what the new system could do, in all facets of the benefits that it implores, he was taken back by what this power from God could mean for the nation and the world. He also explored the interactive bible and was blown away by this and knew that there was no doubt in his mind that he could not only provide proof of the existence of Jesus Christ, but also he could mount an undeniable argument against all other world religions who serve false gods.

With the DTR in place he was full aware that the US could convert all of the other religions in the world to the one true religion of Christianity. After a trip to Ionious, the bill was unanimously passed in the House and Senate once they saw the real and amazing power of God first hand and not just in a book form.

Back on the IU Athenia in orbit around the planet there was great turmoil being seen by the Captain and his officers. The newly crowned female Captain Hamutal could not explain what had just happened to her while she delivered orders to her first officer Nethaniah Nu who was commissioned to execute an order that involved firing a toroburst at the port side engine of the ACT 3 before it went into the Northern territory.

Nearing the border they could plainly see that the ACT 3 was on course for their home base in Olympia. Nethaniah executed the order and nothing happened, once they crossed over into the North's territory they were out of the South's jurisdiction and could not be fired upon so they needed to stop them before they crossed the line in the sand.

Hamutal was in somewhat of an outrage and blamed his officer for not firing the toroburst, "You're telling me that you hit the command screen to fire and it just didn't work? Is this what you are telling me?"

"Sir I can't explain it the burst never fired."

"That is not acceptable Commander, give me a full report of your actions and the weapons officer who was supposed to actually fire upon the aircraft."

If worse came to worse, and it did, the Southern Army could always count on their QUEST Starships to bail them out of trouble if the occasion arrived. Arrive it did and when it was their turn to be the insurance run something unexplainable happened. "Was the burst prepped?"

"Yes sir." Said the weapons officer Ahikam, "I went through all of the normal procedures fired the weapon and there it was."

"We are incapacitated and there is a bubble surrounding our ship, and you're telling me that your actions had nothing to do with this?"

"Yes sir, and no sir, I fired the weapon and there appears to be no discharge of the burst. What that bubble is I have no idea."

"How can you not know what happened Lt. Commander? There has to be an explanation for this action. Hamath get me a full diagnostic on this bubble. Security playback the video of the event, and break it down from the moment that Ahikam hit the screen."

The tall slender looking fellow in the chair at the front of the control room was Ahikam. He was the weapons specialist and knew just about everything there was to know about weapons and shield technology and all of the physics both quantum and mechanical that were behind the interaction of these two fields of study.

With a few taps on the screen Hamath found the database of known shields in the Universe. He then did a spectral and energy analysis of the thing that had encapsulated their ship. "I have something Captain, here it is showing me that this bubble thing is an energy shied however we know absolutely nothing about it because it is not in the Universal database."

"Great! Its an energy shield, I could have told you that. What we need to know is what kind of phase modulation is it comprised of and most importantly how do we get rid of it. Whoever it is that has wrapped us in this thing has us as sitting ducks. You know they could blow us right out of space if they wanted to. We need to work quick if this is a threat to our structural integrity."

"I have something sir."

"This better be good."

"Sir, it is, just listen to what the diagnostics just showed me. Okay the Zero Point Source of Energy is coming out of the shield generator."

"So its not of an alien or North origin."

"We can't rule that out right now, what I can tell you is that the passcode to disarming it is encrypted."

"Great! Where is our IT guy when you need him?"

"I tried all of our past and present codes at the point source release opening and none of them work, so it could be that some alien or worse a Red Stripe has sent code to the DTR to enable one of our shields. There is just one thing if it were a normal shield we could fire through it if need be, with this one though, if we were to fire anything at them it would bounce off of the shield and destroy our ship."

"Freakin' fluffer nutter, well I think its clear that we have to get an IT guy in here that is familiar with the pass-codes of the North and the Zyahth. Once it is solved we go back to normal operations and everything is hunky dori. Yes, no?"

Immediately a chubby man with acne entered the room looked to be a geek that really knew his stuff, "Present and reporting for duty sir how can I help?"

"Well it's about time that we needed you in the control room. You any good at decryption?"

"Spent one whole year on decrypting Zyahth pass-codes during the war."

"Any good at shield decryption?"

"I have disarmed Zyahth pass-codes for General Omega during my time in the war."

"Hamath show ensign Javan to the ropes, I want full inspections of the torotube that didn't fire I have a feeling that there is something going on there that has to do with the bubble that we're in. I also want inspections at the Zero Point source to see if there is any connection between the two."

Hamath gave the ensign a lesson in the locations of the whereabouts that the pass-codes were stored and activated in the AI DTR of the ship.

"As you should know we have a cloned AI system of the DTR so if it happening up here then God knows about it back on Athenia too. I have ran the database of pass-codes and nothing that is on our ship will work, so if you are a miracle worker then please have at it, this is way over my head."

"Well, call me the mother of Helen Keller and I'll do my thing."

"You're that good eh?"

"No, God is though, and all I have to do is ask and it will be given unto me so if you don't mind I will start praying right now."

"Have at it."

Javan said a short prayer for his standards however after the first four minutes he started getting the attention of the rest of the crew in the Control Room. When he finally rapped it up and thanked God and ended his prayer a collective sigh was released by the crew.

"So this is where you type in the code?"

Hamath wasn't even looking at the screen. "Yeah, I told you that a million times."

"Just checking I don't want to send off a barrage of torobursts that would blow us all to kingdom come."

"Well, in that case I am glad you asked. You may proceed."

"Lets do all of the Zyahth codes first."

He typed in a few commands and when he was just about to hit enter Hamath looked at the screen. "No not that one you idiot, that will..." Javan had already hit enter. The jammed toroburst was then expelled from the tube and it hit the shield and much to their surprise it bounced off of the shield and was heading back to one of the cargo bays at the midsection of the ship.

Hamath shouted out, "Sir, I didn't do this it was all Javan."

Hamutal was furious, "Shut up you idiot and put up one of our shields to absorb the impact."

Right away he jumped the divider and landed in his chair hit one icon and blam there was a shield that was formed around the ship and inside the bubble. "Thankfully it absorbed the burst and no one was injured.

"That was a close one, now get to work on making that thing out there disappear."

"Will do sir." Hamath scolded Javan for his ignorance, it was new to him so really he couldn't be blamed for the incident, the blame would fall on Hamath for not paying attention to what was going on however, he would never admit that to the Captain.

"How did you get to the toroburst command line?"

"I did this and this was exactly what you told me to do."

"You moron that is the icon for toroburst firing and this one is the command for the shield access for decryption."

"Sorry, they looked the same to me."

"The same? How big of a moron could you be they are totally different with completely different colors and symbols, why couldn't you tell the difference are you blind?"

"Actually I just got a retina implant in both eyes yesterday and I had nearsightedness and the effects of the prescriptions have not subsided yet."

"Good lord, why didn't you tell me that before, I would have helped you to see which icons you were to work on. I am surprised that the Captain even is letting you go on with the operation."

Hamutal made her decision, "I want a full scale evacuation of all on board the ship everyone is to report to the base." Every one went through the PAST in record time and before you know it it was just Hamath and Javan sitting up there in orbit doing their thing.

"Alright this is how we are going to do this, I will get you to the right screen and all you have to do is type in the commands. Deal?"

"Deal, and really I didn't mean to cause such a stir in the ship."

"I just about had a heart attack when I jumped the divider that's okay now though, lets just do this thing, and get this ship docked so something like this doesn't happen again."

"I am here now, just star hacking away." Javan used all the codes that were in his database of his Scroll Data Pad.

After typing in about 100 16 digit combinations he was getting weary. "Okay down to the last one hope this is it."

He hit enter and nothing happened. "Well I guess now we know that it isn't a Zyahth code then. Now we will move onto the Red Stripe codes."

One thing that you don't hear very much on Ionious is, "Are we there yet?' However with all of these codes to type in Hamath was thinking to himself are we there yet? He didn't say it out loud though so as to not put any more pressure on Javan. He realized that this could take some time and he shouldn't be rushed and now his prayers for patience were being answered.

"Do you have very many of them in your Scroll?"

"Only all that has ever existed."

"Well then get to work." Authorization codes were in full abundance and there was no one on the ship that knew the codes better than Javan. He then uploaded all of the pass-codes that were on his Scroll and made a program to consecutively enter all of them in nothing manual anymore.

The AI chugged away and after about 10 minutes it was through processing over 150,000 pass-codes "Wouldn't we know by now if one of them had worked?"

"Yeah, and that's just it none of them did. Let me see if I have this straight he hit the screen icon to launch a toroburst it didn't launch and then mysteriously a shield appeared outside our ship? Am I right?"

Hamath took a while to answer as he jogged his memory though the events in his head. "Yeah, that's right."

Javan got to thinking, "This all has to do with the toroburst so why don't we set up a program that simultaneously enters in all of the North's codes in congruence with each toroburst. Is this logical? I am thinking that this is some kind of combination lockout."

"Yeah, it makes sense to me so why not? Couldn't hurt."

"Yeah, unless they set it up predicting that we would try the combinations and it would fire all of the torobursts at once and annihilate the entire ship with us on it."

"Okay, here's what we do, we make the program to go through all of the known combinations hit enter then PAST off the ship to safety?"

"Sounds good."

The program was simple but, getting out of the ship would be difficult with these processors that execute commands in nanoseconds.

"If it hits the self destruct combination before we get a chance to leave then we're toast."

"If we get the shield to disarm then we will be toasting on some champagne down at the base."

"I think that I like the latter scenario better than the first."

"I just don't see how someone could have overridden the command to set us up in a trap like we're in. The Zyahth aren't intelligent enough to do something like this so it has to be the North." Hamath said with all certainty as the tips on his soles turned and did an about face after pacing a short path behind the station that they were working on.

"Well lets get to it, and have the program initiation from your Scroll and hit it right before we string down." Javan began working on the code taking his time as he knew that just programming a command could not execute it until he hits the enter key.

"You hear that?"

"What?"

"There it is again."

"What is it?"

"It sounded to me like someone was PASTing back on the ship and now they are talking in the Captain's green room."

"I'll go over there and see who it is, you stay here and keep working."

"Whatever you say." Hamath walked intently in and out of the maze on the control room floor. At the green room he heard voices and they sounded like some of his fellow officers that had come back up to see how we were doing.

When he got to the PAST doorway the slide out door slid open for him and then he saw who it was. "Javan quick to the PAST as they both took off running towards the side entrance-way Javan made it first with his Scroll in hand only to find the PAST already streaming. He didn't have time to reprogram for the address of his destination and if he did he would have to override the existing stream. Then a stun blast from a disrupter jarred the Scroll out of his hand and putting a filthy burn on the impact sight.

His disrupter was in the back so he could sit properly and Javan reached around pulled it out as a stun burst went sailing over his right shoulder followed by a burst that looked to be inadvertent hitting the ceiling above his head. It was no ordinary stun burst though whoever that was firing this had the intention of killing Javan. The rectangular box then tethered out from the ceiling above him and breezed right through him.

"Run Javan, get the heck out of there." Hamath yelled to do anything he could to prevent the magnet from liquifying his bones. He had never seen what a blood magnet could do and he didn't want to find out first hand either so Javan stepped out of the way. When the carbon fiber molecules had turned to liquid in the ceiling the shield then sucked all of the metal and liquid carbon fiber down to the floor where the rectangle shield was.

Metal was now dripping in hot molten clumps from the edges of the hole where the rectangle had pulled the materials from. "I am glad that wasn't you."

"Thanks for having my back." By this time they were all surrounded by Northern soldiers on some kind of recon mission all with disrupters aimed straight for their heads.

Hamath had something to say to Javan, "They either want us or our ship and something makes me feel that its not us."

Then a man with a Captain logo spinning on the chest of his AIIA suit said, "Oh how right you are, we now have you and your ship, the big question is 'What are we going to do with you?'"

"So you're the prick that set up this whole shield thing?"

"No actually it was my IT guy I don't even like programming made F's in the class all throughout my schooling."

"Yeah well by the looks of you it is obvious you didn't make it past the third grade."

"If compliments and imitation is the most sincere form of flattery then what would disrespect be?"

Javan was typing on his Scroll that he had managed to stick with him through the firefight. Javan looks up to see the Captain shining his disrupter, "Disrespect is the most sincere form of you better watch what you do with us because I have about 4 million soldiers waiting for a reason to erase your existence."

"Sabta could you get your dreadful excuse for an existence in here." Sabta was a short pudgey looking fellow that did all of the programming for the North's Quest Starships. A real pushover especially for the Captain.

Humbly and very nerdy he said, "What did you need me for sir?" In all this, was probably the biggest geek you have ever seen accent.

"Pardon the interruption there is something that you should know."

"I was trying to introduce you to the man that is directly responsible for all of the chaos around here."

"What are you going to do with us?" Hamath slowly said with enough confidence in himself that one way or another they were going to make it out of there alive.

All the while Javan was plugging and chugging away on the Scroll at his side pocket, to the soldiers it looked as if he was playing with a set of cards. "Oh my did you two think that I was going to let you live? How noble of you. I think you have mistaken me for someone who actually has a heart. No, no the heart I had was no use for me such as you two are so I just had to get rid of it many many years ago. Don't worry your ends will come quickly I have no doubt about that." The Captain then shined the sides of his disrupter.

Javan was all fed up, he was brimmed and more than ready to speak, "It's about time that you shut your keg-hole What I was saying you invalid knucklehead before I was so rudely interrupted was that I will give all your men 30 seconds to put down their weapons before I press one key that will tear you all to shreds."

"How cute he thinks that he can threaten us, usually people have much leverage before they make such threats as you have just made. You are defenseless and unarmed how could you possibly have a valid reason to threaten us?"

Javan started looking around to the Scroll-Walling as he spoke, "Do you see all of the holes in the wall to the side of you and behind you?"

"Yes, I see them. What are you going to play connect the dots or something? That is really terrifying, if I must say so myself."

"Enough clowning Bozo, your ignorance precedes and defines you as my ship and it will always stay that way this room is equipped with anti terror wallings that can be programmed to shoot anyone in any spot in this room. Of course you wouldn't know that because the ship that you are Captain of the Olympia is so ancient that it has none of our technologies. We are AI and DTR clones where as you probably think that AI stands for active imagination. We have great faith on this ship much greater than that of yours."

"We are always connected to the DTR and never skip a beat. To my point, I will only give you one more opportunity for you to tell them to put down their weapons and hand them over or its lights out for all of you. What's it going to be?"

The Captain looked back over to his men and laughed a horrid evil laugh, "They have no such weapons and even if they did how could they program them if they didn't even know that we would be making our presence known on this ship today?"

Javan reaches further into his pocket and secures the base of his Scroll and pulls it out and said, "This is how my friends. With the touch of this finger on this screen I can terminate your very existence."

"So what the geek has a scroll he probably doesn't even know how to use it."

"I have the power to end your life right here and now and I will use it if I have to." Javan said with intimidation.

"That also means that you will end your life as well." His disrupter was holstered on his left hip, they hadn't the chance to take it from him yet. Javan reached down at his side and brought it up shoulder level. The officers from the North that were gathered around him began to see what was in the window of the cartridge holder. It was some kind of cube that had green stripes on it. They had never seen one like this before they thought it must be some kind of new weapon.

"Not exactly, if I hit the screen and run for the PAST and make it out of here I will do something that I don't want to have to do and that is destroy this ship that I love, so I will give you the ship if you let us just walk away nobody gets hurt."

The disrupter holding Red Striped officers didn't flinch. Their aim was still directly on his forehead. Through the small scopes on their disrupters they could see what the damage to Javan's head would look like as they all gazed through and saw a severed head.

"I will give you one chance to drop your weapons and if you don't. Well we will just have to see what happens next. You heard the ultimatum, now down them and nobody gets hurt."

"It doesn't matter if you have a delay programmed in we still will not let you through the PAST." The Captain of the North said with inflicting inflections.

Looking down at his Scroll he knew that he couldn't hit that icon or they all would be up in smoke. So he did the next best thing and hit another icon. Within a minute the cavalry was there and Captain Hamutal was leading the charge, weapons ready, with a horde of backup to provide some leverage for the South.

The step across the PAST and into the scene caused quite a reaction as she emerged from the streaming particles of light. The rest of the officers followed expeditiously behind, as Hamutal grabbed Javan and Hamath by the shoulder, making sure not to lose her aim on their Captain's head.

The men were safely behind her and the other officers now and she motioned with her disrupter, "Alright drop your weapons, this ship is mine, and you better get back to where you were going."

Clangs and clashes littered the air as the Northern officers dropped theirs as their captain followed suit. The North's Captain held his disrupter in both hands and looked it over with eyes of defeat he clicked it over a notch probably to set it to the safety mode then a little smirk lifted the side of his lip and one last disrupter thudded on the synthetic flooring.

As soon as it hit it launched out an energy burst hitting Javan in the shin, bouncing off of his AIIA suit and landing on a wall as it slowly slid down as the artificial gravity had its way, even on a Starship. Once the officers saw that Javan had been hit the other officers, who had their weapons set to stun, fired upon all of the North's officers leaving them shortly asleep on the cold synthetic flooring.

The gleam in Hamutal's eyes were similar to that of the stare of the faffe as they intimidate their opponent before the Zycetanl is fired.

"Let's round them up men before they awaken, bio cuffs on all of them." Hamutal said looking into the eyes of each of her officers as they all whisked away the fallen, through the PAST.

"Where to Captain?" Sabta said to Hamutal.

"To their new living quarters somewhere deep within the Southern base. Of which I am supremely confident that there will be no dramatic escapes for them in the near future."

Walking over to Javan, Hamutal stretched out her arm for a well deserved hug. "How have you been doing Javan?"

"Just fine, I seemed to have made it out of the house today without the requirements of a crane or of an ACT 1, so quite well indeed to answer your question."

"You have seemed to have required my assistance to make it out of the Athenia alive."

"And for that I am forever thankful."

"To the important matters, has the shield disappeared yet? Or is further attention required."

"Actually it was dissolved after these mongrels entered the ship, so as seeing that your job is done you can go back to your house, but this time remember moderation or you might need a crane to lift you out of your bed the next time you are needed to report for duty."

"Looking forward to some calorie free foods and a ton of exercise. Will do sir."

Chapter 11
The Op

"Things to Consider"

Throughout America's history there have been several assassinations and attempts on our Presidents. The North thinks that if they can assassinate General Omega they can win the war. Think about what assassinations have done to our country in the past and the effect it had on our nation.

Chapter 11
The Op

Stuck like flies to flypaper were the eyes of a very wise General to the Scroll-Walling in his office. He had ordered for all to leave and for none to disturb him as he had business to attend to. General Omega was alone with the lights off, kicked back in his intelli-chair, conducting simulations. He had been at it for at least 20 minutes and there was no stopping him until he got the results that he wanted. Eye 2 Eye can be a very dynamic program when used for specific purposes. He had already set up two simulations and ran them both with differing variables on each and each with differing outcomes.

He figured that if he could produce enough defensive measures that he would find a way to end it all. Things like; never fire until you are fired upon, were some of the parameters that he set in the program. He had used the simulator countless times before during other wars, only never against the North. He never thought that it would all come to this, a madman at the reigns, producing destruction to his base and cities with reckless abandon, and at an alarming pace.

His reliance upon the expertise of Daniel and Ezekiel were paramount in summoning a decent strategy however if he really wanted to know something then all he knew that he ever needed to do was to pray. In the results of the run #2 on the simulator showed him something that he was not altogether pleased with so he did what he always did and that was pray. "Dear Lord in the name of Jesus you know my situation and you know my concerns so I ask you with humility and fervent humbleness to show me some way that will give our side the edge in this atrocious war. I thank you for it in advance because I know your word."

The Holy Spirit spoke to Isaiah and said, "Go to Ezekiel and he will lead you on the right path to find out answers to all of your questions." Isaiah did so and found himself sitting in Direct-view on the front row of the hall.

With clearance codes from Ezekiel, Isaiah Omega was watching the assembly take place that Aaron was heading up. He was silent during the speech and only clapped when everyone else did. Isaiah saw it all and this was something that was so pertinent to their operations that he just had to have some kind of link to the scene that was developing before his eyes.

Back at the base in the north where them men who had just been freed, there was much animosity in an air of angst. Leading the charge was Aaron who had the gumption of a motivational speaker who is hell bent on taking all of your money for his own personal gain. In the main assembly hall, the General Alpha was at the head of the pack behind a hovering podium with millions of Northerners plugged into his Direct-view system who all simultaneously saw flashes of Hitler come forth.

"I have seen our victory and with the help of God almighty we will rise up from the ashes into an unstoppable force that will soar on the wings of justice. For you know that justice was eclipsed and it is still being eclipsed to this day. God cannot stand for this evil that is upon us, that is why, my men, we must take up arms against those who have taken our lives away from us."

His anger augmented his face as he spoke, his words hit their hearts like boiling magma hit the sea. Always forming new land in the intellectual landscape of all who were listening until magma began to boil within them. The real estate of peace that was once tranquil overlooking the ocean now succumbs to the magmatic words of Aaron that in one single sentence could wipe out all that existed before in the land of peace.

"It is one thing to destroy our source of life and it is another to pass legislation that hinders our ability to survive. If you, my countrymen, will side with me I can guarantee that our futures will all be secure without spot or blemish. Sure, we all want peace, it is more about what are you willing to do to attain it. Take up your arms and stand with me

187

in glorious unison, as we all will succeed in unison. God has shown me his plans for this war and I know that they will come to pass."

After his speech ended there was a thunderous applause that roared through the hall with passionate acceptance of the thing that they must do next to regain their rightful place in the world of Ionious. Standing and clapping with them now was also Kedar, right next to Sharon Alpha, the wife of Aaron. After the soldiers were freed from their bondage Omega knew that they would most certainly need Kedar as they were extracted before the other third of the puzzle could be completed.

Kedar loathed every word that Aaron spoke however, one could never tell as her perky demeanor exuded with approval, as deep inside she could only think of what she had to do to further the underground effort for peace. She was not the only one who shared these feelings, as many who were against the war from the North met in secret as they hatched plans to stop General Alpha.

These peoples talked at their own expense to some of the leaders in the Southern Army asking what they could do to help further their cause. The main contact point was to get close to the officers of the North so that they too could obtain the codes that allowed the South to gain an advantage of when their next striking point would be.

After the commotion was subdued Aaron was in the mess hall dining with some of his men that he had asked to talk with. One of the men was a sniper programmer specialist, another was a Marine reconnaissance specialist. They all were very hungry and were glad to have the chance to make a good first impression on Aaron. Aaron was not there to eat however, he was there to recruit, but for what? No one knew but him. His line of questioning was detailed to the situation that he had seen when God revealed the future to him.

The sniper programmer, Peter Pi, was born and raised in Olympia and he went to the best of Colleges and had special training in weapons after his graduation, and had been in this line of work for over 15 years now. Aaron found this out after asking him a few questions about his experience.

Peter loved to talk but he kept it terse and to the point when he was in the presence of a future Prime Minister, as General Alpha had spoke in his speech about overtaking the government and setting up a new regime. The thought of this excited Peter to the point of daydreams.

He imagined himself, while taking a huge chunk of a bite of a blue-cheese burger and red onion, all crunching savoralicly in his mouth, as a major player in this new government. The food seemed to imbue a sense of trust between the gentlemen as they talked about things that Aaron wanted to talk about.

"Yes sir, I am highly skilled in the art of programming pulses to be fired and land on targets through GPS guidance and infra-red signatures to eliminate individuals over 200 miles away. If you want grunt work as a stealth agent I can maneuver with the best of them."

Aaron figuratively strafed in, "I'd like to see you at work."

"Does this mean that I got the job?" Said the eager marksman.

"Lets get this straight there is no 'job' per say. You tell a soul, you're off the radar, and I will find someone else that is qualified. Lets just say that you are some insurance that I just purchased for my new house. Got it?"

The look on Peter's face was somewhat surprised in the fact that he would be chosen, not knowing what was going to be required of him. "What exactly am I to do sir?"

"When the time comes you'll know what to do. Meet me at the Shuffle Cruiser Bay tomorrow at 0600. That is all, now get out of here. I have some others that I need to talk to."

Now it was just Jude the Marine recon specialist and Aaron eating at the table centered in a gargantuan mess hall. The sight of the General who normally didn't eat in there with the others must have spooked some of the others that would be eating there if it weren't for his presence.

They did this partly out of respect and privacy and the rumor mill had Aaron planning out some clandestine operation of sorts, and not a being there in the base knew precisely what it was. That didn't seem to bother the good Marine Jude. After gulping down some Oranos Aaron had questions that only Jude could answer and he didn't feel like wasting any more time in that hall so he proceeded.

"So tell me Major Jude do you mind if I just call you Jude?"

"Anything works. I am pretty laid back so is there anything that you want to speak to me about?"

"I wouldn't be here at this table if there weren't. Tell me how well versed you are in the art of point blank dispersal of a weapon."

"That depends on the weapon."

"Let's say its a blood-magnet, ever shot one?"

"No sir, I am sure its no different than any other charge from a disrupter."

"You're right and wrong about that Jude. The cube does all the work all it is is point, aim, and pull. Do you think you would be willing to use one?"

"If it was an order from you or the DTR there isn't anything that I wouldn't do for you sir."

"That's exactly what I wanted to hear from you Jude, you just might turn out to be not so bad of a Major."

"I just want to help the cause and fight for my planet."

"I can't tell you what you're going to be doing however I will tell you that from the reports that I have read about you you are most certainly the best in the business. I feel confident that you will do the right thing and make the right decision. You and Peter meet up at the Shuffle Cruiser Bay at 0600 tomorrow."

Aaron pushed on the edge of the table as his chair slid back he left his tray there, and weaved through a jungle of backed out chairs much to his chagrin. In his head he was playing out all of his plans and was affably relieved to find that he is gonna win this one. This wasn't all about the Nivio so much as it was about all that had happened since then, needless to say Aaron didn't like the fact that he was taken prisoner. That still abraded him as he blenched at the very thought that they had the audacity to do what they did both at Zeus and at the base.

It was 0600, Aaron had been there for the last ten minutes, pacing and plotting, searching the words, as if he really needed to at all. He knew what these men were capable of, and he also knew what they were to do. Peter arrived and shortly after it was Jude's confident walk that he traced in the Bay with. Aaron went over to exchange hand shakes with the two elites, as Aaron like to think of them.

"You ready for this men?"

Peter said, "I am just ready to do my job whatever that might be."

"You major?"

"I was made for this mission and what's funny is that I don't even know what it might have me doing."

"You okay on that?"

"Yes, sir."

"If you're not I can get someone else."

"No, sir, no need in that, you recruited me for this and this is what I am going to do for all of Ionious."

The General gave them both their orders and from the looks on their confident faces, peppered with small beads of sweat from walking around the Bay in the morning sun, they looked like this was something that they were not expecting. Did this change their mind about doing it? Not in the least, if anything they both liked a challenge and this would be their biggest one that they had ever had.

The AIIA suits both had green stripes that they carefully noticed taking them off the extended arm of Aaron. As they were putting them on Jude had this special clarity consume his head, "This is gonna be good."

"No doubt soldier, it will be, now just execute your orders and you'll be fine. I don't want either one of you to get compromised, this is why I picked you two soldiers they don't know you and they have never even seen your face so they shouldn't suspect anything."

There was really nothing to load except for Peter's rifle extension and that was already hidden from sight so they were ready to make this one a go. The Bay doors slid open, and off they went, in pursuit of possible redemption and with the hand of God. The stomach of Jude was rumbling and tumbling, the eggs that he had eaten were not agreeing with him. This wasn't the only thing that wasn't agreeing with him, he was beginning to have second thoughts about this whole mission. They were nearing the megaport at the west entrance-way and all he could think of was turning back.

His face gave it away and Peter noticed this, "You okay man?"

"Yeah, I am fine. Just a little stirred up, what did they put in those eggs?"

"You've never had any jalapenos before or what?"

"None that have ever done this to me."

"It's the orders isn't it?"

Rounding out a corner with knuckles white on the screen Jude said, "I'll do it but it doesn't mean that I think that it is the right thing to do."

"No way man, this is going to save us from this freaking war that we're in, you see that don't you?"

"I guess, just butterflies, I guess."

"Well snap out of it knucklehead we have an op to do and you are leading, if you can't do this man just tell me because believe me I can."

They finally hovered through the Megaport and now were in the South's territory. "Now to find a parking spot." Jude rambled out over the roar of the underside jets with windows down. They coasted over the fields of green grass to a building that looked abandoned. "Hey isn't this the research lab?"

"Yeah, this is where Uzziah and the crew broke in I'll just park it here."

The Cruiser came to a stop gnarling the grass beneath in woves of circled plant life. Once the craft hit the grass they exited the vehicle and proceeded around to the front where they could make a safe entry that didn't have any stringers in the PAST that they could be connected back to. Scroll in hand, Jude typed in the address, and they both walked through and Jude said, "Without a trace."

Now they were in an empty training room that was selected because of its close proximity to where Isaiah was supposed to be. The room was dark and not being used and the only thing that they could see was the glow of their Scrolls which reflected a sharp breed of colors onto their faces. Peter typed in a program that would allow him to carry out his orders. He throws his head back, as he was hitting the keys at about a mile a minute, then laughs and says, "Insurance!" chuckles some more and, "That Aaron, he knows what he is doing."

Jude was just starting to get nervous, he knew that this had to be completed down to the last dotted i, and the last crossed t or he would be captured. This was dauntingly dismaying his countenance, however this was what he did best, just not in the middle of a hive, if the PAST didn't stream, it could mean the end for him and Peter too. The clockwork had to be precise so Jude hit a key that piped in some of the latest music from Ryan Miles which dossed down his edge, for a while at least.

The DTR streamed in the music to his transcom, "A heart at peace gives the body life. A world at peace makes everything right."

The music slightly faded enough for him to hear the words of the Holy Spirit, "Psalms 16:11, You have made known to me the path of life; you will fill me with joy in your presence, with eternal pleasures at your right hand."

Now that was what Jude needed to hear. His heart rate returned to normal as he found peace within himself that only God could deliver.

The glow allowed them to see around the closest parts of the room that had a mat that was made of some kind of material that responded to their steps. Intelli-chairs lined the outskirts of the room, this could be a hand to hand combat training place. Which the thought of it getting that sticky made Jude even more queasy.

On Jude's screen there was a red line that lead to the position of the General, or at least the tracking of his AIIA suit. They both had seen pictures of Isaiah so they knew what he looked like before hand, and they would definitely be able to spot him in any crowd if need be.

Jude studied the red line that started from his current position, all of the turns and doorways that would take him to the goldmine. Target X was gleaming, staying in one location, now Jude just hoped that he would be alone, and that he wouldn't move. In the dim light they looked at each other, "I am a go, you?"

"Just say the word."

Peter had already been programming and he was as ready to go and take this op on, as Jonah was after getting spit up on the beach. "Let's do this."

Jude strafed with his back to the wall getting a good look at the scene outside the PASTway. He made his move all with a face of belonging, eyes ahead to his next turn with a impetuous glance to his Scroll Data Pad, which was at his midsection. His walk was in between a briskness and solid pace that resembled the other people in the hallway. At the end of the hallway there was a mess hall where most of the soldiers were going to. On the right were several other halls and the third right was the turn he needed to make.

Peter still in the training room watched as Jude made his way, inconspicuously through the hallway. He knew his follow point and Jude hadn't made it there yet, so he silently waited. All the time hoping that no one would enter the room as he fastened the extension to his disrupter and placed it on his sticky suit. Jude was about ten paces away from the turn and that was when things went south.

The lights came on in the room and an officer with the rank of

Master Sargent whisked in the room. Startled to see someone in the room, Peter was sitting in an intelli-chair and rose to his feet saluting, then the Master Sargent asked, "You ready for the next session?"

"No sir, sorry I was just leaving."

"I don't think I have ever seen you in here before."

"I might be back for the next session." Peter said with a troubled grin as he noticed Jude was at the turning point.

Jude passed several soldiers that saluted, two paces away, one saluted and said,

"Howdy Marine." Jude thought of something swift to say before he made his turn.

"Howdy, nice day outside isn't it?"

"Yes it is, have a good one."

"Yeah, you too."

And the soldier skimmed by on his way to the mess hall. Right now Jude was wishing that he hadn't chosen the Jalapeno omelet for breakfast, it was right next to the normal cheese omelets and he didn't even notice the green peppers.

"What a mistake, just concentrate on the op Jude," he thought to himself, ready to make the turn. He looked in a direct line to see if Peter was now getting out of the room. He took it so whiskily that he didn't even see him, and he knew that he would be trailing close, so no worries for now, on that part of the spectrum of the op.

In the training room Peter was now in a full blown conversation that he was conjuring up a way out of there. His Scroll was telling him with flashing icons to make his move and now.

"That's great, I didn't even know where the cow farms were in Athenia."

"Oh yeah, and man this is the real thing, no SWORD needed, different taste but, its worth it to actually eat a steak that's home grown."

"I have to get going, appointments await and I am running late so, yeah, I'll get in on a session some other time."

"Yeah? That would be great."

Another trainee strolled in and that was his exit point as he made it out unscathed. Now the following, with all eyes on his Scroll, as if he had other ones, no actually he had the whole thing planned out and already programmed any variable that could pop up. Peter just hoped he would stay in the same position. He tapped an icon to let Jude know that he was now getting into position. Jude's mind was focused on the next turn, constantly glued to the X. He could see the General from a his direct view that was transmitted to his Scroll.

That same X that was transposed over a real-time view of his head started to move back towards Jude's direction and this didn't look good because the General was now around a group of soldiers and they stopped in the hall then kept moving. Jude thought to himself, "Improvisation," his Marine tactics were coming into play, "I can do this."

Peter was now in position and asked if Jude wanted him to make it on the Scroll in a message. Jude's answer was, "I got this one."

Now the General, clasping an item in his hand, had made the turn and he was coming Jude's way. He made visual on only the top of his head with brief flashes of his rank logo on his AIIA suit through the gathered crowd. To himself, "How can I get a clearing, I might have to do a 180 after they all walk by and get a better look."

General Omega saw Jude walking as he was in the midst of scattered conversations between the group that adored him. Isaiah nodded to Jude as he then stopped and saluted. The group walked by and Jude was a typing, "No clear path, its a go if you are clear."

"Crowded over here you take it." Peter was now halfway to the mess hall and the front of the group was beginning to surface. He had visual and saw the folder in Isaiah's hands.

On the Scroll communication message he said, "I have visual and they are moving to the mess hall."

"When they scatter, take it if you can." Now the General was in full visual, folder in hand, accept he walked out of sight before Peter could do anything. Now the Scroll had to be his eyes or he would get compromised. They wanted to remain anonymous, so there was no use of the transcom talking, it would only give away their op.

So Peter typed, "I think I can take it once he sits down."

"Make it a go."

In the mess hall there were a myriad SWORD's all poised a few inches behind the railing as the soldiers single filed it, all with Peter seeing the new development. The general put down the folder to do some typing on his Scroll to order up something delicious to eat.

"I have direct visual."

"Take it now."

The elongated disrupter slid down the sleeve of Peter and only the tip was protruding out of it with his left hand now inside his right armpit. Silently he thought, "The armpit treatment, I have done this a hundred times." Jude was now methodically walking towards Peter staying to the left for safety, his window was now closed and he left it all up to Peter.

Jude wanted to know, "Did you program in this variable?"

"Don't worry, I have it covered."

The General was now grasping the folder and on an unadulterated path to his seat he had to take it and now. Peter raised up his right arm for a brief moment and hit the icon on the screen, the General was halfway up the first section of tables when it hit him. Isaiah pulled in both of his hands towards his chest and crumpled in a pile on the floor as the folder floated next to his head. Trying to scream nothing came out of the General's mouth except for a faint detection of air, with blood at the gravity side of his mouth.

Seeing it on their screens they both headed to the nearest PAST as Peter typed in the position to the abandon Lab. They were there and all they had to do was make it to the Megaport so they jumped in the Cruiser and Peter plotted the course. "Autopilot is great idn't it?"

"The exhilaration is something that almost nothing can match, if its on manual and you're weaving a path through a forest."

"Yeah, except for hitting your target 100 yards away."

"That was slick man how in the heck did you learn how to program like that?"

"I have been programming things since I was in college. It ain't no thang but a chicken wing."

"Now that sounds good if we can make it back to the base safely."

"Stealth man, we made it."

"You're just lucky that everyone was already in the mess hall and don't forget we're no there yet."

"Oh yeah, what is that in front of us."

"Well thanks be to God, it looks like we did make it."

The Megaport was dead ahead of them and now it was just Cruisin' time. In less than a minute they were on the other side of the planet strollin' and a goin' back to the Bay.

"General Alpha is going to freaking love us."

"He was watching the whole thing with a dual Direct-View, both of us."

They made it back to the Bay with no problems got out of the vehicle and there the General was, just a waiting on the two soldiers.

The General was as happy as he could be, "Soldier, Marine you did it, thank God for you two."

"Thanks for putting us on the op sir." Jude said with a energetic and respectful salute.

"Now Peter do you ever know how to program, man you're the best."

"It was nothing sir, 100 yards away undetected for all they know it could have been an internal assassination."

Aaron looked to his Scroll to see what the verdict was on the other end and all he found was a headline that said, "General Isaiah Omega is dead."

What's Next?

Chapter 12
What's Next

"Things to Consider"

When something God does happens sometimes we wonder what is next. Since God has called you to many great and might things for His Kingdom you must have the courage to answer that call and be used by God. Kedar is used of God in this chapter and sees the fruition of her work manifest in attaining what the South needs to win the war and have peace. Think about some of the ways that God has used you to bring about His glory for His kingdom.

Chapter 12
What's Next?

In the office of General Isaiah Omega there were several high ranking officers watching the headlines that the Big 14 produce. Isaiah was in his chair laughing, "Is the Colonel going to be okay?"

"Just a slight bruise to the sternum, that's all he'll recover fast if we need him."

"I would say that was a very successful operation men."

"So God just showed you what would happen?"

"Yeah, we saw the whole thing coming, so we got the Colonel to get in a cloak suit, after much debated convincing though, he agreed and we were ready."

Isaiah had his arms kicked back in the intelli-chair and looked to be pretty happy. Colonel Zeta uncloaked, walked in the room, and they all just started clapping. "You gonna be alright Zeta?"

He took a few deep breaths and said, "We did it sir."

"To God be the glory." Isaiah said with exuding confidence.

One of the officers standing around wanted to know, "So what's next?"

"Well for starters, they all think that I am dead, and we will keep on making them think that and I'll do my job as usual, and God willing, we will see peace sooner than you think."

Colonel Zeta that was still a little shaken up wanted to know about, "What is our progress on Kedar?" This was a matter that the

General was always privy to no matter who was receiving the direct view on her.

"She is set to attain the last code that we need to get a hold on Aaron's direct view. Her entry point is a brief window of time where she will be a guest in the Alpha house. She will have three minutes to use her skills that we trained her in for this. She will get on his Scroll in his office and figure out what the characters and fonts are."

"We need that because you know they will hit us when they think that we are at our weakest." Zeta said seriously and sternly.

In an up tempo attempt to quench this hot matter Isaiah said, "We have already outfitted the Shield Cage in all of our ACT 1's so whatever they bring we will have an answer. This does not mean that we shouldn't keep praying and running our parts of the simulations. I just ran a simulation one with the same parameters and variables that said that I would be assassinated and with the Shield Cage we were victorious. I also ran one that took into account my living on and one with my death we won when I was alive and we lost when I was dead. There is no way to know though, what they are going to do next until we have Aaron's direct view."

While speaking in tongues Colonel Zeta said his thanks and praises for the good God that we serve, "We must give thanks and praise in all of our prayers and never lose our faith that God will do what he said that he would do with Kedar and Sariah."

Zeta's hands were lifted with one slightly higher due to the timed release of the pain pill that had not gone into effect yet. All the while his worship never ceased.

The eyes of Isaiah were shut, as his hands were clasped firmly with his head tilted downward. "We all should pray for Kedar now, for she needs the hand of God to be with her if we are going to get this one." The six men in the room all started praying and speaking in tongues in their request for Kedar to succeed.

She was a beautiful woman especially when she was in her Sunday dress and as Kedar would never dress to disappoint she looked oh, so glam, arriving by PAST at the entrance room of Sharon Alpha's house. Aaron Alpha was away on duty and it was just the two women that had the run of the day. Esther was away on a field trip for school exploring the Universal mountains. There was a constant voice in the mind of Kedar and it was none other than the greatest hacker in history Ezekiel

Epsilon. He would be assisting her in attaining the third piece of the puzzle located on Aaron's Home Scroll.

Her nano-fiber twill dress brushed against the corner of Sharon's kitchen table that was illuminated at the touch about the crumpling of the waist section that left tie dyed pleats of light glowing for the next several moments. It was a new technology that allowed interactive touch response illumination that reflects mood and momentum. She quickly 180ed with russet hair bouncing in the spin all to twirl comfortably and curl around her soft ivory neck.

By any standards she was beautiful, no matter what she was wearing, be it a moment before the lights go dark at bedtime or an arising in the morning with fluttered frizz, any condition her eyes always told the story, and her facial features reflected a warm and sensitive heart.

It was this sensitive heart that lead her to choose sides in the war that seemed within her grasp personally to have a positive impact upon. This job or duty that she was about to do was quite hard on her emotionally because she still teetered on whether or not this was the right thing to do in God's eyes, deep down she knew that it was and that this method of reaching peace was much more diplomatic than the brute force that Aaron exerted with his Army.

Her doubts were always relinquished by the recalling of the video of Ezekiel's dream that God had given him, that she had seen in her recruiting. This was something that had chosen her, more than she had chosen it, something that had happened to her that she can use to make a difference in this world about.

As she turned she saw Sharon sitting with a cup in her hand drinking some sort of tea that was very aromatic that filled her senses as her nerves were calmed by her assurance in God. Sharon had a full cup to drink and asked, "Would you like for me to make you some?"

"Sure," was her response, wondering how she could slip away for a moment. "I have to use the restroom."

"Go ahead its down the hall past Aaron's office, I'll have it ready by the time you get back."

She could already see victory in her grasp, "Thanks, it really was nice of you to invite me over."

"Don't mention it, you're always invited over here you know that."

The nerves began to creep in as she became very anxious about making it a quick sweep. She had the tools to do the job it was just a matter of time now so she made her exit to the hall that was a few rooms away, dress glowing at each contact point with the objects on the way. God spoke personally to her as He sensed he heightened anxiety and heart rate. "You are in my will never doubt your calling, I have called you to play this part you know the truth and you have seen it, never forget that."

Everything started to click as she paced slowly and surely towards that Scroll. Passing the edge of the main hallway the outskirts of her dress caught a breeze on the Scroll-Walling that illuminated a brightened glow of pinks from obfuscated to cotton candy light she was now focused and her mood was reflected. Taking a right she now could see the entrance way and she hurriedly moved towards it.

Upon entering she took in the view of the video playing of Isaiah Omega being assassinated, the sick prick must have had it as a screen saver art as some trophy for taking out the General. On the main desk there were holographic pictures that were playing of his wife and children, with no Scroll in sight. Where was it? Ezekiel said his home Scroll would be there and it wasn't.

In her transcom she heard Ezekiel talking, "Put on the glove and touch the walling." The glove was firm fitting and as she touched it, it had some touch slack to it and gave a little, this was somewhat different that her other encounters with wallings.

Immediately a keyboard appeared on the desk, this was odd, and she knew that this was his normal method of working in the office. It wasn't there before she touched the walling so the room itself must be a SWORD dynamatomically creating the keyboard. She didn't have time to figure out the mechanical occurrences.

She had done the capture of the passcode several times and thought that she could take it from here. She oriented her eyes to the icons on the walling and clicked on the settings one that had gears on it that were rotating as she moved over it. Direct view was on the screen and now with a click it would be revealed to her, as Ezekiel watched on.

She clicked and there it was her target, in grasp, with another click it was to be uploaded to the card that Ezekiel had made for her that was identical to Sharon Alpha to bypass the location drop security and to her delight the small card lit up as the passcode was received and immediately transferred to Ezekiel's Scroll. She clicked once more and...

"What are you doing in here Kedar? I thought you were going to the restroom." Kedar's heart rate went through the roof how could she possibly explain so she retraced her thoughts and wasn't sure what that last click did to the wall that was now to her back as she was facing Sharon at the doorway.

There could be anything on that screen just behind her and that worried her. Her cover could be blown, so with class and poise she said, "Nothing, I guess I just got a little intrigued by seeing the video from the hall."

She didn't know if Sharon would be upset with her being in her husbands office, the card now was out of sight and blending in with her dress as it attached in her swoop to turn to see Sharon. Thinking that she would ask more questions she prayed that everything would be alright.

"Well your tea is getting cold, come back to the kitchen and we will share some memories okay." Sharon took the turn back into the hall, and as she was even with the doorway Kedar glanced back at the room and the walling, ironically much to her surprise it was Omega getting shot. Ezekiel must have overridden the walling, thank God for Ezekiel she gleefully thought.

"I heard about the news and that really is terrible and all did Aaron have anything to do with that?"

"Oh honey, in our marriage we have rules to keep the work at work and leave the home life at home."

"That's good, I guess if it works for you and keeps y'all happy, and together then it must not be that bad."

"It's not at all, I would hate to have to hear him go on and on about all of his things that he does at work, so when he's home its just us and it works like that so that's just what we do."

By this time they were already in the kitchen and Kedar was seated on a monkey stool, it was a seat with the back made to look like a monkey's head and torso with the arms and legs as arms of the stool. Sharon sat Kedar's tea in front of her and she took a sip to a heightened sense of pulsating heat to the tongue. Reflexively it went back to the table where the steam was drifting upward disappearing into the fragrant air.

"Here are some holopics you can turn through them if you want, most are of Aaron and I."

Kedar had already accomplished her goal, and really wanted to get out of there just in case anything happened, she decided to stay for a while though.

She flipped though some pics and found one. "What is this?"

"Oh that's just Aaron rubbing my dogs."

"You have pets? Where are they?"

"No my feet you know my dogs, hushed puppies don't walk They are hushed and I don't talk, at least when I am in bliss with the rubdown."

Witty Ezekiel was watching all of this and said in the transcom, "I've got dogs too I call it flatulence and they bark, I bet my dogs stink worse than her dogs." Kedar bubbled up a laugh that she tried so hard to keep down.

"What's so funny?" Sharon wanted to know and Kedar just shrugged speechless.

"It's none of my business."

"No, its fine actually its my business someone said something in my transcom."

"Oh well, you can talk in another room if its really important."

"I really should get going, my business calls."

"Okay, it was nice having you."

"Yeah, thanks for the tea."

Sharon had her Scroll out and said, "Do you want me to?"

"No, I got it." Kedar typed in her address and was away swiftly through the stream.

First to her house, she changed clothes, got something to eat, and then immediately to the south base where Ezekiel would be anxiously awaiting. When she made it to his office she peeled the card from her glowing dress as she said, "Got it right here."

"I got it too, take a look at this."

On his scroll was the direct view of Aaron Alpha. They weren't sure where he was up North they knew it was him when he talked though. She was so glad that she could help, "Sweetness, this thing really works?"

"Uh, yeah it does."

"So what is he planning?"

"Nothing yet, I have been direct for almost an hour and its all routine. We'll know something whenever he does though. We can't thank you enough Kedar."

Reflecting on what had just happened Kedar had something to tell Ezekiel, "You know you really saved me back there."

"I found the passcode to the PAST for that room and saw her coming so I just changed the scenery somewhat."

"She is still a good contact and God only knows what could have happened if you didn't."

Kedar was kind of wondering what to do now that she had completed her operation for the South after all she does live in Olympia. "Did you see what was on his screen saver?"

"He is an evil man that refuses to believe the truth, he needs God to change his life is what he really needs."

"Yeah, a revelation would help and this could all be over."

Ezekiel was thinking about it all, "Somehow, I just know that he will get his revelation of the truth in God's timing."

"It would have to be God, we both know that no one can convince him otherwise."

There was a brief pause for thoughts and Kedar got to thinking about, "Isaiah Omega, what's he doing today?"

"He's always busy you know that, especially now that we are waiting on the next strike. We could go see him though he's a few rooms down."

"Okay."

Sharon's card attached itself to Kedar's hip on her illuminating dress and she was ready. She thought that she would leave it with Ezekiel accept he already had it uploaded so she could give it to Isaiah though. Ezekiel trailed and noticed the bright flashes of light and color that sparked as she brushed up against the doorway to his office. "Nice dress, my wife has one of those, they are great for dancing close."

"Can you tango?"

"Rose and all."

"Cool." Kedar said as they entered a busy office with people tracking in an out like it was some kind of recruiting station. "As the other side of the pillow. Hallo."

"Sir we got it." Kedar peeled the card from her side and handed it to Isaiah. He placed it on his desk and his head motioned for them to get behind him, as he was sitting at his desk.

The General was very pleased, "Thank you Kedar we couldn't have done it without you. Guess what I am watching?"

"The afternoon news?"

"News before it happens, this is General Alpha, Colonel Eta, and Colonel Nu's direct view."

"How in the world did you get all of those?"

"Turns out Ezekiel here already had power set up in the other two Colonel's rooms before they escaped and we got the third piece and that was all that we needed." Isaiah said as he hit a key on the screen so that they could see it better and it holographically popped out to a bigger dimension. It was three direct views all in different places, doing different things.

Ezekiel was ecstatic, "This means we have it won."

Isaiah was fast with a reproach, "We play defense here, all this means is that we know what they are going to do before they do it, and that's it, we still have to thwart all of their offensive moves and be one step ahead. I've got three soldiers listening and if anything happens they let me know first hand."

It was mid-afternoon on the Northern base as Aaron took to his green room to talk about his strategy for their next move. There were Colonel's and Captains in attendance all chatting before the presentation that General Alpha was about to deliver.

"Soldiers we have a tough task ahead of us and there will be a zero tolerance policy for everyone on this Op. If completed it could be our first wave of attacks that would make an impression literally in the face of this conflict. We have a superior advantage here today due to the fact that they are short a General."

There was applause and some whoops involved by the men in the room after that statement. "Right now they are in the process of rebuilding and reconfiguring their ranks. They are also in a mourning process that will result in the funeral to be held at the Erebus Cemetery for the late General Omega."

"I can't help but to say that we had a significant hand in making that happen if any of you were not aware Peter a sniper of ours, who is not with us today, made the shot which ended the rule of reign of the General and now they mourn his death. In attendance of this funeral there will be all of the heads of state and ranking leaders. That is why it is our primary goal to bomb the funeral once they get to the cemetery. Making it happen will be the duty of you soldiers who have stood by me for all of these years, of which I am grateful, and know that you will prove to succeed. If anyone wishes to add anything now is the time."

"During the 21 gun salute there will be some ONOA's flying above should we take them out or could you tell us the plan?"

"The plan is simple we hit them hard with some torobursts on the ground which should be enough to kill all in attendance, and by the time that the ONOA's get there we will take them out by launching some more firepower as they fly over. Bang bang show we're doing here. We're taking three ONOA's and one ACT 3 should be all that we need, others will be in stand by a few minutes away at the border."

By this time the General Omega was, of course, watching on a Scroll-Walling with the designated soldier, Ezekiel, John Lambda, and Kedar standing near.

The General had something to say, "Its just a matter of making this thing happen. John lets set this thing up call out the men and relay the orders."

The Captain of the North's Air and Naval Force, Thad Tau was deeply engaged in correcting all of the problems that the ONOA's had and active on the one ACT 3 needed to get up in the air. "Go to the SWORD and make the part."

"Which part?"

"The one for the turbine you moron."

"Does the material matter?"

"Of course it matters, for goodness sake let me see your Scroll." Thad yanked the Data Pad from the pilots hand and started typing something in. Some of the guys that were also pilots thought it was funny that the Captain had to do his job for him.

So Thad interjects back, "Enough, can't you see this imbecile cannot do this on his own and we are due up in the air in 30 minutes. Get a grip people." They stopped laughing and a part, the part appeared in the SWORD 3000.

The SWORD 3000 was used primarily for creating aircraft parts and it certainly did the job when the Captain had put it to use. "Now install it." He barked out to the fledgling pilot that didn't know a plasma coil injector from a pinwheel stuck in the ground.

I guess all he knew was the controls of the cockpit and depended on the mechanics for all of the useful stuff at least that's how Thad saw it. "How do I get past the overflow bypass?"

"Do I need to get a mechanic in here for goodness sake, didn't they teach you this in training?"

"I guess I was asleep in that session."

"Lazy bones, how in the world did you even get to be a pilot? Seriously."

"I passed all of the tests."

"What did they grade on some kind of dunce curve? Because you are being a complete moron here."

"I don't know how to assemble it sir."

"For goodness sake give me the freaking thing and I'll do it for you." Thad jerked the injector from his hand and began disassembling the thing and had it installed in less than a minute, he knew his stuff.

"Any of the rest of you need some help?"

"No, sir." Came from the other pilots.

Within ten minutes all of the ONOA's were repaired and ready for takeoff as the flight programmers were poised and in position to give it over to the pilots. The xum programmers exited the hangar and were in the ready room watching their work in action.

All of the pilots mounted their aircraft and got comfortable in the cockpit. Once the programmers were done there was not much else that needed to be done as the pilots entered in their clearance codes on the screen.

The ACT 3 was already hovering outside the hangar waiting for the word to get a move on it. It took a head start after the Captain transcommed the pilots as it was a slower moving aircraft. Thad said to all of them, "You have your orders now lets make this quick and we'll all come home to our families and have a nice dinner."

Now, they were left out there on their own, and they all knew what they needed to do. The ACT 3 pilots had already crossed the border by the time that the ONOA's whizzed by them. It was a simple triangle formation just the three of them and they were right on time. The head pilot of the leader was talking to his co-pilot, "Easy money, they think that it requires no intellect for us to just go out there and execute another xum program."

The co-pilot nodded, "Yeah, you know we don't get paid enough to do all of this manual labor like this." Lights in the dark sky permeated their minds as they entered the city of Athenia. It was a beautiful city when it was dark outside all of the glitter and the glow could be sensed from miles around. What they saw was just a bright glow from the altitude that they were at. They then took a nose dive to intersect their drop point engines were at full speed as they barreled down through the various atmospheres.

The pull up was counteracted by the inertial dampeners as the full force of the G's that they were pulling would have otherwise left them conked out. All of their external lights were off so they could enter in stealth mode.

"You ready for this?" The pilot asked. The co-pilot hit the icon and a barrage of torobursts were delivered to their target point.

They waited to see the impact that the weapons would make on the ground and several enormous explosions occurred about a mile up from the ground. "What the?" The pilot wondered, "Did we hit them?"

"I can't tell."

"I think they just exploded in the air."

"Hit them again." They fired even more torobursts at the site this time.

"What do you have on the visual?"

"I am not sure but there are six ONOA's coming straight for us."

One section the screen showed starburst cannons all firing to thwart our attack. On the other section of the screen there was a formation of six aircraft approaching at an increasing speed and they were firing right at them.

"Intercept the bogey with some starbursts." The co-pilot manually typed something in and then hit the icon as bright flashes of red littered the dark sky. Explosions followed with more being launched from the oncoming aircraft.

"We have to retreat."

"Roger that, typing in the coordinates now." Unfortunately for the pilots it was too late and they had run out of starbursts to combat the onslaught. A toroburst hit their cockpit and immediately it went up in smoke.

The other two were still at high altitude and swooped around to get back to the hangar all the while they were being followed at least until they got to the safe zone. If they could make it without getting hit.

One pilot prayed, "Dear Lord please allow us to get back to our wives and families we don't need to die here like this, I thank you for answering my prayer. In Jesus name I pray amen."

Two were nearing the safe zone when the South ONOA's reached their altitude it was too late they had no jurisdiction and specific orders not to fire. The four pilots would live to see another day.

"Thank you God." One of the pilots said as they flew away back to the hangar. The ACT 3 pilots were soaring just above the skyline and were intercepted as they got to the target point. They released some torobursts, but it was to no avail, as they were hit shortly after they made it over the target point.

The large bulky aircraft hit a building next to the cemetery and went cratering into the ground. Southern soldiers were all on it and went in and took the pilots as prisoners, as there were no others left on board. As the pilots were being shoved into the Cruiser they noticed a huge hole where the funeral was supposed to be. So one of the pilots with fresh bio-cuffs on said, "Victory, we got them." He knew that Aaron Alpha would be watching his direct view.

Aaron clapped his hands together and was pleased out of his mind with the op, and said, "What a way to crash a party! Can you believe it? One of the torobursts made it through the starburst cannons. We got them all."

On the Scroll there was a very bleak and disconnected scene surrounding the crater. Some of the MP's had put up some FOLED glow tape encircling the disaster area and the mourners were crowded around with various artifacts and poems that were put at the base of the fence. With hands clasped it was obvious some of the people were praying and the glow tape lit up their faces.

A FOLED sail was hovering over the scene giving more light for the people and when one looked up they would see the message, it was a scripture and it said:

"Jeremiah 22:10 Do not weep for the dead king or mourn his loss; rather, weep bitterly for him who is exiled, because he will never return nor see his native land again."

Aaron thought this might be a message to him about his pilots that were captured. Knowing Aaron though, he would definitely make a fight about it and an attempt to rescue his men.

"Right now they are in shock about the events that have just

transpired and they would not be ready if we were to attack them."
Cocking his head to one side Colonel

Grant Eta said, "Why attack? They are defeated sir."

"Why attack? If we fail to capitalize on this opportunity then when
they get time to reorganize it would be too late and they would be at
full strength."

"Their strength is gone, is it not? We eliminated all of their highest
ranking officials."

"They have over 2.7 million soldiers remaining in their Army and
various forces, all they need is 24 hours to promote their officers and
they will be as strong as they were before. That is why we need to attack
and now. Their chain of command is broken and it would be like the
American news, only one camera to tell the story of the events that take
place in an entire nation. We have direct view and direct news from all
points of view and they are accurate."

He continued, "With the DTR giving the orders it can see from
all points of view however it cannot plan a counterattack on itself. It
will defend itself it will not counterattack its own people. The DTR is
not divided, people, it does not just hit the self destruct button. If they
were to re-form, their chain would be back in place, and they would
be just as strong as they were before General Omega was killed or any
of the others."

Chapter 13
The Service

"Things to Consider"

Do you have any friends that you would like to see come to know Jesus? I know that I most certainly do and I wrote this chapter as a testament as to what God can do with those that are willing to heed the call of the Lord on their lives. Many hear about the gospel but not all choose to accept it and believe. Think about ways that you could do more to bring more of your friends to church to get them saved.

Chapter 13
The Service

Struggling for position the blast grazed his arm and blood began to flow. Hobbling, his breath was getting away from him and hyperventilation was taking over, he reached for his loyal disrupter and all he got was a handful of micro-fiber. Waddling like a duck he wobbled behind the corner and saw many bursts flying past him mostly green and some red. He crouched in a shadow in the dead of night however this darkness had more activity and people exchanging shots than he had ever seen in the interactive theater.

His efforts to flee were feeble thinking. He had already had taken a blast to the femur and the puddle of blood, only one minute there, thwarted any thought of hope that he might have. It must have hit the femoral artery, if he didn't find an escape, and fast these fleeting gulps of air could be his last. Endeavoring to find a PASTway he scanned the building that must have been a hundred stories tall. To his right there was a canopy entrance only about 20 yards away. The light was dim and scattered in the darkened mist.

The blast that hit his left triceps was minimal and only burned an excruciating hole in the muscle fibers past his outer wear. Adjacent to his position was an outer PASTway that kept firing green energy blasts around its corner.

On the other side and across from the green bursts was two towering giants with green stripes chugging it across the way to make it to a clearing. As they reached the angle inception point, red bursts billowed out in rapid succession hitting the AIIA suits. This did not impede their progress as they made it to the clearing behind the PASTway.

He knew that the Army wore AIIA suits with the green and red stripes but his only AIIA suit was shed several blocks back and he was now in outer wear with no digital protection. Mark was an American that had been on his way to see a friend downtown at his apartment when he saw the red stripes landing.

He decided to get on his elbows and his his knees to crawl to the canopy entrance since his bleeding wouldn't stop. The hyperventilation had stopped to some degree and now it was labored breathing with his head down watching the micro-twill on the ground part, and light up as the heat from his breath activated it.

Thoughts were racing through his head as his grinding exertion on his touch points were now getting raw. He was now ten yards away and the light from the canopy was getting brighter. He knew that if he wanted to make it he would have to pick up the pace now that he was in a lit area.

The Northern soldiers could be coming around the corner any minute and speed was his painful and only option. Now his elbows and knees were bleeding from the friction created by the miro-twill this didn't matter anymore as he knew he could make it.

Mentally gathering himself, he spoke inspiration that would carry him faster through the light. Right, left, right, left, went his elbows as his knee trailing behind scraped against the skyscraper gouging out a gash that left blood on the porous material that just soaked it in as it was designed to do with the rain.

Now only three yards away he kicked it into high gear, mentally blocking out all pain throughout his body, it was pure will now. He thought that if anyone could save him or help him now would be a good time to use the transcom, that Melinda always praised about, so he activated it mentally.

Mark did not know God and was a sinner and that is putting it mildly. He was not a Muslim, no not at all he just had never been saved. His live in girlfriend was saved though, and talked to him about Jesus and about how He could change his life. He never really listened, he worked too much and partied too long to ever give God a chance.

Static filtered in through his transcom at first it was all white noise, it was the first time that he had ever used it and the sensors had not fully formed in his brain yet. He also heard footsteps coming from around the corner then they halted so he pressed forward. Grind after painful grind, he felt his bones being scraped across the material. He knew that he did not want to hit his knee with the building again.

Now a few feet from the front steps as his elbow raked across the new materal micro-twill that was much less abrasive. The static was now completely gone and he could hear someone talking. He hadn't heard anything like this before so he knew it was either God, Jesus, or Holy Spirit. He began to listen. It was a deep voice very wise and learned, and it also had the quality of vocal perfection that stirred something deep within his soul.

"Proverbs 8:17 I love those who love me, and those who seek me find me. 18 With me are riches and honor, enduring wealth and prosperity. 19 My fruit is better than fine gold; what I yield surpasses choice silver. 20 I walk in the way of righteousness, along the paths of justice."

Then he heard another voice very fresh and full of somber life, "You must seek me and I will show you things that will preserve your life and give it new meaning. You are at a turning point in your life and if you choose to seek me with your whole heart you will be spared as one of my servants mighty to defeat any enemy and you will help bring justice to your world. You must go to the Cathedral."

And then it stopped.

Amidst the talking in his transcom he now heard footsteps that were getting louder and then a burst sailed right into the blended material. It hit and then slid down landing on his back and burning a hole through his shirt. Hustle, he had to hustle, it was right in front of him and he had to make it. He flipped over and reached for his scroll and typed in an address to get him the heck out of dodge.

Just past the top of the display he saw a red stripe and a hovering disrupter that swayed to the left and right. Someone was running right at him. He keyed in the last number and when he did he saw a large brunt head hovering over him that extended his arm and fired right into his face.

Making several swimming motions he started screaming as he came to himself and checked for wounds. Everything was fine, he then tried to remember what God had spoken to him right before he got shot. All he kept seeing was the burst coming right at his face, that red glow that exploded upon impact and then the white.

"Babalicious, you awake?" Mark said to his girlfriend Melinda. She just rolled over in bed and went back to sleep.

"Babe, you have to wake up. Something just happened."

"Tell me about it in the morning I am going back to sleep." The covers went over her head and she tosseled around a bit. Mark decided that he needed to see his dream so he prodded around the floor next to his bed until he felt it.

He started the sequence right at the femoral artery hit, looked around, noticed it was Athenia, and walked over to the guy that hit him and said something to him, then he sifted forward.

"There, there it is." He was in the dining room by now and Melinda couldn't hear him. He played it from the beginning of the talk from God and then to the part where Jesus talked about going to the Cathedral.

He knew what he must do if he is going to survive on this planet. He didn't want to wake her but he knew what he was going to say when she did.

Hours later she came in the kitchen and he already had breakfast made. Sleepily she said, "Whatcha got cooking good looking?"

"Something great."

"Eggs, aww you made them the way I like them." She thought about how she once thought the eggs were called Sunday side up and humored herself knowing now they taste almost the same.

As he dished them out on her plate Mark said, "I am going to church with you today."

She was already sipping on some coffee and when he said that she took a huge gulp and it got stuck in her windpipe so she started to cough. In the cough she said, "What? You want to go to church with me? Well, that is an answer to prayer. Praise God!"

"I have to, I know that there is going to be a word from God for me."

Wiping her mouth from the coffee she said, "I have been wanting for you to go with me for years. What has happened?"

"Last night I had this dream where I turned on my transcom and God spoke to me."

"You finally turned on your transcom? Ever since we got here, you know how I talk about that."

"Only all the time I know, Jesus said for me to go to the Cathedral with you today. I don't know if I am ready to receive Jesus but I know that there is going to be something that I have to hear. My life has to change."

She got to thinking it over for a while in between the eggs and bacon, "So you don't listen to a word that I say and now you are listening to some dream, great just great."

"Just be glad that I am going."

"Don't worry I am, I just wished that it was me that you were going for, I know I shouldn't be like this and I am only thinking of myself here."

"No, it was you, in the dream, you were the reason that I even turned on my transcom on in the first place. I was wondering yesterday, daydreaming about something that you had said about it and there it was in my dream."

She sipped again and moved her finished eggs to the center of the table, "Dreams happen like that a lot."

Now sipping on his coffee, tons of cream, and a heap of sugar today, "I know, I am starting to notice that."

"I love you. You know that?"

"Do you know that I love you?"

"Yes, my babalicious."

"I never knew how much my life would change just by taking up the courage to go over and talk to you at that game."

"I did notice you above all your friends, you have always been the life of the party, and you really stood out in my mind. Now you're the life of my day everyday."

"You were so hot the guys thought you were out of my league."

"Who were we playing that day?"

"The Pirates and Cubs May 9th 2027."

"And there hasn't been a day since that we haven't been together."

As she curled a strand of hair looking up into his eyes. "I pray that God really ministers to you today."

"What time is it? We have got to get ready if we are going to make it on time."

They both looked at the Scroll walling and saw that it was just an hour away. "I get the shower first." Mark said leaping with joy to a run into the bedroom towards the adjoining bathroom.

Spinning in her chair Melinda had other ideas yelling across the house, "No, you don't, I have to shower first so that you can shower while I am doing my hair."

"Okay that's fine I will concede. Just this once though next time its all mine."

Poutily she whisked out, "Fine, we'll see what happens next time you want some of my good cooking."

"I got fingers too you know." He said fingering one by one through his army of suits deciding what he would wear, he had to look good, her friends at church had never seen him before. She didn't even have to tell him, he already knew what she would say about what he would have to wear.

Fifty minutes later they were in prime condition to present themselves to her friends at church, although this was not his primary reason for going. He had long since keyed in the address to Jeremiah's Cathedral which took him several times until he finally just looked it up in his bible. Cathedral wasn't an easy one either, luckily he had a voice activated dictionary on his scroll which always came in handy for his presentations at work.

Now to just walk through and be presentable for a few minutes and then to wait to see what the pastor had to say. At work he was a shark, looked good, did good, and made good. He had some serious confidence even at his new job in Athenia, this church thing kind of threw him for a loop, though. Before they stepped through he had to know, "What do you think?" His hands went up and down as if he was presenting himself on The Price is Right.

"Good."

"Just good that's it. Let me put it this way, what will your friends think?"

"Believe me you will be the best looking guy there."

"Really?"

"Babe, you are better looking than fifty percent of this world."

"Yeah but they're all aliens."

"They're human just like you ancient Greeks. Did you somehow forget."

"No, no, just making sure to make a lasting impression on... oh great what are their names again?"

"Don't worry I will do the introductions."

"Better than fifty percent huh? Well that makes me feel good."

"You feel good, you look good, now can we just go?"

"Yes, and if I didn't say it enough in the bathroom you look absolutely beautiful."

"Babe I wasn't wearing anything but underwear in the bathroom."

"Yeah well, you clean up nice, suit or no suit."

"We are going to church you are going to have to take of the mind set of the flesh and put on the Spirit,"

"That is what you call that thing right?."

"What?"

"Your suit thing."

"Yes, Mark. Mind of Christ, alright?"

"I'll do my best."

Mark took a deep breath and they walked through. This Sunday the entire Cathedral was covered in scenes from the interactive bible with moderate sound coming through the walls. One scene was Jesus talking in Mark 15:16. Beaming through on the side of Jesus was several of the illustrations, the one that he noticed was with the woman that had been bleeding for twelve years touching His garment. This depicted how He healed the sick. It showed her before in her illness and it reminded him of his dream that he had just seen and brought him back to the words of God in Proverbs.

He had no idea what Proverbs was, this was something that Melinda would have to explain to him. They went through the isle and sat next to some of her friends. Now for the introductions he thought, and afterward when they all said goodbye he would have to repeat all of their names, why did she have to have so many friends? They were all very beautiful so this might not be so bad.

She said, "I would like for you all to meet my husband to be, Mark."

One of the girls sitting next to Melinda said, "You better get a hold of that Mark."

"I am, slowly but surely."

"I have heard so much about you and now we finally meet, well I am glad you came." She told him all of their names and he did his best to get the name with the face.

At work he met new people all the time so it shouldn't be so hard accept they all had biblical names that he had never heard before so he just thought of them by their last name, Iota, Delta, Kappa. This was much easier his way.

Melinda knew that the worship service was about to start and wanted to clarify something with her husband. "You know that when I say fifty percent that the other fifty percent are all women and they don't count so you are better looking that the fifty that do."

"Best looking man on the planet?" Mark smiled and looked over at her beautiful eyes.

"Yeah, that's what I was getting at." She had this like duh look on her face.

"You know I have the best wife on the planet, and hottest too?" He put his arm around her and squeezed.

"Am I now? That should get you places Mr." Her eyebrows raised accompanied with a sensual smile.

They all talked until the worship began and when he heard Melinda sing he thought man she can sing and how glad he was to be with her, and to ask her about her voice later. He didn't want to bother her when she had her eyes closed. She never mentioned her singing to him before, he had heard her sing but not like this. Now he was getting to see the side of her that he had heard about.

The miracles and scenes transformed into angels clothed in glory and out of their mouths came bright and glowing letters of the words that they were singing. These letters moved as one looks at them reverberating and dancing zooming back and forth. The sound was like a choir in heaven and a thousand voices all proclaiming their praise to the holy one, the great and deserving one.

As Jesus proclaimed in his ministry,
I am only one of the three the holy trinity,
we all play our part in the body of Christ,
may yours resound vibrantly in your life,
Standing in your presence I never want to part,
Let my worship to you become an art,
Make my thanksgivings exalt you from my soul,
I accept your blessings now your spirit flows,
your word in my heart exclaims,
reflecting your nature proclaims,

your amazing blessings and grace,
in healing my spirit in this place,
your love suffices all my needs,
I know your word and sow my seeds,
in your everlasting love that transcends,
all things and enters my heart to see it never ends,
Here I am to worship you,
becoming one with your word,
breaking through any resistance,
seeing only you oh Lord,
Satan cannot touch me when I worship,
This is one on one communication,
There is no interference from the darkness,
As it is shattered by the light of exultation,
My burdens are lighter,
As you take me higher,
Into the light of your glory,
I want to know your story,
Of love and grace,
In your arms I embrace,
How you lived how you died,
And paid such a great price,
So that I could be free,
In awe of you I see,
Amazed by your sacrifice,
Knowing your grace will suffice,

Looking around he saw people weeping with their hands in the air and didn't know why they were crying. Maybe they will stop their tears by the time that the pastor starts to preach or his words will ease their burdens. Why are all of their hands lifted? Maybe I should raise mine but I don't want to start crying. I wonder if that would happen if I started to sing, what am I thinking I can't sing.

I better just stay put until the songs are over then I can see what this guy has to say. It just said to go to the Cathedral and it didn't say anything about the singing or preaching I wonder if I am supposed to be singing too. Maybe God would give me a voice, all of these people can sing, maybe they won't hear my awful voice.

Church is really draining, maybe because this is my first time, I bet it isn't always like this. And then again I have never had a dream like that, I have never even heard from God accept when, well I guess that was God, that lady's life that I saved from her stepping right into that bus. I wasn't even supposed to be at that corner and God made a way I guess that's how Christians talk. That's how Melinda always talks, that's how everyone at my new job talks. That's how everyone on this planet talks. Church is like a whole new vernacular, it really is, I wonder if I could ever talk like that and really feel those words and everything would just make sense.

Nothing here so far is making much sense, I do like these screens on the pew, I didn't bring a bible so I am guessing that its on that screen. What is this? The interactive bible? Maybe that's what all these people are looking at and that's why they are crying.

I don't know much about the bible, but I do know that Jesus died on the cross and if these people love him that much they could be there at the cross watching him die. I know I would cry if that were Melinda up there dying. Why don't they just blink out or something? Nobody should witness what Jesus had to go through. He started listening to the songs again.

The triumph in his blood,
The freedom in his love,
The grace in his forgiveness,
The glory in his holiness,
Stepped into my life out from my darkness,
You broke in and started shining through,
You took this heart that was just a big mess,
Turned it around and I reflect it back to you,
Singing you shine in glory,
Your life is holy,
You took the keys from life and death,
Took away my sins there was nothing left,
Filled up my heart and you blessed,
Gave me new life and nothing less,
Than all of you,
Singing, all of you,
wanna be more like you,
do the things you do,
and you'll pull me through,

This life this flesh got nothing for me,
All I want is more of your glory,
Shine on through into my heart,
I reflect the rays and darkness parts,
I am a testament of your everlasting love,
Saved by grace from my savior above,
Singing you're all I need,
I can get through anything,
Its gonna be great,
Doing figure eights,
Eternity is calling,
I am living,
In your word,
All I have heard,
Brings me close to you,
I am gonna make it too,
When all this world brings me down,
There is inspiration in the sound,
Of the hope that is in your voice,
and that's when I begin to rejoice,
Then I know just what to do,
Lift my hands and praise you,
For all you've done,
Never had so much fun,
I have got the word and I live,
This spiritual battle is all down hill,
Breezing through the boulders that were meant to kill,
Every sinner needs a savior if you will,
Call on his name,
Never be the same,
This ain't no game,
No one to blame,
Singing you are the righteousness of the father,
You are the only never another,
Sent to Earth to be our savior,
Always perfect like no other,
This music isn't so bad, its nothing like the music that I listen to. Positive and uplifting as opposed to just Rock and Techno babble

they never have good words like this stuff. This is like reading that Ed Young book that Melinda gave me, only they sing it. I guess its more about how you get through your problems and who you turn to when you are going through stress. Everyone goes through bad things its just that these people have an answer and its God. I never have an answer for myself, well my answers are all self centered I look inward and they look to God. You know what I could do that, I don't know much but I really think that I could do that.

There is nothing like surrender,
Lift up your hands to a perfect savior,
Give it all to Jesus the rock on which I stand,
When I go through hell the rock of Jesus is where I land,
He is holding on to you,
Even when you can't,
He will pull you through,
Listen to his words and his plan,

The music began to give into the presence of God and different people were all singing different things in the spirit. How do these people do this? None of them sing the same thing but they all are in perfect harmony. I guess God is on these people maybe that's why it all works out so beautifully. Melinda began joining in on the movement and she was singing incredibly beautiful.

This is kind of embarrassing what if someone sees me with her and she is doing this. Wait everyone here is here to hear from God so this is a normal thing to these people. Nothing to be worried about this happens every Sunday I guess. He started to listen to her sing.

Glory to God who meets my needs,
In his presence darkness flees,
I will embrace this eternal light,
God is there to fight your fights,
You might just see a boulder,
God sees a million pebbles,
What everything could be,
Nothing is impossible to thee,
If you are hurt you qualify to have a healer,
If you play with heart you qualify to be a winner,
If you are married you qualify to be a father,
If you are a sinner you qualify for a savior,

Don't ever think that you are too bad,
That Jesus won't save you and all you have,
He died that we might have life,
And live more abundantly in his glorious light,
Just open your eyes long enough to see,
That Jesus died for all of us for you and me,
Give your sins away and take up your cross,
Follow him in your ways and your thoughts,
    What would Jesus want with me? I am no good I have no talents
or abilities nothing I can give back. In business there is always give and
take something for nothing just doesn't work in the business world.
Maybe this Heavenly Kingdom isn't like the business world or maybe it
is. If I give him my heart he gives me new life and forgiveness, I wonder
what that imparts? Giving him my heart and everything, does that
mean that I always have to put Jesus first before I make any decisions in
my life? This is something that Melinda and I are going to have to talk
about. And what if I sin after I get saved what happens to me then do
they just throw me out of the church? Or is his forgiveness everlasting
without end?
    One of her friends is singing now, great what is her name? Iota? No
different dress. Delta? No different eyes. Its got to be Kappa. I wonder
if they would be upset if I forgot their first names?
    Oh well I am sure that Melinda can remind me after church. Man,
Kappa can sing too, wonder what she is going to sing about? What
kind of voice is that Alto? No I think that one is much deeper, its got
to be soprano, like an opera singer at Carnegie Hall or that lady on
Broadway.
    Phantom of the Opera yeah that's the one now that lady can sing.
I am thinking too much I really want to hear what she has to sing
about.
    There is such love in his grace,
    It knows no bounds and is always there,
    It has to be that feeling when you see Jesus face,
    Forgiveness to which nothing can compare,
    We mess up and fall down again,
    His forgiveness is there to pick us back up,
    No matter what we've done no matter what the sin,
    This is above anything I've ever known this love,

He was perfect in his life,
I am so far from that,
I am a wretch that deserves no plight,
He forgives me anyway and makes clean all that I have,
His blood frees us from sin,
His blood makes us whole again,
Triumphant is his blood,
Washes away our sins like a flood.

I wonder why He would just keep forgiving me every time that I mess up? Melinda says that he sees your heart and if he knows that I am doing my best and that in my heart I have the best of intentions that he will just forgive me if I go crazy and mess up again.

If I mess up then if I get into the word, it could help me, and keep me from messing up again. I think I have a good heart, I don't ever intentionally mean to ever hurt anyone or mess up anything for anyone else. Yet sometimes I do do that and if I knew more about the bible and how God works I could learn not to do those things that hurt others.

The angels and beautiful scenes of the heavens were all changing with the music, that's all it was now no singing just soaking in the spirit. Oh wait, I think that's the pastor, Stephen right, okay he is getting up and going to the place where his Scroll is, some kind of podium thing.

He spoke, "Just let the spirit move and soak in his presence." He lifted his hands and closed his eyes. Mark was now just scanning the room and watching some of the walls. What in the world? That is my dream in text and video, that is God talking to me. Proverbs 8, what in the world is that doing on that wall. I have to ask her about this, I don't think that any of these people want to see me get shot.

Will it get to that part of it? Maybe its is just showing the word from God. Is this why I am here just to see my dream on the wall in front of all of these people.

Okay most everyone has their eyes closed so no one will see it and that's a good thing. Its only one of several dreams being played and they are all in Athenia and its dark outside, same as my dream, that's odd. Okay now this is a time where I can use what Melinda taught me about taking every thought captive and obedient to the knowledge of Christ.

Somewhere in the bible it must say something about not being anxious, worried, or concerned. This is just a pebble that looks like a boulder.

His transcom was on and he activated the controls and searched for anxious. On the screen in front of him was a verse:

Philippians 4:6 Do not be anxious about anything, but in everything, by prayer and petition, with thanksgiving, present your requests to God.

I like this bible this is some great advice, I have prayed before so this should be something that I can do. The pastor is getting ready to speak.

"Please be seated in the presence of the Holy Spirit. This is a time unlike another that we are facing today we are at war and it is not just any war it is a war that we did not choose and that we did not bring upon ourselves. In Ecclesiastes 3:8 it says: a time to love and a time to hate, a time for war and a time for peace."

"God has predestined a time for war and also for peace, they seek war and destruction and they shall see destruction brought against them unless they turn from their evil ways. We however, seek peace and those that seek peace and pursue it shall surely have it. The time that we are in now is not peace it is war."

"In Deuteronomy 28:2-7 it says: All these blessings will come upon you and accompany you if you obey the LORD your God:

I am sure that many of you are much like me, I love to obey the Lord when he speaks to me and I hear him and if he tells me something to do, I do it, sometimes without even thinking about it. I know that this pleases the Lord and I am pleased that I could be of service in the simple act of just obeying. I get the best feeling in the world when I hear God talk to me and after I have obeyed I just get all fuzzy inside knowing that I was able to help out the creator of the Universe. You say well what do we obey? First let me tell you about all of the blessings then you will find out what and how to obey God.

Verse 3 says You will be blessed in the city and blessed in the country.

4 The fruit of your womb will be blessed, and the crops of your land and the young of your livestock--the calves of your herds and the lambs of your flocks.

5 Your basket and your kneading trough will be blessed.

6 You will be blessed when you come in and blessed when you go out.

Basically all of the areas of your life will be blessed if you simply obey. When you walk through the PAST you will be blessed wherever you go. Your descendants will be blessed. Your children will be even more intelligent than the generation before them. They will be more obedient to you and to God and for that they will have multiple blessings. The fruits of your labor will be blessed. God will show you how to do things better than they were doing before. God will give you new revelations and new technologies new ideas. The food you eat will be blessed and this will bless your health you will not get sick. You will be blessed in every area that you could possibly fathom, you are just going to have a blessing attack.

"Now is the part about the fate of our planet. Verse 7 The LORD will grant that the enemies who rise up against you will be defeated before you. They will come at you from one direction but flee from you in seven."

"God has shown me, yesterday in fact, that they are going to attack and this time they will not only attack our bases no, they will attack our city. I have already had several people tell me about the dreams that they had last night of a war that was being fought on our streets. These were very brutal dreams and perhaps you are here because of a dream that you had. Several of the ones that I have talked to were on our walls during the moving of the spirit. I did not plant them there, it was God that revealed those dream on our walls, and I was surprised to see them. Can I see a number of hands in the congregation today that had one of those dreams last night?"

Hands went shooting up, Mark was not sure if he should or not, somehow he knew that the word was about to come and it is destiny that he is here today. He was glad that he was not the only one, almost half of the men raised their hands, so up went his.

"Men you are not alone, some of you are not even Christians, and some of you were instructed to come to church today in your dream. I respect your courage men there is much valor in your hearts in making your decision. Your dreams were very vivid and gruesome some of you saw your own death, and if you do not want to see that come to pass men, women we must have a call to arms to prevent this attack. Our leaders are already in the planning phase of averting this from happening."

"This is a call to arms not in the physical, we will leave that up to our military, what we will leave up to God is our spiritual intercession. I am calling for a fast for all non-enlisted citizens to pray and intercede for those who will fight the good fight against the evil that has become of the North Army."

"If any of you had a dream last night and you know where you were I urge you not to go to that area of town today or tomorrow. At this point we don't know when the attack will occur all we know is that it is coming, and we must be ready. If any of you need help in finding out precisely where your dream was contact us after church and we will access it for you."

"8 The LORD will send a blessing on your barns and on everything you put your hand to. The LORD your God will bless you in the land he is giving you.

I do not know if that lad that God is talking about is the North's land or if it just refers to a land of peace. This we will find out about when it comes to pass.

Now verse 9 The LORD will establish you as his holy people, as he promised you on oath, if you keep the commands of the LORD your God and walk in his ways."

"So I urge all of you to keep his commands and walk in his ways. The commands that this is talking about is not to memorize all of the laws this is rather a call to love, because when you love in all areas of your life you obey all of these commands. For these are the commands of Jesus. So do not live by the law, rather live by the grace of God and the love of Jesus."

"Just as there is a time for everything, now is your time for a turn around, you can stop those horrific dreams from coming true by just recognizing this truth in your time of turn around. Our turn around is here and now. If we intercede on behalf of our soldiers to aid their enlightenment of God's omniscient knowledge we can defeat our enemy to the North. Obey Jesus, become a prayer partner, join us as we fast for the knowledge, and enlightenment of our officials and officers."

"You must know that in all of this there is an answer to this war and it is Jesus, do not despair rather hope in the promises of his word. Do not pay any attention to what the circumstances look like, how will we defend our city? Our city will be blessed and remember that all things are possible with our God."

He continued, "He can do all things and you can do all things through Christ who strengthens you. We will be victorious and we will be redeemed from this conflict, do not think that you will die just choose to live in the knowledge of the promises of having eternal life through your salvation in Christ."

The war we fight is not in the physical it is in the spiritual rather 2 Corinthians 10:4 The weapons we fight with are not the weapons of the world. On the contrary, they have divine power to demolish strongholds.

5 We demolish arguments and every pretension that sets itself up against the knowledge of God, and we take captive every thought to make it obedient to Christ."

"People, listen to this, we are not physical human beings trying to have a spiritual experience. No, rather, we are spiritual beings attempting to master the human experience. Above all we are in the world but not of the world nor is it in us for we are spiritual beings that had an existence with God before we ever took our first breath of oxygen."

"He knew us before the foundations of all worlds near and far. If you have grown weary in the course of this war I urge you to take all of your burdens and put them all on Jesus. He has already died on the cross for all of them. He took the weight of the world's sins and bore them on the cross from which he died and rose again."

"And in that one last dying breath when he went to hell and took the keys to life and death and the veil was torn so that now we can have open communication with God. The miracle in his death and the mystery of his resurrection amaze us all to this day. And never a day goes by when we should not be eternally grateful for what he has done for us on Earth 2000 years ago."

"This war has consumed our lives for months now but it has not taken away our lives. We still hurt, we still have failures, I urge you not to look at those things. Rather we should realize that He was wounded for our transgressions, bruised for our iniquities, and by his stripes we are healed."

"We are healed from all of the hurts that are inflicted upon us in this life. We are healed from those wounds that we face that might be an illness. Jesus bore those wounds so that we could be set free and healed for now and evermore. There are no illnesses that can take away our will to serve God. He will heal us so that we can live to serve Jesus another day."

"Whatever you are going through God is going to bring you out of and make you better than you were before you ever got afflicted. God is there for you and he never lets go of us no matter if we cannot bare to hold on any longer. There is hope in our savior who paid the greatest price that anyone could pay. To know Jesus is to know hope and love and promise through his word. He will give you a peace that passeth all understanding."

"If you have not accepted Jesus into your heart and you would like to now please come down to the front and someone will pray with you."

Mark came for a word from God and now he is giving his life over to Him. He took those steps down to the front of the church and somehow knew that this was what he should be doing. He said to the prayer partner, "I want to have that peace in my life, I want to have freedom from my sins."

"Only God can give that to you and it is through Jesus that you can have that peace and freedom. Only Jesus can free you from your sins." The person praying for him was pastor Stephen Beta, he took him through the sinners prayer and Mark cried for the first time in a very long time, as he accepted Jesus as his Lord and savior.

Chapter 14
The Test

"Things to Consider"

Throughout life God gives us many tests that bring out our character and form new identities in Jesus if we choose the right answers. Just remember have a great character is good but the biggest test of your life is to accept Jesus as your savior and go to Heaven. That is the test of life will you accept what you have heard about Jesus and go to Heaven for all eternity or will you not listen and make the worst mistake of your life and burn in Hell for all eternity. It is entirely up to you on that decision and I hope you make the right one. Everyone has an eternal life it is either spent in Heaven or in Hell it's up to you.

Chapter 14
The Test

Dashes and dots of white speckled the deep awaiting blue in this midday sky and there was an image of Omega on the screen, at both sides, that sparked a calm assuredness in the hearts of the anxious soldiers of the Army. From the podium Isaiah cleared his throat modestly with a fist move to the mouth and then a look out into the sea of green and harder to see green stripes that blended in with the green field. The soldiers heads were not cloaked, well most of them weren't and for the ones in the front he could see the passion in their eyes and a love for their world and the one true God.

The speech had never been spoken before and would be fresh and new to these soldiers that were looking for any kind of righteous inspiration. That is exactly what they would find on this sun filled breezy day that couldn't have been more than 75 degrees out there. If the heat were to get bumped up their AIIA suits would respond. The mood in the crowd could be summed up as ready and restless most of these men and women had not seen the bitter grief of what a war can do to the morale of a person in the heat of battle.

Nonetheless no matter how war can affect someone, these soldiers were different, they had the word of God planted deep within their souls and knew its promises and laws. Even if it ever turned brutal and heart wrenching they would always know that God the creator of the Universe had their back, and that was a good feeling to have. The General was waiting for Daniel to get there before he started so he

233

focused his eyes on two soldiers in the front row and he could hear what they were saying. Eyes forward the man said, "You got any gum?"

The other soldier backed up as much as he could and covered his nose with his hand. "Goodness gracious, what in the heck did you eat that is rank? No, its worse than that its BCS rank. There should be a scale of death that measures how bad that breath is."

"Do you have any gum or am I just going to keep making flies drop?"

"I don't know let me see, these things have a million pockets, seriously what did that to your breath?"

"I just ate about a pound of Hagus and garlic for a garnish."

"Why in the world would you eat something like that? Hagus reeks man, and whoever heard of garlic for a garnish man somebody really pulled a stinky prank on you."

"Nope no prank, lost a bet."

"So you just ate all that?"

"Yeah, pretty brave right."

"Brave? Was it over a woman?"

"Yeah, didn't get her transcom ID." The soldier handed something over to the stinker. The guy looked it over for a second, it was a stick of white gum and a white pill.

"What's this?"

"Breath bleach gum and a Neutrafresh. Good breath comes from within."

The other men were all at ease and talking to one another when Daniel came walking up the steps to the platform.

Immediately then all went to attention as Isaiah spoke up, "Back at the UA academy I had this professor of history and he was someone that I could always go to for help if I needed it. He had this reputation for being a flunker, he would do anything he could to flunk students or so the students thought, actually the students just couldn't hang with his degree of detail that he took in making the tests. He was an outstanding professor during lecture or talking to him in his office, when it came test time he was hard nosed and you better have studied hard or you would flunk like a lot of the students did."

"He let us know of when the test would be a week in advance so I studied his lectures and the book with an uncommon thoroughness. When it came test time I thought I was ready, so I went to class sat down and he gave us a refreshing of notes and all that was just fine. Then he started reviewing things that none of us had heard of before. Someone asked him what he was doing and he said its in the book that means you should know it. Now we got scared and knew this was going to be a horrendous test."

"He passed out the test to everyone and told us to begin and when I got the test I and in total misery, reluctantly turned to the first page. Much to my surprise and delight noticed all of the questions were answered next pages all were answered. Then it came to the discussion questions and they were eloquently answered better than I could have done. And when I got to the last page it said this is grace. The professor said congratulations you all passed the test with flying colors and you all will get an A+ for your grade."

"The students started jumping and yelling for joy. He said what you have experienced here is grace and God gives grace to all that accept Jesus into their heart. Doesn't matter if they deserve it or not if they are the best person in the world or a putrid sinner if they accept Jesus he gives them grace in return you have passed the test."

"In the test of life if you accept Jesus then when you get to Heaven God will say to you job well done my good and faithful servant you passed the test. You may enter into Heaven for all eternity just for accepting Jesus into your heart. You know what soldiers? Everyone that was there for that test never forgot what grace was. If you have accepted Jesus into your heart as your Lord and savior you too know this grace that I speak of."

"You may not know this soldiers but we are going to be attacked once again and this time it is going to be here, at home, in downtown Athenia, and we are facing some of the toughest times that Ionious has ever known. Let me tell you something, tough times never last but tough people do. In the heat of battle when it comes, and it will, know that God is on your side. When you make a decision the Creator of the Universe conspires to make it happen. That which is behind you and that which is in front of you, pales in comparison to that which is inside of you. The strongest and most courageous person that you would ever want to be on your side and that is Christ within you. As we go into battle there are some that might be anxious or worried about their weapons like the Blood-Magnet that naturally strikes fear and worry in your heart unless... Know that the carnal mind has great worries, the spiritual mind has no time for worries or fear."

"Their Army is great in number, in training, and in skill. With all that they have going for them it might look like a mountain to you, know this, if you master yourself in obedience to Christ then you can conquer any mountain and any Army. Some of the greatest battles will be fought in the secret corners of your soul. God says that he is the Alpha and the Omega the beginning and the end know this, God is with you always from the beginning of this thing, and He will see you through it to the end. Peace never attacks you but troubles will, to attain peace and breakaway from the troubles that surround you, you have to seek peace with your whole heart and it will be yours. Go with God and in a heart of peace."

At the office of Aaron Alpha trouble was mounting as a Nivio Engineer entered his room to give a report. "Soldier, what do you have for me today?"

"Nivio report sir." Aaron takes the report on his Scroll and the Engineer swiftly leaves the room, like something was bothering him, you could see it in his face.

Aaron throws the Scroll on his desk and yells, "Get back in here soldier." He heard him halfway down the hall and reluctantly made an about face. Slothfully walking back he shakes his head in disgust.

Aaron takes one step out of the PASTway looks down the hallway sees the guy and says, "Don't leave this room with a report like this you should know better than that. We need to talk."

In his office Aaron says, "Did you even take a look at this report or did someone else write this? Because if you wrote this report and you think you can just walk out on me you might just need to find another line of profession."

"Sorry sir, I will do better next time."

"Yeah you will, now you're telling me that we are out and we cannot last another 24 hours with our current supply?"

"Appears so sir."

"Could this be an error?"

"Manually checked and double checked it myself a few hours ago."

"Where did this consumption come from?"

"Don't know sir. It was just depleted. Don't know how."

"What is the turnaround time on the Odyssey deposits?"
"One week sir."
"How much?"
"100 Kilos."
"What? We have already depleted that much and that's all that we have left? That won't last two weeks."
"War's consumer more energy, it takes time to refine it sir."
"Don't talk to me about war, you have never even set foot on a battlefield. What about the East Mountains?"
"Two weeks."
The General became very angry at this and started to boil over but he kept it all inside until he told the Engineer to leave. "That is all, I'll take it from here."
How could this happen? We have two ranges that we can pull from and the earliest that we can access them is one week. This is just unacceptable. Something must be done. "Grant, get in here!" The General said into his transcom in a somewhat stifled rage. If Grant and I talk I know we can figure something out.
Grant showed his face not knowing at all what he was walking into. Very chipper he said, "You called sir?"
"24 Hours till shutdown."
"What happened?"
"That's not important, what is though is how are we going to last another week with no refined Nivio or Vionium. Our ban on Vionium still set?"
"Never lifted. They are voting on it this Wednesday." Grant said to the General checking his Scroll.
"We can't wait that long. What do you think about moving some muscle around on Congress?"
"Do what you have to sir, I'll back you in whatever you decide to do."
"It's done then, get them on my transcom."
Hacking away as it required Grant got to work. In minutes he had the President pro Tempore, Moses Mu, on the line for the General. "What can I do for you General?"
General Alpha had Moses on his Scroll and was watching him talk as General Alpha said, "We have a problem."
"I'll see if I can help."

"We need Vionium."

"General you know that is restricted to the South. Don't you have other mines that you can pull from?"

"We need some and now. We need at least one week supply for our base and for all of our territory."

"We have a vote on Wednesday and you can just wait until we find out if the Senators think that you should have access to it."

"Well then, I know what I have to do."

"Sir we cannot just move the vote date up to fit your demands, you should have planned you consumption better. I am not going to just let you fuel this war."

"Here are my demands I want one week supply. I am asking you to inform the rest of the Senators that you have one hour to meet my demands."

"If the demands are not met?"

"We will get to that if it comes to that, I am hoping for you that it won't."

Now all they could do was wait and Grant began talking to General Alpha and they decided that if it should come to that then they would have to be ready. The General said, "We are going on full alert prepare to attack the North wall of Athenia and the Universal Mines be ready and on standby."

Chaos erupted in the base as everyone was going to the locker rooms and hangars. Aaron and Grant saw people running past their doorway immediately. Aaron's secretary came running in and said, "Sir, its a madhouse out there something crazy. How are you doing sir?

"Not good but it could get better within the hour."

"How is Esther?"

"Just as sweet as ever."

"She's takes after her dad." Aaron just smiled, she was always giving him nice compliments like that. Maybe that is why she has lasted so long around here. Somebody has to cheer the guy up every now and then. And with her its on a constant basis because he is always going through something where he needs some uplifting words. No one else is going to do it. I am sure that his wife does when he gets home but it is always good to be good to the people that ensure your livelihood.

"I just wanted to let you know that at 1:00 pm on Tuesday you have an appointment with her at her school. They are doing a presentation that I know you won't want to miss."

"I won't forget thanks for reminding me."

"Don't worry I'll remind you again on Tuesday."

"Thanks you're a sweetheart."

"Bye, I'll be praying for you."

"You too, Bye now."

Grant was curious about what this presentation was. "Sir that is very noble of you to attend your daughter's presentation in the midst of all this chaos around here."

"I would do anything for her no matter what's going on in my life."

He got nothing about the presentation, oh well I am sure that it will be good whatever its about. Now to this whole situation about Congress. I wonder if we'll still attack if they give us the Vionium?

The stirring and prompting of the Holy Spirit was there upon Grant Eta. "What I know is that God is bigger than this circumstance that we are facing here today Aaron. All things work together for good for those who love Him and are called according to his purpose. There is going to be a resolution and whatever and in however manner that this plays out we are going to believe God. We know that He rewards those who diligently seek him."

"He won't withhold anything from those who walk uprightly. If we don't get this Vionium we are going to have to put out a conservation measure that all of us must adhere to until our shipment arrives."

Halfway around the world in Isaiah's office Daniel said into the screen, "You're not walking uprightly Aaron and that's why you won't get any of our Vionium. You better just get prepared to live on reserves for a week."

The President Pro Tempore was on the transcom with Isaiah as Daniel was saying that. They were all watching what was happening at the North's base. "I knew they would not accept it and I asked them anyway. They all rejected the ultimatum and prepared for Wednesday's vote. I knew that they wouldn't go for it in any way not even one day's worth of it."

"There is just no way that we are going to fuel their war." Isaiah said grasping his Scroll.

"I said the same thing he is a madman he really is and to think that he would think that God is on his side. We gave them the evidence and I cannot wait till God steps in and resolves this whole thing. Hold on its time I am about to give him the news."

"General Alpha I have consulted with the Congressmen and they refuse to meet your demands, you should try conserving the energy that you have left. You will have to wait until Wednesday for the results of the vote. I wish you the best."

"You will be sorry for making this decision."

"It wasn't all me the other Congressmen all said no."

"It doesn't matter who it is they will pay."

Bomb the downtown area, kill everyone in sight and march through the city and conquer all, he was thinking in a mad rush. Furiously he typed and said this to Colonel Grant Eta, "Here are the orders see that they are carried out." His face red, rapid heartbeat, hands and head sweating he punched his desk sweat moved with the momentum of the direction his hand was going in before it hit, injuring his hand probably fracturing or even breaking something.

"Will do sir. You okay?"

"Get out of here!"

Immediately the plans went into effect as the alert was now full blown attack. If God is on my side then who can be against me. He never thought through it all that he might be the one in the wrong here. Nonetheless the city that they loved was about to be rubble and there was nothing that they could do about it. Here it was war at its best and now all of Ionious would be watching as I crush them for what they did to our territory.

Renown for his inspirational speaking and getting his troops motivated to do what was right in the eyes of God Isaiah did what any citizen of Athenia would do. "You all know what to do, if they want to bring it lets make sure they don't get too far." The soldiers in the room relayed the orders that was already on their scroll and went marching out to complete the tasks.

The ancient Greeks used a hoplite phalanx that really was just a wall of men with shields and spears. This was their method of warfare before they were taken by the ancients and in some sorts the hoplite phalanx would live again if Daniel had anything to do with it. He finally got his orders and just had to smile as he unplugged and opened his eyes from the interactive bible, to find out that his prototype would now be put to the test. Shields were his thing, and in the bible interpreting dreams was, so now what he had to do was use his skill of the shield and combine it for interpreting the enemy's next move after they see what they can and can't do with the advent and use of what he had worked so long for.

In his mind it was here the Titanomachy, the war of the Titans, some refer to it as the Clash. No matter what you call it there was a major battle going to take place here and if Daniel would have his way, this clash would have them scratching their heads when they see what he had been working on. He just used what already existed in the city and took it to his advantage.

When Casey and the crew got the word that they had a go his heart skipped a few beats and then he considered what it would take to get the job done. He was now a full blown pilot promoted and trained from the request of Colonel Grant, obviously he had made a lasting impression and that made him feel good. Feeling good about himself and the work that he did wasn't a normal thing it was something that just happened on rare occasion and when it did happen everything just started to click.

"Boosters on?"

"Check."

"Program ready?"

"Check."

"Hangar clear for takeoff?"

"Check."

"Controller giving a go?"

"Check."

It was now second nature and he had this flying thing down and had a good grip on the weapons too. He was good at handling any situation stressful or not if he had the knowledge to get something done accomplishing the task would be easy for him. After going over his checklist he asked his co-pilot in a very non formal way, "You ready for this?"

"I sure hope so."

His co-pilot was in control of writing the program and some of the weapons aspects and had good instincts for on the spot changes, you know going with the flow.

"Lets do this."

They were airborne in minutes and heading straight for the border somewhere Casey never made it to in his first flight with Grant. He knew that he was skilled and ready for anything that came his way now. The way this order system worked was they would just get to a location and get their orders on the go. This didn't bother him one bit, it did spark some anxiety to know exactly what it was that they were going to be shooting at. Maybe they were just dropping some jumpers out, you never know, you just have to trust God no matter what is asked of you and when you do get the word, do it to the best of your ability.

In the distance Casey saw a fleet of ONOA's heading for the border they were just specks on the scanner and dots in the sky. There were so many of them that they just made this line in the horizon that kind of curved with the shape of world. Casey had already made an impression and don't think that the primary reason that Samuel his co-pilot wasn't because of the indelible impression that he made on his superiors. Originally he was trained to be a ONOA programmer for their UAV operations and when Casey heard that there was a position up for grabs with her she made sure to take full advantage of the situation.

They had been friends back in college, Casey had so many degrees it wasn't even funny, although his outrageous humor had captivated the hearts of Grant and with the several others it was his laughter that was contagious especially to Samuel. If you could make Grant Eta laugh you had a job and his credentials only helped to support his decision to become a pilot.

So pretty much they were Bo and Luke or two peas in a pod, they were close and perfect for each other. The thing on Casey's mind was not what they were about to do, which was indifferent in his eyes no, it was just life, oh yeah and, "What why can't we get a hold of them is there anybody out there? I need some feedback here and nobody's giving me anything."

Samuel looked down to the screen and just below the console and said,"You can't have everything."

"I will have this though, all they said is we will get them when we get there, that is not good enough we need some feedback here and we're not getting it what tha heck?"

His lip twitched like an Elvis twitch seeing Marilyn sing to Kennedy and Samuel dared to utter, "I will do what I can, just calm down Casey. You ever take lamas class? Well if you could just do that now it would help."

"I am not married bonehead."

"Don't gotta be married to have a baby or to make one." Sam jokingly said to ease her tension.

"I don't need to think about making babies right now."

"We got like 20 minutes, so why not think about making babies?" Sam again just hung that one over the plate ready for it to get ripped to shreds.

"First of all my name might be Casey but I am not a girl got it?" He shrugged.

"And you're a guy too so we couldn't even make one if we tried."

"Good Lord. I have a question for you bonehead you know the rock that you crawled out from under did they have room service? Or did they have call girls? You could have been under a rock in Rock Vegas saw that one on the Flintstones."

"Don't you know that I am a decent person here and mind you a Christian so no, no, and uhh no, prostitution is a sin and none of that stuff happens on Ionious you know that."

"Yeah, but it is the first profession ever recorded in history and that includes Biblical times."

"What did Jesus tell them you know the whores? Go and sin no more. Got it?"

"You are uptight. Man, just trying to lighten up the mood a little."

"You know what you could do for me right now?"

"Shoot."

"Get me the order delivery time."

"You're still on that? Man are you on some kind of medication. Here take this."

Sam handed Casey a pink pill that had dark pink holographic letters circling around it that said, "Chill."

"Seriously, a chill pill what is this junk?"

"Its not junk just take it and you will feel just fine."

Casey threw it at the visual screen it hit that then bounced and hit the consoles and landed right in his lap. Very sincerely Sam made sure that he was looking right at him and said, "Its just Tylenol, I did the graphics. It will take the edge off. And if you're interested there were some hotties that I saw get in the back, when they all were boarding, nurses I think. I could get them up here and we could talk?"

"I just want the freaking itinerary is that too much too ask?"

Casey prayed a whole lot more than Sam and now was the time to do just that. Silently, "Dear Lord, I have no idea what we are going into and I really need to feel your presence right now and if you could just tell me what is going to happen. Am I going to make it out of here alive?"

The voice in her head was Jesus, "I have not given you a spirit of fear but of love power and a sound mind. Fear not and know that I am with you, always. You will survive I still need you to witness to the other Americans."

She didn't take the pill and now she was glad about that, because that was just what she needed to hear. Her anxiety and paranoia was calmed and now she could think straight. "I don't mean to be rude in any way but what we need to do here is pray all the way through this and ask the Holy Spirit to guide us or there is a possibility that we might not make it back today. I don't want to hear anything else from you okay just pray."

"Okay man, sorry, I'll do what I can to get that itinerary."

"Forget that, my trust is in the Lord I don't even need that anymore. Ever watch Star Wars and how Luke was going to drop that missile on the Death Star?"

"May the Force be with you."

"Yeah, the force is the holy spirit and when he turned off the electronics he used the force so what we need to do is use it, the holy spirit. Do you know how to pray in the spirit?"

"That would definitely be a no."

"You can pray and listen to Him though?"

"Of course I am good at that."

"Okay, that's what we're going to do from here on out I need you to just listen and talk out loud even we can both do it. I got a feeling that we are going to be dumping all of those guys in the back and then fighting like hell to get out of there and if we are going to make it then we are going to have to pray so lets get to it."

They were passing the border and in sight was the Athenia, way off in the distance they could see the tips of the skyscrapers, it kind of looked like Lando Calrisian's sky city from this distance with the clouds in between the tower tops.

"What is the altitude of our drop point?" Casey wanted to know as he made some calculations on the console.

This was the easy stuff for Sam. "10,000 Padiwan."

"Padiwan? More like Jedi Master." Casey exerted his rebuttal.

There were more calculations for Sam to do and after a minute he had something figured out by the way he was pointing at the screen. "I just know they will be waiting at that altitude we have to go underneath the rest of them if we want to have a chance."

"Can you do it?"

"In my sleep."

"Make the adjustments."

He did his thing and Sam just added for assurance, "This is really going to save us you know that."

"Yes knuckles, I saw the whole simulation, it looked logical."

"What is this? You sound like Spock now."

"Spock is cool. Have you seen any of the remakes?"

"Only all of the them."

"There is one where the real Leonard Nimoy is in this ice cave where Kirk finds him after being chased by this huge monster the abdominal snow dragon. Kirk says something like I need to go back out there and Spock goes, that would be highly illogical with this eyebrow raising voice, man it was just like the first Star Trek. How we doing on time?"

"ETA 3.2 minutes. Time to start praying?"

"Lets get some more info first. Scan for bogeys we need to know what we're flying into."

"Listen man we can see in the spirit faster."

"Go for it Jedi Master."

When you first close your eyes there is just blank or light creeping in, but after you pray and it takes over and you communicate instantaneously then the real dynamic art of the spirit sight starts. "Holy Spirit give me eyes to see. I need to see any bogeys on our course heading." It was clear skies there were some above none on his heading though so it all looked good for Sam.

The Holy Spirit talked to Sam silently, "You're clear for a drop off and turnaround unless any of the firefights above you see you at that altitude. I will notify you if they do."

"1.3 minutes till orders arrive."

"Are you ready?"

"As I'll ever be."

"What if?"

"What if what?"

"I don't want to think about it I just hope its drop and turnaround."

"Ever think that we are not in formation?"

"Doesn't matter now."

"I guess we'll just have to wait."

"Not long .2 minutes."

Here they were at 8,000 ft. and not far from where the others had already dropped. They were far enough in front that the dropped jumpers had already passed their altitude. They got the orders and it was not what they were thinking that it would be.

"Dang it, what is this I didn't even know that was on the agenda."

"We have to do it, what we don't know is if we will make it back or not."

"Yeah, I know that I am making it back, Jesus said I would. You better pray about it."

"What? I am with you I have to make it back."

"We are going to the Universal Mountains you never know what could happen over there."

"You're right I better pray."

"You better hurry we are dropping like now."

The jumpers were all going about ten at a time, there were hundreds of them and then they were gone. Dustin was one of the jumpers and he was doing a swan dive and loving every second of it and he was going to wait until the last minute to hit the button. When he did, he was way past the others and about 2,000 ft above the towers. He got to looking around and saw this ring around the city wall and he was curious what this was.

All he saw were buildings and he was preparing to land on one of the walkways when he felt this wall hit his legs. "Jesus help me." Now he was sliding down some embankment that was transparent he could see the buildings below him and what in the world was going on. His heart rate spiked and sheer terror was in his eyes. "What is this?"

Now the embankment was getting steeper and he was going faster and faster, passing the outskirts of the city then he could see the wall and, Thud! He hit something and it seemed to be grass and mud. He started to get up and slipped yeah it was mud. Then he wiped his eyes from the mud that cluttered them. "You okay?"

"What is going on why am I here? I jumped with about 200 other guys they were all...Oh no!"

Thud! Thud! Splat! They were all hitting the mud like raindrops or more like grown men that weigh about 260 pounds with 100 pounds of backpacks on hitting the slush at about 15 miles an hour. Not a pretty sight.

The soldier that had been there and watching the whole thing said, "Listen we all did the same thing it seems that they put up some kind of shield over the whole city."

"Can't we just run to the waiting ACT 3's?"

"Look over there through the mist."

"Are those our guys?" In great hope of what he thought he saw.

"Nope."

"Great!" The detached sarcasm couldn't be any thicker. He then started watching the soldiers get closer. "Isn't that one of our ACT 3's?"

"Sure is."

"Are they here to pick us up?"

"Nope that one barely made the turnaround before getting shot down."

"Just Great! So pretty much we're screwed."

"You could say that."

The other thing, as you know that there were many that Dustin couldn't figure out, was what in the world this outer wall shield thing was doing there? For some reason the guy that just so happen to know everything about the situation would also know about this but might get somewhat deterred if he asked another stupid question decided that he would have to answer this last one for himself.

So he goes up to the shield and punches it with his fist, and that was not the response that he was looking for, as it could have fractured or broken any number of bones in his hand. It was a lot sturdier than it looked. So the walk right through the thing didn't work, and he could see the South's soldiers coming to get all of them, so he pretty much figured that it was some sort of cage that they just stood around and collected jumpers. So he never asked the question, and isn't there supposed to be no such thing as a stupid question? Well Dustin now realizes that yes that would have been a very stupid question and he was very glad that he didn't ask it.

In the air was Sam and Casey and they had just dropped off Dustin and the rest of the guys that were supposed to get dropped off in Athenia which now were all sitting ducks. Now Casey could be at ease, even though he was not, about the fact that all they had to do now was to fly for 1300 miles and drop off the rest of the jumper nuts at the Universal mountains. Well at least she knew what and where she was supposed to be doing right now this should, underline, should, make her more at ease. This was not the case dear Watson it seemed to be elementary confusion and anger with a pinch of sadness just to get the red out. We now resume the conversation before Dustin and the nuts jumped.

"Okay, I am gonna pray." Sam said and well, this time he actually meant it so he started. "Dear Lord make me a bird, no no, Dear Lord I am flying all around this new world to me and I just want to know if I am going to die tonight please advise thanks and amen."

The remark that Casey had was very cunning, "Signs say yes. What kind of prayer is that? You should have gone with the bird one, at least that one is from Forest Gump and who doesn't like Forest Gump?"

"That prayer was to God and I accidentally messed up I say that line so much. And also I have no idea if God likes Forest Gump or not."

"Please, here is some advise, goodness you are talking to the creator of the Universe not Dear Abby, goodness Gump have some gumption about you. And of course God likes Forest Gump."

"Okay, I didn't know, I feel so inadequate around you, you know so much about God and all."

"Actually, I don't know that much, only what God tells me, and about Gump that was just a hunch I have no clue if God likes Forest Gump or not. You probably should ask Him and don't worry about messing up in a prayer it happens to the best of them."

"Thanks, that makes me feel a lot better."

"So are you going to ask Him or not?"

"About what?"

"If he likes Forest Gump or not."

"Oh, do you really think that I should?"

"Well, it never hurts to ask, you know that there are no such things as stupid questions with God. I have never, in all of my asking God for things, come across a time where God said that my question was stupid so I think you're good to go."

"Okay, here goes, Dear Lord please do not strike me down for asking this but, do you like the movie Forest Gump?"

"Sam, I love the movie, there are many great scenes that bring glory to my Kingdom from it."

Casey had to interject, "I told you not a stupid question. Did you actually think he was going to strike you down?"

"You never know it sounded like a very stupid question."

"Enough, God does like it, next subject."

Casey got this look on his face like he was in great anticipation to hear what he was about to ask. "Okay, I got one for you. How did you get saved?"

"It happened before we met in college you know that."

"I know, but you gotta tell me how you got saved."

"Okay I'll tell you, if you really want to know. It started my freshman year in College..."

"We were all just hanging out at this Mexican food restaurant near campus and I was having a horrible time in Calculus and I was studying before the food got there and my friends were all making fun of me for not making good grades in Calc. Two tables over completely unbeknownst to me at the time there was this table of girls and she must have seen how they were treating me and how it was affecting me. So she as beautiful as she could be, came up to me at the table and asked if she could have a word with me.

"She pulled me aside into the foyer waiting area and we both sat down her name was Lauren and we started talking she said the reason that she first noticed me was because I was tall dark and handsome and she said that she didn't mean to bother me but that there was something that she needed to tell me. I said sure go on and she said, I have a friend and her dad oversees the Lottery and this Friday there was going to be a drawing and I have the numbers if you will just write this number down you can have everything that you have ever wanted because it was mega-millions

"She asked if I was interested and I said why did you choose me she said I just saw what you were going through. You are going to have to call me on Wednesday so here is my number and then I will give you the winner. I said sure that would be great and she was very good looking just beautiful. So Wednesday comes around and I call her and she says that something has happened, and that I can still get every thing that I have ever wanted but the Lottery is being overseen by someone else but that she could give me something even better. I said that I was interested and I agreed to meet her under the tree on campus.

"We did and she looked so beautiful I was asking myself, what I did to deserve this or how lucky did I get? She said that is just it we don't deserve it and we should feel special because of what He has done for us. I wanted to know who did what and she said that you can have everything that you have ever wanted just wait until the next life after you die and in Jesus you can have a life better than you could ever imagine with this mind. There is just one thing you have to accept and believe in him in this life for you to see him in the next. I said I was ready to believe and she said what I needed to do and I accepted Jesus that day and I have been following him ever since."

"In witnessing you have to have answers for all kinds of people from different backgrounds. Some people think so abstractly and wonder why would anybody die for them? And if believing in this makes them go to heaven and why would something like that make them go to heaven? I have to tell them its like this you go to history class and you believe that Washington died for his country and JFK died probably just because he was a Kennedy. Its kind of like that, Jesus was like a Kennedy he was destined to die like JFK was just because he was the son of God. And to top it all off he died like Washington not just for his country but for everyone that has ever existed so they could be free from sin. He died with the weight of everyone's sin on his shoulders, the weight of the world so you could go to heaven. So that when Washington died it wasn't all in vain he went to heaven because he believed in Jesus and so did Kennedy.

Casey was flicking this new chill pill up in the air watching the word spin in the twirl and listening to Sam when he thought he had something to add, "As you were talking I can just tell that you have this incredible passion to see the lost come to know Jesus and that all may know of his love and grace. I have found if you just let Jesus rule every aspect of your life that people will be saved by your love for the King. I developed this outgoing personality where I could just go up and talk to anyone about the love of Jesus and have them saying the sinners prayer in a matter of minutes. Whereas some of my closest friends were atheists, and it took years for them to see the light, once they accepted Jesus they were radically transformed and new creatures in Christ. This calling that God has on our lives is not an easy challenge and it takes our constant prayer in the spirit to battle the evil that does not want to see these people saved."

The tone in Sam's voice went into TV personality mode he was so convicted by this, "When the fight gets to be too much for us to handle what I do is just get in the word and keep praying in the spirit and find new scriptures to battle the thing that is conflicting me."

Casey hit the roof of the cockpit with the chill pill, "If we fought for souls back on Earth with the Americans with the intensity that we are fighting with in this war, man, there would not be a lost one among them."

The coordinates that Sam was checking on were right on track and they had some more time to talk, "Why don't we help the guys back home you know?"

Casey caught the pill in his mouth then launched it on the screen in front of him. "One way or another this war is about to be over and when it is I am going back and I am going to join Houston with the fight no matter what."

With his finger, he traced the flight path on the screen in front of him. Sam's mind was in a few different directions mostly thinking about home though. "I want what we all want, and I think that if we had this technology back home we really could save those beasts in the East."

He was thinking about home too when Casey flicked a glowing holographic pill into the bottle. "Ever think about this? They just want to kill us and all we want to do is save them from eternal damnation. Hell forever for those guys that don't accept Jesus, I have been saved so long I really don't think about hell too much but man those guys just can't see the light."

There were a ton of Islamic jokes that Sam was thinking about after what Casey said he didn't say any of them though. "I swear and promise that this technology will convert those guys, transcom, DTR, Interactive Bible man this is powerful stuff and could convert any non-believer."

They were now getting close to the drop off point at the Universal Mountains. Sam's eyes were following the landing procedure not that he had to, it was always just pretty cool to see what all goes on in the aircraft during the landing. There were not that many defenders at the drop off point and they could land safely without any obstacles in the way. Casey said, "Everything cool on your side?"

"It's all good in tha hood Obi Wan."

"We gonna be clear for takeoff?"

"The heavens await."

Thick as a clump of bio-spray the tension in Aaron's room was ready to be broken. Aaron was getting in reports from the programmers that were busy on the new project. Hit or miss on most of the locations on the addresses that they were trying to barge into. Not all of them were going through, there were a lot of bad reports, well mostly bad reports however there was one programmer that was a former Athenia student that was hitting everything that he keyed in. General Alpha said, "Thank the heavens above because we have got plenty to be thankful for men."

There was a collective sigh of relief by some of the men in the room and Grant Eta was one of them. "Are we up to a thousand yet General?"

"Grant we're not even up to 50 yet."

"How many programmers do we have working on this?" Another Colonel wanted to know.

"Plenty have quit with no luck at all and right now we are down to about 34."

"That's it well then how many open doors do we have?"

"Twenty-one."

"We haven't got a chance at even making a dent in their city sir with all due respect."

"With all due respect Colonel our men are doing the best that they can, they are good at what they do and unless you have any other bright ideas about how to get into a city that has a shield dome over it then I am all ears."

"How is the Olympia doing?"

"Have you not heard? She is out of commission? Besides that our Act 3's have already tried firing at it and there is no use. It would take days for our Starship to even make a dent in it."

"What the heck happened?"

"We'll not go into that right now Colonel, there are more pressing items at hand."

"How are we supposed to get a million men through twenty one PASTways?"

"We are just going to have to make due with what God has given us for the time being, and right now what is happening as we speak is the Athenia student is training other programmers to do what he has been successful at, so by tomorrow we should have over two hundred open doors. If we want to get there though, I have said it once and I'll say it again, we are going to have to start praying."

"So we do have a lot to be thankful for."

"That is what I said and that is how good our God is. If you don't think it is God I can tell you the story about the programmers that we have and it is God people."

It was the same PAST that they all had used, however today its use was somewhat different. There were a group of soldiers ranging from Private to Corporal standing around it. Each with different things inside their packs, some had SWORD's for medic's stuff, and others had shield array setups, all had something even if it was just more ammo. Their Staff Sargent was checking the packs to make sure the right guy had the right stuff. Every now and then he would find someone with something that they were not supposed to have. He just discarded it on the floor and kept moving to the next guy. At this point no one had gone through the PAST they all at least thought that they were ready for what was about to happen next.

The Staff Sargent was getting anxious to some mad degree. "Alright you bunch of ballerinas what do you think this is a Ball that we are going to. This ain't no song and dance you maggots, you could lose it out there and its going to be your own freaking fault. You're about as prepared as a kitten in a too-too taking on a wildebeest with a blood-magnet."

One of the Private's that was as skinny as a pole and not a telephone pole more like a straw decided he would be the moron that would give up some prey for the slaughter. "Sir, I have heard that they won't shoot back. So what is there to be worried about?"

Pacing up and down the open path that was between them and the wall the Staff Sargent rifled out, "Which one of you scum sucking maggots said that? Was it you? You Mamby Pamby looking maggot of a worm?"

"No sir!"

"Well then which one of you too-too wearing ballerinas said that then? You clown nose bozo toes looking freak?"

"I did sir!" Said the toothpick.

"Let me ask you something brain boy maggot, have you ever taken a wasp's nest and shook it up and put it on your head?"

"No sir, I am not that stupid sir."

"It seems to me you are here, you brainless maggot, when we go into their city into their home its going to be like you took down a wasp's nest, a wasp's home, shook it up and just put it on your head, for each sting on your head or body that's one soldier down and those Kamakazi Harrey Carey maggots will sting you a million times whether they die or not, you soldiers are expendable. We have millions of you and if all of you morons go out there and get stung they won't flinch and neither will we. Any more questions maggots?"

Everybody didn't even move their heads they just looked around making sure that there wasn't some complete idiot that would speak up. Luckily there wasn't and then that brought on the thing that they were beginning to fear, walking through. They had no idea where they were going there was no intel on the address it was just like any other PASTway they all just hoped that it wasn't into a wasp's nest.

"I just want to motivate all of you to breathe, when you stop doing that well I'll just say this it ain't good. Got it maggots? We need you out there all of you are vital to this campaign. So let's go out there and getcha some."

The soldiers got this feeling in their stomach's that made it turn and then they saw the PAST stream from the top, over the other soldiers heads, a sparkling green that made it even more real to them. The first soldier walked through then the rest proceeded through the stream and some of them had their data pad in hand so if they were going to die as they walked through, they could contact their wives back home.

The first one through couldn't see a thing and there was no fire from the other side so for the minute it was safe for the others. They began packing in all seeing complete darkness as their AIIA suits were the same lack of light. "You good buddy?" A soldier asked another.

"Not a scratch." He checked his suit with the glow of his Scroll data pad.

They began to whisper in the dark, "Somebody turn their suit on light mode."

"You do it. I am not that dumb."

"Are you deaf? Somebody turn theirs on so we can all see."

From the pack there was one soldier that had what it took. "I'll do it."

There was a noise from another room and a plasma burst that lit the doorway for a brief moment.

The Corporal breathed a whisper. "Hold on there pilgrim, not yet. I am going forward to access the situation."

The soldier that spoke moved his data pad to the doorway and began to see what was on the other side. The other Private put his suit on a dim glow so that they could see somewhat in the room. There were no other noises from the room in front of them. A few gathered around to see what was on the screen. There were 14 soldiers in the next room that were planning on the Alpha's walking through the PAST in the Omega room. However the programmers got the go for the adjoining room and they were one step ahead of the Omega's.

In the Omega's room there were DNA sensors that would trigger blasters that would kill the Alpha's automatically if they were to enter. Down the stairway were 10 soldiers that were ready to blast any that made it through the blaster sensors. All that watched clinched their disrupters and with the glow shining the others did the same as they proceeded to get out their data pads to see for themselves.

There was a Private in the back, the same guy that just spoke up to the Staff Sargent that also got ridiculed, he began to pray silently. "Dear Jesus we need a solution here and only you can help us or we will have to turn around. Lead us, guide us, show us what to do."

While the Corporal was devising a plan Jesus began speaking to the Private and said what that they should do. The same Private that had been praying began typing in what Jesus told them to do on his data pad and then forwarded it to the others. By now they all had theirs on and when they got it they all looked to the back of the room and the Private smiled, and modestly waved, like yeah its me. The Corporal thought that this would be more successful than the plan that he was going to use.

Most of them agreed with it, but because he was the dunce that just got ridiculed they were not so optimistic about following through with the plan even though it was from Jesus some of them doubted. The ones that disagreed whispered and made angry gestures then the Corporal said, "God is not a respecter of persons he can choose the weak to lead the strong he did it all through the bible either you guys jump on board with this or you can go back if you feel safer."

"I am going." One of the doubters said and another followed, other than that, they were all with the plan. So they all got to work on it getting out all of the components out of their packs and assembling them just as Jesus had instructed them to do. When it came time for them to throw it in the Corporal did the honors and then the fun began.

The Corporal standing at the door entrance held out the flash looked back at the guys nodded and smiled and prodded the door just enough to toss it through. Total chaos erupted in the next room as the flash went off blinding everyone in the room. The South's soldiers known as Omega's were ordered to wait until they made it through the door before firing and it was too late they were all momentarily blinded now.

Minutes and shouts went on and they recovered their sight to blurry vision. The flash that was made in one of the SWORD's had a compound in it that triggered the DNA responses of several of the men and set off the blasters which disintegrated the nano-mesh alloy door.

The North soldiers were all in position and there was one standing right behind the now open doorway so the Omega's began shooting all that they had right at the Alpha soldier that didn't flinch an inch. One of the Alpha's said loudly, "Are you crazy get outta there you're gonna get shot." The plasma bursts just hit and slid down the shield array placed right behind the door.

The Alpha used his booster boots to float to the ceiling to a corner of the room as the shield slid open. When it slid open an Omega fired some shots that hit one of the Alphas in the arm as he sunk down on the shield. The Omega's then did what they could to began to find out what was going on in there. The first Omega snuck past the door only to be blasted by a neutral stun shot from the Alpha Private that was sitting on the shield just above the doorway.

The same thing happened until one of the Omega's slipped through and got a few shots off as the Scroll Walling was activated and lit up the room. The Alpha AIIA suits were all set to blend mode, and it was tough for the Omega's to tell where they were.

Quickly the assailant was neutralized by several of the floating Alphas. The other Omega's saw what was happening and knew that the room was a death trap so they decided to throw in a gyro-blaster. This would adhere to the floor and shoot in all directions at once to penetrate the shield.

The lounging Alphas saw that their shield was taking some hits and the SWORD techie programmed a flash that would make the Omega DNA to that of an Alpha soldier. Another Alpha Private did the honors of setting the blasters to stun on his Scroll Data Pad. The Corporal threw the new DNA reversal flash into the room it took effect and the Omega blasters obliterated the remaining Omega soldiers with stunning green plasma bursts.

The next room and the stairway was now secure and they had to make some choices about how they were to get to the Parthenon. There was no turning back now they had to proceed with their orders and could not return to that PASTway. If they needed a way back to the North base they would have to find another way.

The secured room was someone's residence and there were tables and chairs with lounging furniture scattered about the room, lit with Omega logo's on the Scroll Wallings. Once they were all in the room the Corporal accessed the injuries and it was the Private that spoke to Jesus that got hit in the arm. It singed his suit and the impact just left a bruise.

"You gonna make it buddy?"

"I think so, with God's help I will."

"That was one great idea soldier."

"Wasn't my idea Corporal it was Jesus, I just prayed and he talked to me."

"God is good."

"Yes He is Corporal, yes He is."

There was a subtle nod from the Corporal and a look into the soldiers eyes that foreshadowed the possibility that the same thing could be waiting for them on their way to the Parthenon. They all got the move out nod and a feeling that they are going to be depending on Jesus quite a bit in this journey. The proceeding feeling was that of one that they all were almost nothing without their savior. This just made them even more thankful for the grace and guidance that He imparts.

Down the modern stairs that felt like they had shocks on them all lit from underneath the men passed at eye level sconces on the Scroll Walling that lit their view even more. At the base of the stairs there was a doorway to the walkways outside that were bright with the visual gift from their star. Scroll data pads were out and in full effect scanning the exterior of the building out on the walkways. There was much activity and it was mostly Alpha's that had already made it through their first test, thankfully.

Their Staff Sargent was just getting the word about their news on their recent accomplishment and now they were instructed to wait on new orders before moving forward. The Corporal found out that things were new concerning their mission and that the Sarge would have something else for them to be doing before they went to the Parthenon. Private Chi began to pray and Jesus responded with this scripture from Isaiah 30:18 that said, "The LORD is waiting to be kind to you. He rises to have compassion on you. The LORD is a God of justice. Blessed are all those who wait for him."

Chapter 15
Will you Listen?

"Things to Consider"

God can talk to us in many different ways. Through other people like pastors or friends or through events that take place and it is up to you to listen. If you don't listen and act upon it there maybe dire consequences to your inaction. Right now we don't have on Earth the technology in this book to hear from God so it can be tough to know if you are actually hearing from Him or not. I strongly advise you to get in the Bible and learn as much as you can because that is the main way that God speaks to you and it is up to you to listen.

Chapter 15
Will you Listen

He had run them all and there was not anything that could make him any happier than finding new uses for his new technologies. Sariah came into Daniel's office where he was running the simulations and said, "Daddy I have been working on some new songs." There was one thing that made him happier than finding new technologies and that was his beautiful daughter Sariah she was the apple of his eye and could do no wrong, she was perfect to him. And she loved apple-juice as she took a sip, Daniel loved cooking up some new blends on the SWORD in the kitchen.

"Honey, I would love to hear them I am just working on something right now." Daniel was busy tinkering with something new, and he was on the verge of finding out how to get it to work.

"Daddy will you listen to me sing?" Her beautiful brown eyes looked up at him and she softly said, "Pleeeaaase." Using many syllables this art of the Daddy daughter relationship just melted his heart and he had to take a break and hear her latest.

"Sugarbear I am so sorry, what was I thinking sure I want to hear you sing, what have you got?"

"I have been working on singing in the spirit and I was thinking that we could sing a duet." She swayed with her hands together and her shoulder to her chin brown eyes looking up.

"Do you have the songs on your Scroll?" He hadn't sung in the spirit in a week and was looking forward to sharing this experience with Sariah.

She threw her hands down and smiled in the cutest way, "Daaady, just listen to me and let the Holy Spirit guide you."

"I know that its just been a while since I have done a duet so work with me if I am horrible, okay sweetie?"

"You're not going to be horrible Dad you just sing about Jesus."

"Okay lets go."

Sariah closed those precious eyes and turned her head heavenward and took a deep breath and started.

"Holy is the Lord God almighty,
you create all things with your glory,
I will praise your miraculous works,
I will worship your amazing words,

Her voice was soft and so sweet, and her pretty eyelashes graced back and her eyes were on her Dad, so that he would join in on the singing. So with a humble heart he began.

"There is no one else like you,
in the Universe and your creations anew,
I could never find someone with such grace,
such a beautiful thing the cross you alone can save.
Give me strength and your knowledge to seek,
give me hope when all is bleak,
let your love shine and your glory proclaim,
you are you were and you will always remain,

His voice was Tenor and he reached some Pavarotti notes as his praises declared the goodness of the Lord. It was all extremely powerful hearing him sing and this affected Sariah as she was ready to take over and she began swaying to the music that was extrapolating from the last melodies sang. Their musical technologies were very advanced and reacted to the melodies that are being sung.

You are my rock and my fortress in you I trust,
forever you are merciful forever you are just,
you move your people like you move a mountain,
springing up from the depths you rose again,
Though valleys may come I can always see the top,
your dwelling is magnificent I build my house on this rock,
you are enthroned in everlasting glory,

let this servant sacrifice to tell your story,
Your words are in my heart and praise on my lips,
you have brought me from the depths I am thankful for this,
your works are a river of miracles I will praise,
your words are water to the soul you have saved.

Normally she was a very tough girl and there were few things that made her cry. After she sang the last verse there were tears in her eyes as she began to think of what it will be like in heaven and of how thankful she was that she is saved. She was a very sensitive and precious girl and her Dad saw her crying and went over to give her a hug.

"I love you, you know that right."

"I love you too Daddy."

She kept on crying and her Dad said, "Sugarbear its alright." That was all that he said and she still remained crying embracing the presence of God. After a while her Dad was able to comfort her and they began talking about her presentation.

"Would you like for me to recite what I am going to say Daddy?"

"Sure precious, can I give you a few tips?"

"I don't mind. It would help a lot, sure critique anything I say Dad I know you have good judgment in speaking."

She started out by giving the imaginary crowd the cutest curtsy holding the edge of her beautiful dress, her knees bent, and she bowed her head, and then looked up and her smile curled to thunderous applause. Her Dad was clapping with sheer joy ready to hear what she had been preparing for all semester. So with no further adieu she started and she was so excited about it her Dad sensed the magic that the crowd would feel from just seeing her talk. Her first introductory paragraph went without a flaw and Daniel had some suggestions.

"I am sorry to interrupt, but would you like for me to critique you as you speak or after the presentation?"

"Speak up anytime you think I need work on something."

"Sure thing sweetie. Okay you are doing great, I think that if you enunciated your words a little clearer and just speak a little louder it would be superb."

"Like this?"

She began talking with the same energy and enthusiasm only paying close attention to the way that she talked and it sounded quite sophisticated.

"Just a little louder baby girl."

"Okay."

Using her diaphragm that she had been taught to use in choir she really sounded out and could be heard, he was sure, by the back of the room wherever she was going to be speaking. Now, she had it going her speech could rival the Prime Minister with all of her eloquence and clarity that he delivers on a daily basis in front of Congress. Someday she could be a Senator or even the Prime Minister if that is what God has called her to do in life. For now she must concentrate on the task at hand and that is this speech that she will be giving to her classmates and also to General Alpha.

Her Dad saw her talents in speaking and knew that she could do whatever that she wanted in the government if this is what God wants her to do. "Beautiful sugarbear, just great!"

Now she was nearing the main point of the speech and she wanted a buildup to be very thought provoking so she used her skills in her drama class and her beauty shined through. When she spoke the power point words, it was on point, and on tact, her case was thoroughly valid and her Dad Daniel sensed that this would move anyone to emotions no matter what your beliefs were.

"Very well done Sariah, magnificent."

Now she only had a few more paragraphs to go and she wanted to backup her statements and she illustrated them extremely well with hand movements and gestures. As she concluded and left the remainder of the speech to her friend which was just the final paragraph she curtseyed and again thunderous applause erupted from the music program that was also a simulated audience.

Amidst the claps and cheers she heard the most important one of all and that was her Dads. "So how did I do, overall?"

"Without any doubts the best speech I have heard in a long time. You left no doubts as to your case, you presented the evidence with punctuation and eloquence and delivered a resounding point that all should know by now."

"Thanks Dad, you know you really helped me out after a while I am going to go and watch the presentation again mixed with Esther's video and see where I need to improve."

"Sugarbear do you have a minute?"

"Sure Dad, what is it?"

"There is something that I want to talk to you about. Don't get me wrong here sweetie your speech was wonderful and if it is successful you could be an instrument used by God to change the tides of this war. If you don't though I am still going to love you and just know that there might be something that I can do or that General Omega can do to bring peace back to this planet."

"There are some people that are just so thick headed that no matter what you say you can't change them, these people only look at the outside and they don't turn to God for answers, or what they call God is made by man. We both know what you're speaking about is right but these people that look to this man made God won't so I just don't want for you to be disappointed if General Alpha doesn't listen. Okay sweetie?"

"Thanks for telling me that I wasn't sure what would happen with the war after the speech. I will do my best for God and not for any man."

"That is one of the wisest things I have ever heard you say." Daniel hugged her and gave her a kiss on the cheek. "The speech is tomorrow and there is something that I want for you to have that I made for you."

"What is it Daddy?"

"Now listen, I know things that no one else knows about this presentation and if you clip this to your dress you will be safe and just know that I will be right there watching you so there is nothing to be worried about I will protect you if I have to."

Daniel handed her a small pink clip that would match her dress for tomorrow and Sariah looked at it intently with her big brown eyes and started to wonder what it did. She pressed the diamond on the top and began to walk to the kitchen when she neared the door she saw beautiful streaming pinks and purples all around her. It was a shield that was activated if anyone got near her that would keep her safe.

She immediately ran to her Dad her dress swaying from side to side as she jumped into his arms and said with elation, "Dad you're the best. Are you going to tell me how it works?"

"The energy frequency modulation emits a shield…"

"Daaady what does it do?"

"Okay whenever you wear this you are protected, I love you and I don't want anything to happen to you if there are any Alpha's there.

It detects intent of those around you and is activated if an intent is directed at you. So if an Alpha soldier decided to, God forbid, tackle you or shoot you it would automatically be activated and nothing would harm you."

"You really are the best Dad. You made this for me?"

"Yes sugarbear, I know things that no one else knows about your presentation and I know what could happen. The bible says to not fear because God is with you always so when you deliver your speech do not be afraid I will be with you and so will God and I just added a little insurance that everything will go as planned."

"Can I wear it wherever I go?"

"Its yours wear it anywhere and you will be safe."

"I noticed that when I bumped into the wall it reacted, is it supposed to do that?"

"There is an elasticity shield inside that conforms to your shape if you are to run into the shield if you hit something like a wall. If you see someone shooting at you or going to tackle you just crouch down and the shield will go solid on the outside and you will not be harmed and safe. In the bible it says that God is our tower and safe refuge just think of this as your safe refuge."

She was so excited that she gave him a big sugarbear hug and a kiss and Daniel just smiled with jubilation. "I am just glad that the Lord has given me the knowledge to make something like this for you, God is so good, remember that in all things that you go through. God is good to those that honor Him and you do so you will always be blessed."

"What is that smell Dad? Is dinner ready?"

"Smells like leg of lamb to me. Mom must be on the SWORD."

"Lamb my goodness that smells so good, you know that's one of my favorites."

"Mom knows the best recipes on the planet. You want to go eat?"

"Sure." She looked in his eyes already in his arms and squeezed his neck pulled back so she could see his face and smiled and said, "I love you."

"Sugarbear I love you too."

He put her back safely on the floor and they began walking towards the kitchen from his office with her out in front her saw her hand and grabbed it lifted it up and kissed it. "I will always make sure that you are safe and protected God has great plans for you Sariah."

Knowing her existence as a daughter that is just in grade school the thought of doing great things for God or the Government made her blush. "Daad don't make me embarrassed."

"I am not I just know that God has great plans for you and that someday you will be a great woman of God no matter what you decide to do or what God calls you to do. Seek you first the kingdom of God and His righteousness and all these things will be added unto you."

"I love how you know the bible so good Dad."

"Years of living in the interactive bible you learn the bible word for word. You can look forward to learning what the bible means to you in your own life and how you can use your knowledge of it to help others."

Her Mom was busy putting plates on the table and when Sariah saw her Mom she went running to give her a big sugarbear hug. "Maaoooom tell me is it leg of lamb."

Zeph picked up the plate with the food on it and displayed it to her, there was a perfect leg of lamb cooked tenderly that permeated the air with an aroma that made the senses heightened for Sariah. "I have the best parents in the world. Guess what dad did for me."

In the cutest and sweetest way that she knew how to show her mom her new protection clip she said, "Hit me."

"What are have you lost your mind?"

"Do you have a mirror?"

"Yeah." She handed her the mirror. Sariah look intently at her head.

"Nope its still there. Haven't lost a thing. Now will you just hit me?"

"I am not going to hit you sweety."

"Will you at least tackle me?"

"No sweety."

"Well then how else can I show you my new safety insurance? I know, Dad do you have a disrupter on you?" He reached for it and handed it to Sariah she then handed it to her Mom.

"Okay, Mom I am ready go ahead shoot me."

"Daniel, what have you done this time?"

"Honey, she is just trying to show you what her new shield clip does."

"Shield clip?"

"Yeah Mom its a shield clip. THE Coolest thing ever. I just ran into a wall and it has this elasticity inside thingy that allows me to not get hurt if I run into things or if something tackles me or even shoots at me." She then pressed the jewel in the clip on her dress and asked her Mom, "Okay will you just hug me?"

"Sure sweety." She leaned over and went to give her a hug and her arms met a beautiful pink and purple streaming shield. "Daniel this is amazing."

"She has a big presentation tomorrow and I want for her to be safe so I made it for her."

"Babe, that is so good of you. How does it work?"

"I am glad that you asked. Okay the energy frequency modulation emits a shield..."

She immediately stopped him in mid sentence and said, "Baaabe! You can tell me later. The food is ready, lets eat."

Dad and daughter resoundingly both said, "Great, Jinx you owe me a Oranos."

Daniel just laughed and said, "I said it first sweety."

"No Daad I did."

"Okay, you win I'll get you one from the SWORD, fair?"

"Sure Daad." She said lovingly. "Get you one too it was pretty close."

He went over to the sword and typed one up and brought them both to the table and said, "I am hungry and thirsty here is your Oranos, drink up. Last one done is an Alpha."

They both grabbed for their cola and started gulping of course Daniel finished first and then he responded to the triumph and said, "You're the Alpha sugarbear."

"I am from the South and I will always be an Omega."

Daniel bowed his head and looked over at Sariah and smiled at her comment. "Lets pray sweety, Dear Lord we come to you in the name of Jesus and we thank you so much for this beautiful day and for all that you have blessed us with. We ask in Jesus name that you protect Sariah in her presentation tomorrow and make her words change the minds and hearts of the Alpha's and especially the General show him the truth and make it known to all the truth of General Omega. We also ask that you anoint Sariah to grow to be a great woman of God someday that she can be a servant of your glory and bring others to Jesus. By your love and grace we thank you and ask this in Jesus name."

They ate the tender delicious juicy leg of lamb had many laughs and even some meaningful conversation which was the norm at the dinner table. Then it was time for Sariah and Esther to get together to work on the presentation together. When Esther got there it was startling to say the least, she walked through the front door particle streaming and all and Daniel and Sariah had a plan for Esther that she would soon find out about.

Sariah said to Esther, "I am so glad you could make it today, there is so much going on, okay first of all our pet tragle Cooley chewed up my favorite holographic projector base and broke it and now my Dad is getting ready to punish him." Esther snuggled up to Cooley, the cross between dinosaur and cat, that was on the floor and started scratching behind its ears.

"Sugarbear, I am looking for it I'll be there in a minute." Daniel shouted out from another room in the house.

"Hurry up Dad! Esther is already here."

"Okay, almost ready."

Esther wanted to know, "What is he getting?"

"You'll see."

"This is a very pretty clip on its collar."

Daniel barged into the room. "Where is that rascal?"

Sariah said, "Right here with Esther Dad."

"Well let him go we gotta do what we gotta do."

Esther saw the disrupter in Daniel's hand. "What are you going to do?"

"He's been a bad little tragle and we have to shoot him."

Esther was outraged at the idea and she had to stop this from happening. "I cant let you do that Mr. Delta." And then she threw herself out in front of the tragle.

"We just gotta do it, he ate up the brand new projector that I bought Sariah."

"Please don't Mr. Delta, please." Sariah winked at Esther without Daniel seeing and pointed to the clip and she caught on to what was going on here.

"We have to Esther."

"Okay if you must."

"Now just stand back Esther everything will be alright."

"Yes sir."

She walked over to where Sariah was sitting on the couch. Now the girls were getting ready for a laugh to really let Daniel have it. Daniel readied his position and pointed the disrupter right at the tragle and fired. The blast was absorbed by the energy shield that was activated by the pink clip.

"See Esther, this is the new clip my Dad made for me will protect me and keep me safe. We love our tragle and we would never hurt it you must think we are crazy. We are going to go practice now okay Dad?"

"Sure girls you just go on and do your very best." As they were walking to Sariah's room Daniel reminded them. "As if it were for God."

Sariah's room had everything that a girl could ever want all the glitter and technology. "I just love your room Sariah you can really decorate."

"Thanks, I put up this one yesterday its pretty cool I guess."

"So how have you been its been a while since I have seen you."

"Good, God is always good to me and my family. My Mom and Dad have been getting along so great I am so proud of them. It's one thing just to tell your wife that you love her but my Dad is always showing her that he does in doing the things that she honors. My Mom does the same thing she thinks the world of my Dad, she is always telling him that he could do anything that he sets his mind to if he keeps his eyes on God and asks for His guidance. She is always reminding him of all the good things that he does for her and that he does in life. He really needs the support with this war going on and all it can get pretty depressing for him sometimes, well most of the time really. That is when my Mom isn't around. He really needs her love and support in his life or he wouldn't make it. And of course I am always there to be a positive reminder that God loves him."

"With your Dad's job, it sounds like he has it pretty rough."

"You have no idea, there is this evil woman named Martha at work that is always putting him down and telling him that he can't do anything right and that he should just quit on what ever he is doing. She is so evil she is a mental manipulator and is always messing with his head, she never lets him talk and give his ideas, she always cuts him off before he can ever say anything. She never says anything good about him, when he has an idea she always tries to take the glory for it so she can get a promotion."

"There are just some people that are just plain evil and don't know how to serve God they just serve other people and are not in God's will. The job of the wife is to serve God and your husband and your Mom knows how to do that. If you love God then you're just naturally gonna love your husband if he is a good man and your Dad is. I saw you wink at me I knew you and your Dad were just playing around with the disrupter and all."

"It was set to stun and my Dad makes the best shields anyway so I knew it would work. It has to because it has to protect me." Sariah clipped on the shield device and then extended her hand way out and then pointed back to herself. The shield lit up and went to the beautiful streaming colors that matched the pictures that were on the Scroll-walling behind her from Esther's view.

"Can your Dad make me one?"

"You're not that special."

"Why not?"

"Sure, he could make you one I guess. I'll ask him okay?"

"Okay, do you want to get to work on the presentation?"

"Yeah where do you want to start?"

"At the beginning I guess."

They rehearsed for over an hour and then Esther went back home not without thanking Sariah's parents for letting her visit. Sariah's Dad commented on how well mannered Esther is and that he was glad that they were friends. He then said it was time to go to bed early today because of the presentation and all tomorrow, so he went into her room read her a story and said a prayer over her and kissed her goodnight and said that he will program her Scroll walling to wake her up early. He was the best of Dad's, as far as being a good Dad can get, well he was the best Sariah thought, as she went to sleep.

When she awoke she found some of her favorite direct view moments of her and her parents on the walling and she was so glad that he did that so she would be in a good mood, and not worry too much about today. She was very intelligent when it came to judging peoples actions and determining where there heart was. She also knew where Martha's heart was when she would be evil to her Dad and it would make her very angry that someone would be that evil to her Dad someone that she loved.

When her Dad would tell her about the insipid things that Martha would do she would say things like, "Well, she just has an evil heart." She knew that his woman was not a good person and also not a good Christian either, so she would always tell her Dad to fire her and be done with her evil ways. And all of her ways were evil even though she put on a good front for other people when it came down to it she was of Satan and not God.

Sariah was up and about and getting ready for school when she found a note that her Dad had left for her on her dresser it said:

Sariah I love you more than anything and I know that God has a calling on your life. I pray that your presentation goes wonderfully and that it changes the heart of the officials of the North Army and government. Also, that God will anoint your words so that all will hear and know that it is God. May you and Esther do your very best, so that you and all will be blessed by what you have to say. Seek God first and His righteousness and all these things will be added unto you.

Love,

Dad

Don't forget to activate the shield clip that I gave you.

It was getting late and she was now ready to go so she went into the kitchen to pick up her breakfast and lunch and see her parents before they left for work. Daniel was wearing his usual casual clothes to work today and Mom was dressed looking very nice.

Daniel was sipping some herbal coffee and looked up and saw Sariah looking just beautiful in her new pink dress and said, "Sugarbear, you look great I just know that you are going to do wonderful today, did you get the note?"

"Thanks Dad, and yes I got the note, that was very sweet of you to think of me and don't worry I have been praying about this, so stay close you are both invited if you want to go."

"We will be there, here's your lunch we'll be praying for you." Her Mom said as she left for work.

Daniel's coffee cup was done and Sariah had her lunch in hand and was ready to go so she looked at her dad like, this is it. Daniel had some positive words for her, "Be strong in the Lord never give up hope you're gonna do great things today I already know. Mom and I will be there for you and guess what?"

"Whaat Daaaddy?" She said with those big brown eyes.

Her Dad was sitting there on the chair and had two clips in his hand both different colors of green and he held them out for Sariah to see. "I made a clip for your mother and I to wear today, Don't worry about a thing you just go up there and speak what the Lord has given you." Daniel saw her pink clip that was there on the table and picked it up and said, "You wear this and you will be safe no matter what happens don't be afraid of anything."

She clipped it to her dress and pressed the pink jewel. "Thanks for all your support you're the best Dad a girl could ever have."

Just before she went through the PASTway her Dad said, "I love you sugarbear."

"Love you too Daddy."

When she got to school her friends were just getting there too and she wasn't late so she sat down at her desk and flipped up her Scroll screen on her desk. The teacher was going through her desk and then started typing on her Scroll data pad as the words showed up on the Scroll Walling behind her for all of her students to see what the itinerary was going to be for today.

Sariah was checking the walling to see when her and Esther were going to give their presentation and then she found it and it said that they would be the last ones to go. She thought that this would be great so she could see how the others did on their presentations, so she was fine with it. She looked over her notes until Esther finally got there, and sat down in the desk beside her. Esther was part of the integration students from the North she was also the General's daughter.

The first wave of students had already given their speech and all was going fine, then General Alpha walked through the PAST. It was his first time back to the South since he narrowly escaped from being a POW. All the other parents that were from the South had a severe hatred for this man and just stared at him as he made his way to the side of the room.

When Daniel and his wife arrived you should have seen the look on General Alpha's face. He thought Daniel was dead, and now here he is alive, in person, something must be going on he thought. Daniel winked over to Sariah as he settled into the other side of the room close to the front where she would be speaking.

Finally it was Sariah and Esther's turn to go and they arose ladylike from their desks with datapad in hand. Smiling as bright as sunshine they made their way up to the front, curtsied to applause, then typed in something and the walls were surrounded with images of the Zeus mountains and General Omega sitting at his desk talking to some soldiers. The movie on the walls would go along congruent with their speech.

Esther began the speech by introducing herself and Sariah to another applause and elation on the faces their parents. Daniel began praying for protection of his daughter and a change of heart of General Alpha.

"The very first words of the bible were, "In the beginning was the word." There are thoughts behind every word spoken the creator of the universe thought before he spoke he did not just speak the words without thinking. Man develops their own methods of systems that try do determine what the thoughts are behind a mans words however man is flawed and man cannot take into account every variable or experience that someone goes through to determine the thoughts behind another man's word. Man looks at the outside while God sees the heart and knows your thoughts. Today, we have a technology that can record a person's thoughts called Direct View. We also have the DTR that makes this possible. What happened on the day that the Zeus Mountains were destroyed was that the DTR was programmed to give the order to fire upon those mountains not General Omega. General Omega did not give the order for the QUEST Starship to fire upon those mountains. Here is a forwarded movie of the events around General Omega following up to the events that took place that day. Never once did he give any orders for this."

"Also, here is the movie of the ones that programmed the DTR to give that order and the events that transpired with them before that proves that they were responsible for the attack and wanted to start a war for their own gain. These are the facts presented to you as they occurred only a fool now would think that General Omega gave those orders. So I ask are you an fool? I hope you are not."

The speech ended to mixed applause from the North in attendance however the people from the South all erupted in applause and whistles and screams. One of the Dad's from the South screamed aloud with his hands cupped directing his voice at General Alpha, "What they have said is a fact they presented the truth now you evil people from the North are killers."

A yelling match then ensued which led to soldiers storming the room as Sariah was running to her Dad on the side of the room, frightened to death, and was shot but didn't get harmed and her pink clip emitted a shield that protected her. Daniel, his wife, and Sariah were not getting shot at to no avail due to the shields and they narrowly escaped out the back PASTway to safety.

The melee ended and General Alpha and his clan went back to their house to convene to discuss their next step in defeating the Omega's once and for all. General Alpha called for his leaders to meet him in his office to setup orders.

There was a stern seriousness about the look of Colonel Grant Eta as he entered the room. "General I came as fast as I could."

"Thank you for making it, have a seat."

"Thank you sir."

"Let me tell you what I have been thinking, here recently my daughter gave a speech and it has come to my attention that we might shouldn't even be in this war in the first place. Let me tell you why, I wouldn't even listen when General Omega pleaded his case that he didn't give the order and I wouldn't even watch the video of the dream from Ezekiel Epsilon. Someone messed with the DTR and made it give the order and it wasn't Omega."

Colonel Grant looked at him like he had lost his mind there was something that he was already cooking up and now it was just a matter of getting the okay. "General none of that matters because tomorrow Congress votes to give us Vionium and I know for a fact that it is not going to pass. I just got wind of the preliminary results of the vote and it is unanimous that they keep the ban."

"We don't have a chance and here is where my plan comes in. I say we send our best troops into Athenia and take Congress hostage hold them up and make them vote for us. It's all done on data pads with a security code that is entered with the vote. The DTR won't know that we are holding disrupters to their heads and we win the Vionium and we win the war. Either way you look at it we win."

"I am not so sure that this would be the best thing to do." General Alpha commanded.

Another soldier that was there said, "It might not be the best thing to do but it is the only thing we can do. If you don't know this it is blackout for all of Olympia if we don't get that vote. We have to do this sir. Does anyone else agree with me on this?"

"I vote yes." Another Colonel said.

"I vote yes." A soldier spoke up.

"We have to do this its the only way." A Captain said with respect.

"I agree." Said the Captain in the back of the office.

Everyone in the room accept for the General agreed so he compromised. "Okay I will agree but we can't just storm in there until you give me enough time to find out more about this with Zeke. Agreed?"

They all said, "Agreed sir."

"Now to go find this Ezekiel Epsilon. Colonel Eta I need you to head up this operation so get to it. I want him here within the hour."

"Yes Sir, dead or alive? Or does it matter?"

"Alive you imbecile, I have to talk to him."

"Sorry sir, I didn't know."

"Sometimes I think that you are so poor that you can't afford to pay attention. Now shut up and go get Zeke. We will setup camp here bring him back to me. Listen I trust you and I would give the shirt off my back for you if you mess up I am here."

"Will do sir." The salute was kind of frustrated and then he left to do his duty no questions asked.

Chapter 16
Conflict with Congress

"Things to Consider"

When we finally accept Jesus into our hearts it is our job to get the word out and witness to others so they can get to Heaven with you. In this Chapter General Alpha has the task of getting the word out about his newfound belief and it turns out to be a very difficult task. Think about ways that you can witness and bring others to Christ.

Chapter 16
Conflict with Congress

The various array of mountains that are found on Earth are quite beautiful, its just that you have never seen a mountain like the one that General Omega was on. It was one of the base camps of the Coeus Peak of the Universal Mountain Range. The mining operations were very far away and this camp was springing full of life in this time of year. There were signs of the change of season on the various asunder of giant trees that speckled the landscape. The leaves ranged from the full spectrum of colors and you never knew what kind and color of Nivos were going to be soaring through and above them.

It was Wednesday morning the day that Congress would be voting later on that afternoon and General Omega had to clear his head and have some alone time to think. Many people have places that they go to think and for General Omega this was one of his favorites. It had everything, an incredible view, and the air was intoxicating with the leaves, and bark sap bringing forth a scent that could rival Ruth Omega's cooking. When Ezekiel had contacted the General he was perched in his nest of a different kind of house, one that actually had more windows than walls. He got the word to meet him there with chimney smoke billowing, so there they would be two peas in a cheddar pod with a ma-g-sniff-a-cent view.

The depths of contemplation that the General was going through could be very similar to that of Jesus in the garden of Gethsemane praying. Just before Zeke arrived the patterns of his contemplation were prayer, answer, conversation with Jesus, plead, then dig deep for virtue, all cyclical. When he did arrive, this is what he heard from the General, "All good things in life are from you and if they are not then it can't be from you. I have given all I have and now I need you to show me the way, my ways are not your ways so show me what to do, what to say. You know this planet and what it can become so bring us back to the way it was and the way that it can be."

Not knowing if he should interrupt the General sensed him in the room and said, "Zeke! What a blessing, sit, anything to drink?"

"Thank you sir, I believe that I am the one who is blessed, and I can get it, just stay there, you don't have to stop for me." Zeke went to the SWORD and began typing in an exotic. "Jesus will give you the answers you seek."

The General confidently smiled and took a sip of hot Odyssian Coco, "I have been in this too long good friend. Do you bring me news of some sort of heavenly relief?"

The exotic was very pungent at first imbibing, and after very smooth and fresh. He sat with drink in hand as the bitterness was washed away and a cool creamy fruits slid down his throat. "Your prayers have been answered and they want me."

"Go on."

"Direct view on Alpha has him talking to Grant Eta saying that he is thinking about calling the war off. He might want to make some sort of negotiation for Vionium if he agrees to cease fire."

"What in the world changed his mind?"

"His daughter Esther and Daniel's daughter Sariah. They gave a speech and now he isn't sure if he should have ever been in this war."

"Two girls did what none of us could do."

"He will use anyone sir, that will walk in His will."

"What does he want with you?"

"Details, he wants to see it all for himself, everything, the dream, direct views, there are things I know and can explain that no one else can concerning the DTR. He trusts me. I am here to get your opinion."

"For Heavens sake Daniel, go and don't even put up a fight. If I were you I would just walk in there before they get you. They are coming for you I presume?"

"General Alpha has sent Grant Eta to find me."

"Do everything that you can show him the truth and he will listen to you."

"Thank you for everything sir I better be leaving he has also agreed to take control of the vote unless he gets the information from me so I better be going now."

"Godspeed Ezekiel Epsilon." He finished his exotic drink and sprang for the PAST he was on a mission now.

In his office he picked up his Scroll Datapad that contained all of the access codes to the DTR that would allow him to give General Alpha all of the necessary information. He typed in the codebreaker to grant access into the General's home and proceeded in that direction. When he arrived there were armed guards that began questioning him.

"Lean forward for an identification scan here, keep your eyes open."

Another guard that had a disrupter to his gut said, "You have no authorization to be here give me one reason why I shouldn't shoot you dead right now."

"I am Ezekiel Epsilon and I have urgent business with the General."

"We will just have to see about that."

With the disrupter firmly in place the guards walked Zeke into General Alpha's office. "Sir, I am sorry to bother you but we seem to have an intruder that claims he is Ezekiel Epsilon."

"Zeke, come in have a seat." General Alpha motioned with his hand for Zeke to sit over in front of his desk. "That will be all men, as you were."

While the guards were walking out one said to the other, "That really was Ezekiel, my goodness, he doesn't have long to live if he is seeing the General." They were oblivious to what had happened before with Colonel Grant.

Back at the Alpha headquarters they got to know one another. "Where is Colonel Grant Eta, Zeke?"

"I am not sure."

"Did Grant not bring you here?"

"I thought I was here to give you the information that you requested."

"Yes, yes, so lets get to it we have other plans in the works unless you deliver."

"Just tell me what you want to know, I will deliver."

"You can start by telling me if General Omega gave the order."

"No, he did not it was the DTR."

"So you have evidence to back this claim."

"It is not a claim it is a fact."

"The evidence Zeke."

"Sure." Ezekiel whipped out his Scroll and on the wallings around them was the day of General Omega of the day in question. "Here it is."

"This could take forever. Do you have a transcript of his words on that day?"

"Right here, transferring it to your Scroll."

General Alpha began looking it over and there was a considerable amount of information to review. "Very good Zeke, now if you could get the video together of the DTR overthrow while I am reviewing this and just wait outside in the living room. My wife and guards will make you feel at home."

The same guards came to get him, this time it was with a great respect as per the General's request. "Make sure that he has everything he needs."

While General Alpha was deliberating Colonel Grant Eta walked in. "Sir I have not found Ezekiel however the troops are prepped and ready to go when you give the order."

"Don't worry, Zeke is in the living room waiting and I am looking over this transcript so if you would just give me a minute I will be with you shortly."

"Sir, the time is approaching they will vote in less than two hours. We can't afford to waste any time."

"I am reviewing this and there isn't going to be any need to send any troops so you will just have to wait."

"I can't wait sir, the entire North will be out of power if I don't, I am going to give the order if you won't."

"No, you will not, I will have you arrested if you do."

"Watch me and see what you do. All I have to do is give the troops a go and they will be off to saving our campaign."

"I am not ready to make that decision yet Colonel Eta."

"Then I will!"

"No you will not!

The Colonel ran out the PAST to alert the troops, things were now being set into action. General Alpha exploded in anger and ran to go and get him back accept the stream to the PAST had already dematerialized. Now what Alpha thought, he had to get more information from Zeke and in a hurry. Running for answers he found Zeke sipping some Odyssian Coco on his couch.

"Tell me more about the DTR Zeke we don't have much time Colonel Eta just gave the order to attack the Senate voting today."

Sitting aside the cup of hot Coco Zeke began to talk with a nice chocolate brown and marshmallow white mustache, "Okay the DTR was taken over and re-programmed to give orders to destroy the entire planet and after it gave the order to demolish the Zeus mountains, I intercepted the signal and gained control of it before it could have done any more destruction to the planet. The Nivio deposits were just the first of a string of events that were about to take place that would have killed us all that is why I am thankful to God that I was able to stop it before it could."

"I need to pray about this for a minute is that okay?"

"Sure."

General Alpha was beginning to understand the repercussions for his actions and felt convicted by the Holy Spirit so he prayed, "Father in Heaven, I come to you with a repentant heart asking you for your forgiveness for what I have done to the South. Please tell me if what Zeke is saying is true. I ask this in Jesus name."

God who knows all things and is omniscient responded to his prayer, "Aaron you have seen the transcripts for yourself, you now know what no one could persuade you of before. General Omega was telling the truth and you were in the wrong for what you did. You have free will and I could not stop you from what you did to the South. I forgive you however you need to get the forgiveness of the South most of all and do what you can to end this war."

"Goodness gracious, you were telling the truth the whole time, I am such a fool. Listen I am sorry for everything that I have done to destroy you, and I pray that someday I can repay what I have taken from you and your people."

Zeke jetted to his feet and said, "No need to be concerned with that now, what we need to do is stop those troops from getting to Congress."

"I agree. Lets go."

General Alpha was typing and running at the same time to get an open PASTway to go to the base. They ran through to find Colonel Nu awaiting them and his orders. General Alpha spoke up, "Where is Colonel Eta? And where are those troops?"

With a stern wondering eyebrow Colonel Nu said, "Sorry sir, you just missed them they left for the Senate several minutes ago."

"Great, tell everyone on that mission that it is canceled, repeat kill the mission."

"Sure thing, sir." Colonel Nu typed in the code to break the news to all of the soldiers on the mission. "General Alpha has given the order to kill the mission repeat kill the mission. Please respond."

The three of them waited for a while and nothing there was no response. Alpha wanted to know, "Zeke see what you can do with the DTR it seems that we're not getting through."

"Yes sir." Zeke did what he could to override the DTR but it was no use someone must have taken control of it again. "Sir I have done everything that I can, nothing is getting through, we are going to have to manually give the orders."

Everyone that they saw on the base they relayed the news to stop the attack. By now the commissioned troops were already running down the streets of Athenia or shuffling their way across the city in a cruiser making their way to the Capitol. All that Zeke and General Alpha talked to at the base were instructed to bring the news to those troops.

They both passed one room with a guy that had his feet propped up on his desk just lounging with chaos going on around and the General wanted to investigate. They trotted in the office and found a friendly face. General Alpha greeted the guy, "You sorry lazy maggot."

The soldier that he was talking to was none other than Captain Uzziah who promptly sat up straight in his intelli-chair and stood up when he saw the extended hand of General Alpha. Saluting him first Uzziah said, "Nice to see you too General."

"Looks like you have everything under control in here."

"Yes sir, just doing some research."

"Let me guess heel to desk pressure?"

"Is there something that I should be doing for you sir?"

"Actually there is, you up for a mission?"

"Anything you need me to do sir."

"Good, I want for you and your crew to go to the Capitol and stop the attack. Can you do that for me?"

"Most certainly." Uzziah said certainly with a stoogy high pitch to it.

"Alright, go get them you knucklehead. And take the Shuffle Cruiser you might need it."

"Sure thing sir." Uzziah had this cheesy grin on his face as he walked over to the General and saluted him.

"Well get going."

"Oh yeah, yes sir. I..., we will do our best."

"I know you will. Strength for the journey!"

"Strength for the journey." Uzziah left and was already getting the guys together on his datapad.

They all met up in the locker room in the base and Uzziah gave them their orders as Ahaz was chomping on some eggs. "Listen up pansys and bozo's alike, we have orders to go to the Capitol in Athenia, and stop the commissioned troops from taking over the Senate, and yes we will be taking the Shuffle Cruiser. So get your best dresses on and load up."

The eggs were very tasty and Ahaz was itching to drive this time and he thought that since he did such a good job the last time that he should be the driver. "Uzziah whaddya say you let me drive?"

"No way, we all know what happened the last time you drove when we went through the Megaport."

"Yeah, but what about our last mission where I almost saved Shaphan on the ACT 1. I fell at least ten feet and man it hurt. And what about my dancing I'll dance for you guys again."

"There will be no dancing this time bozo, although you really can cut a groove and quite funny at that. However what if the General were to walk in again and you were dancing he might not be so forgiving or understanding. You danced your hump right into General Alpha."

Shaphan was remembering that incident and started to laugh, "It was pretty funny though Uzziah."

"Yes it was." Uzziah saw the eggs that he was eating and he noticed that there were a few eggs that were still in the shell in a container beside Ahaz. "Ahaz you remember the puzzle about the rooster?"

"Yeah. Listen I have never even been to a farm so how would I know about hens and roosters?"

"That's okay this requires no knowledge, here's what I am gonna do to see if you get to drive the Cruiser."

"You're gonna let me drive?"

"That will be up to those eggs right there. Here's what I am gonna do I will let you drive if you can balance an egg on your head for ten seconds. What do you say?"

"I don't know how to do that."

"Come on Herman Munster you have a head as flat as a road. You could do it." Amos piped in some inspiration.

"I guess I could."

Uzziah wanted to give some positive words to help him make up his mind. "I'll even hold my hand over your head so if it falls I'll catch it."

When Shaphan and Amos heard this they burst out laughing. They both said, "Yeah, Ahaz you should do it, do it for your wife that you dance for."

"She does like eggs, and she would be proud of me. Alright I'll do it."

Uzziah gave him the instructions, "Alright, flat top I am just going to put this here egg on top of your head and then Shaphan will have a clock on the Scroll Walling in front of you to time you, when you get to zero seconds then I'll take the egg off. You get four attempts."

"Okay lets do this."

Uzziah had the egg already in his hand and motioned over to Shaphan to get it ready and then he placed the egg on Ahaz's head. He took his hand off and the countdown started ten, nine, Ahaz was sweating as the egg began to move. Uzziah's eyes glanced over to the guys and then he slammed his hand over the top of Ahaz's head and the parts of the egg got all over Uzziah's hand and it fell down Ahaz's head.

Uzziah was wondering what happened shaking the mess from his hand. "What the heck?"

Ahaz started laughing, "I knew what you pansy's were going to do when you started laughing. So I put the raw eggs under my AIIA suit and Uzziah grabbed the boiled eggs. You guys are so dumb."

Shaphan thought that was hilarious, "Uzziah you got out played by Ahaz, and he is the dumbest one out of all of us, no offense Ahaz."

"None taken, moron." Ahaz resembled the remark.

Shaphan finished, "Now you really have to let him drive."

"Alright, alright Ahaz, I guess you can drive."

"Ahhh yeah, way cool Uzziah this is going to rock." Ahaz then began dancing his dance and scooting his hump across the floor. "Its getting away, its getting away." As he made it all the way over to the lockers. With his eyes closed, "Bring it back, bring it back."

He scooted hump first, slapping his rump all the way over to the bench, hit it, and bumped the raw eggs container on the floor. Then his knees hit the bench and tumbled over the bench and his head landed right inside the round container of raw eggs face first. He then stood up with the container on his head and the eggs were dripping down his suit and all over his face. The guys started whooping, laughing so hard, Amos was wheezing.

"Way to go Bozo!" Shaphan said with his hand on his side.

Ahaz heard them laughing standing there with the eggs on his face he took the container off his head and there were white shells and yellow egg yolks all in his hair and on his face, and dripping through his beard. He saw the guys laughing at him and he just wanted to know, "Can I still drive?"

They laughed even harder and Uzziah spoke up, "Now that is funny, yes, you can drive. Alright pansy's load up, and Ahaz wipe that stuff off your face, you're making me hungry. And next time you might want to bring eggs to the office, scramble them first, and didn't your Mom teach you not to wear your food?"

"Yeah, it was supposed to be an egg shake."

"Clean up and get ready to drive you knucklehead."

"Yes sir, boss."

The guys were all waiting on Ahaz as he washed up and got on his AIIA suit which was surprisingly clean. After a while they were all in the Shuffle cruiser and taking off for the Megaport. Proudly, Ahaz was behind the controls and he wanted to convey to Uzziah that he was thankful that he let him drive.

"You know that I'll pay you back for letting me drive, you can come over for a bar-b-que. Heck my wife and I could invite all the guys."

"Will there be any eggs at the bar-b-que?"

"Yeah my wife makes the best egg salad, I'll get her to make a batch for you."

"As long as you weren't wearing them first."

"Oh no boss, that is the first time that anything like that has ever happened to me."

"As clumsy as you are you have never spilled anything on yourself?"

"I don't do the cooking boss, my wife does."

"I might eat the egg salad if I watch her make it."

"Its really tasty, she puts celery in it and everything, its the best."

"Just concentrate on your driving and don't hit anybody, and if the mission is a success then we'll talk about a bar-b-que. If there is any beard in it I'll..."

"Boss, I said you can watch her make it."

"Its not your beard that I am worrying about."

"Boss my wife doesn't have a beard."

"Are you sure she doesn't have facial hair?

"No boss just clean soft skin."

"Well make her wear a hair net."

"Sure thing boss."

"You know I am just messing with you Ahaz?"

"You are boss?"

"Yeah, you have a beautiful wife and she is so nice, I like that woman, she is really good for you."

"Thanks boss, I know she is the best, isn't she?"

"She sure is Ahaz, here's a tip for you the next time that you dance for her."

"Whats that?"

"Keep your eyes open when you're 'bringing it back.'"

"I'll remember that."

"I just know you have a nice house that your wife works hard to keep clean and I don't want her to do more work than she has to."

"That's smart thinking, I'll tell her you said that."

The megaport was approaching rapidly, Ahaz was coming in too fast to control the entry point and if he hit either side post it could be catastrophic to the Shuffle Cruiser. The soldiers might not survive such an impact and there would be few other men that could get to the Senate in time to stop the overthrow. Uzziah saw what was happening and immediately hit something on the control board.

"Ahaz, I thought you might get carried away with this driving and talking thing. There. Autopilot is on."

"Gee, thanks, do you know how far away from the Senate we will be?"

"Athenia is much larger than Olympia little buddy. Its going to be a good ten miles across town before we get there."

General Alpha was also in a Shuffle Cruiser and was approaching the Hill. "Uzziah, communications are down, you know that, you need to have your whole crew start praying and now. I will talk to you once I get there."

"Roger that Sir, we'll get right on it."

Ahaz was well versed in the bible and he knew how to effectively pray and when he spoke the words, "In the name of Jesus." He was instantly taken in spirit to heaven and brought before the Trinity on the Heavenly Throne.

God was sitting in the center seat clothed in incandescent majesty glowing and shining and streams of light went forth as he spoke to Ahaz, "My son there will be a great conflict that will take place today unless you can prevent it from happening. You will arrive safely at the Senate I have already foreseen this happening however, there is something that you must do to prevent lives from being lost. You must speak to Colonel Grant Eta and tell him that I have spoken to you and say these words, "This is the Lord of the Universe and these people here are all my people and they are precious in my sight. Call a stand down before all lives are lost and Ionious ceases to exist." If you tell him what I have spoken to you there is a chance that no one will be killed. Now go in the name of Jesus and for the peace of all of Ionious."

By this time Uzziah had scooted Ahaz over and was running the controls as they were already across the border and through the Megaport. Uzziah began slapping Ahaz again and hoped that this time that he would come to. "Ahaz wake up little buddy, you were supposed to be driving. Wake up this is no time to be napping!" Just before he slapped him one last time Ahaz came to himself with bright eyes only to feel the sting of a swift slap to the face.

"Uzziah I was in Heaven."

"Naps usually are." Uzziah uttered as he shifted places with Ahaz so he could take over at the controls.

"No, I was literally in Heaven and God gave me a word to speak to Colonel Eta and I have to tell him this."

"Just a minute there buddy, we have a good four minutes till we arrive. Can you remember everything that you were supposed to tell him?"

"I think so."

"What do you mean you think so?"

"I remember..."

"Go on."

"I can't remember."

"Okay then just tell me what you do remember."

"I saw God and he said that everyone there is going to die unless I say these words to the Colonel."

"Well then what are they?"

"Something about...ughhh! I can't remember a thing."

"That's great, now listen to me do you trust in God?"

"Yes of course."

"Okay maybe God will reveal it to you when you get there and actually speak to the Colonel. Now just keep your trust in God and you will be fine and no one will die. Pray silently that God will be with you."

"I can do that."

"Good now just concentrate on what you're going to do once you get there."

"Sure thing boss." Uzziah had elected for a touchpad control interface and was weaving in and out of traffic. Mostly pedestrians and they were all Alphas on the run. Ahaz wished he could stop to tell the other Alphas that there was a stand down but he knew that it was more important to get to the Colonel at the Senate.

Meanwhile at the Senate Ezekiel Epsilon was in the Shuffle Cruiser using some sort of override to communicate with Matt and Cody at the DTR control center. Ezekiel was worried about all of the new soldiers that were popping up around him that were ready to take over the Senate. Ezekiel spoke into the manual dashboard mic to talk to Matt who was in charge of repairing the systems.

"Hey there Matt, we have a serious situation here and there are more soldiers mostly Alphas that are sprinting up the hill to the Senate with their disrupters set to kill and if there is anything that you can do about getting the transcomms running again that would be just great."

"Listen you aren't the only one that is calling in over the manual towers I am already working on it so if you could just give Cody and I some time we should have it back up in about twenty minutes."

"Time is what we don't have did I mention that they are all set to kill. They need to know that the General has already issued a stand down so get to work now." The sound of distant energy blasts hitting objects rifled through Zeke's ear. "As soon as you can."

"I am doing my best, just remember patience is a virtue."

"Well remember this, death awaits every man and it is approaching rapidly."

Matt was typing a mile a minute and getting nowhere and he just ignored that last comment that Zeke gave him. He couldn't afford the pressure, what he could afford was someone with some knowledge about the DTR that had some patience.

The thing that Cody was doing was supposed to draw energy from the reserves and activate the transmission. They began talking as they did their individual tasks. Cody went first, "You know here Guru Marconi, what we need is more power it seems that the reserves are depleted. And if I've got my wits on straight."

"What kind of podunk redneck town are you from?"

"Wisconsin and the name of the town is Reddink."

"So its not podunk its a redneck town called Podink."

"Kind of, if you put redneck and podink together its called Reddink."

"Whatever my point was, it's head on straight. The proper phrase is, 'If I've got my head on straight' you brainless circuit sizzler."

"Head on straight? Why would I not have my head on straight I am human not some kind of bot. Do you know how many milennia its been since this planet has had bots or androids."

"Data on Star Trek was an android and his head sometimes had to be on straight."

"The back of Data's head was the only thing that came off not his whole head."

"No, Data would say something human like that though."

"You're not getting it though. The uplink to Data's posatronic matrix was though a flap in the back of his head they never detatched his head, you moron."

"Its an android thing, you know head on straight, maybe its spiritual head, you know spiritual thinking and not of the flesh."

"I think its wits on straight."

"Okay we live in a creative dictionary society not limited to past phrases or definitions so fine its wits on straight with you."

"Yeah wits on straight. You know correct thinking?"

"Why do you have to be so brainless? I was just trying to tell you some proper English phrases."

"I am not brainless. I resemble that remark to the fullest."

"You're so brainless that you don't know the definition of resemble. Or maybe you're so brainless that you meant to say that you do actually resemble that remark. You're a confident in your own idiocy."

"What does idiocy mean?"

"It comes from the word idiosyncrasy, it means to have traits common to peculiarity, you know it just defines all the dumb stuff that you do and calls it idiocy, quite coinient in the creative dictionary society."

"I have played scrabble and I know that coinient is not a word."

"It is coiningly poignant."

"Are you some fresh out of school literary Professor?"

"It's Guru Marconi to you."

"Okay oh Great One Guru Marconi, we need more power from the reserves to start the process of booting up again."

"You're the energy guy Cody that's your department why don't you do some research and see if we can bypass the reserves that are on site, and tap into the outer grid. My Dad once said to me that you can do all things through Christ who strengthens you. You might want to start praying."

"I am in a hurry here."

"Pray while you work, in the bible it says to pray without ceasing. You should do that while you work, it can't hurt." Matt said to Cody as he was readying the system for the final segment of the new installation.

Cody began praying and as he was praying the Holy Spirit started talking to him about his work and it seemed that there was no way to get to where he was wanting to go. "I am doing everything that I know how to do and I just can't find it. Wait...okay here it is now how do I direct the energy back to the DTR?"

"Let's get Zeke in on this one."

"Sure thing."

Matt tapped the key and spoke into the mic, "Zeke if you're there we could really use your knowledge."

"I am here what do you guys need?"

"Cody has found the place where you can access the outer grid accept he can't find the acceptance signal to re-route the energy stream. Can you help?"

Just as Ezekiel Epsilon was about to talk into the dashboard an Alpha soldier came up to his Cruiser. "Sir, there has been an incident you need to come quick."

"Sorry men, I have to go and check this out I will be back with you later."

As Zeke was exiting the vehicle Ahaz and the men show up in the Shuffle Cruiser next to him. The vehicle comes to a stop as Ahaz peers at the magnificent structure in front of him, looks around the cab and says, "We made it ladies, all in one piece."

Uzziah makes a move to exit the Cruiser as the door slides aside and he registers Ahaz's comment. He then looks over to Ahaz, puts his hand on his right shoulder and says with all sincerity, "Ya did good turtle, ya did good."

Ahaz's mind was elsewhere though, "Ain't it beautiful, I've seen pictures and tons of video, but, man, this is amazing."

The hand on his shoulder taps a few times for support, and Uzziah says, "You better be going to find Colonel Eta big guy."

"Right, he's gotta be in there somewhere." Ahaz steps down to the granite from the seat of the Cruiser and starts to go towards the grand entrance of the steps and sees Ezekiel Epsilon several paces in front of him. Sprinting for a short jaunt he approaches his six and says, "Excuse me, Ezekiel Epsilon, you are Ezekiel right?"

"Yes."

"I was wondering if you could tell me where Colonel Grant Eta is?"

"I am not sure, there, soldier, something has happened and I have to be going. You will have to find him yourself."

"Right, thanks Ezekiel."

"Just pray that it is nothing serious, okay soldier."

"Will do."

The three other soldiers from the Shuffle Cruiser now catch up with Ahaz and Ezekiel. Uzziah overheard Zeke saying something about it being serious, "Could you tell us just what has happened Ezekiel?"

The Alpha soldier next to Ezekiel spoke up before Ezekiel could say anything, "It's the General, General Alpha, Uzziah. You guys need to follow me."

"What has happened? Is he okay?"

"It's not good, just follow me and I will show you."

"Sure thing."

The men were now at the Megaport entrance to the Senate, and they walk through the doorway into the foyer that is covered in beautiful marble, with streams of gold and silver amidst the gray and blue formations that reach to the ceiling of the portico. They hear much yelling and loud voices coming from inside the main room. The Alpha soldier takes a left and avoids the vocal fight going on inside and proceeds to the left wing doorway.

The Alpha soldier remembered that Ahaz needed to find the Colonel and said to Ahaz, "Listen, you might not like this but the Colonel is in the main room."

Immediately Ahaz does an about face and turns his head over his shoulder and says, "Thanks." He then goes into the main room standing a few steps inside the main doorway, to find Soldiers with disrupters dug into the Senators heads, who are crouched on their knees at their respective seat, encircling the grand room. At the front of the Senate floor near the speakers seat is a row of Omega soldiers with disrupters pointed at the Alpha soldiers.

An Omega soldier, inherently clad in the norm greens and Omega insignias and ranks, displayed from their FOLED AIIA suits, has his disrupter set to MAX Stun and motions with these words that Ahaz blairingly hears, "Put, it, down. Now! You useless violent punk!"

The Alpha soldier that the Omega was talking to dug the barrel discharger end of his disrupter into the Senators head drawing more blood. "Not a chance, freak! I have orders and this doesn't move until we get our Vionium. Got it!"

The yelling match was getting nowhere and struggled on as Ahaz focused his attention more on the other Alpha AIIA suits seeing if he could find out where in the heck the Colonel was. Ahaz sheepishly takes a few steps forward past the last row of seats and notices that the Senators all have their hands behind their backs with porous yet glossy, red bio-cuffs sprayed on. He notices an Alpha soldier at the front of the room talking to a high ranking Omega soldier with a closely juxtiposed Senator, with tears streaming screaming something to the Alpha soldier. Ahaz thinks that he might be able to find out where his target was, if he could talk to this soldier, so he gingerly crouches and waddles down the main isle just above the tops of the seat backs towards the front.

His central objective is to get to the soldier without getting hit by a plasma burst if a crossfire ensues, which it most certainly could, for all his senses could tell, by the way tension in the room was escalating. Row by row, Ahaz inched closer towards the front, checking for fire down each row mainly fixing his disturbed sights on the trigger fingers of the hyperactive itchy Alpha soldiers. A sick feeling overtook his stomach as he caught a glimpse of a Senators despondent eyes, void of all hope in the situation. No, he had to keep going, "Good thoughts." He said to himself, or he was going to hurl.

The front row was approaching and over the top of the seat backs he could see the soldier. "Almost there." He made the turn and heard the Senator that was screaming at the soldier that he was going to a bit better, and it was not good. The soldier just ignored him and kept talking to the Omega soldier as he heard the Alpha soldier that had his disrupter buried in his temple saying, "I am only going to tell you this once more, wait here and everything will be fine, and we can all go home."

"I will not vote for you!" The gray haired Senator then looked up and spit on the soldier.

"Keep it up. Don't think I won't." He wiped the spit from his face.

Ahaz knew he had to keep going, so he did waddling towards the front right edge of the seats where the soldier was, which was also right in front of the spitting Senator. Once he reached the edge he got a better look at the soldier and it was Colonel Eta. He was so relieved he stood up and took quick paces over to him interrupting his conversation. "Sir, I have orders..."

"Who are you?"

"Ahaz sir, the scout team of Uzziah, sir."

Out of the corner of his eyes Ahaz saw someone coming right for the Colonel. Fearful, frightened, and on edge his instincts took over and Ahaz tackled the approaching person as pain and electricity shoot throughout his body. The two men both go limp entangled then separated as they hit the marble floor.

"Private, really, did you have to shoot them."

"I was aiming for the Senator, the last thing I want is more friendly fire."

"Just great, do you know who that was?"

"No."

"Never mind, what was it set to?"

"Max Stun."

"They will be fine. Leave them to me, go check on General Alpha."

"Yes sir."

The soldier left and Colonel Grant Eta bent down to see how the men were recovering. "Ahaz, you awake yet?" He shook his shoulders and looked into his blank eyes. Ahaz mumbled something then life sprang up into his eyes as he caught on to the face of the Colonel.

"What in the world?"

"You were hit by a disrupter."

"Naw, really? What was it set to? Man, this hurts." Ahaz grabbed his bicep and let out a scream, looked at it and shook his head.

"Max stun."

There were blood bubbles in a small area on his bicep that looked something like shingles. "Does it always do this?"

"Sometimes, get up. Can you get up?"

"Yeah, I think so."

The soldier was back from seeing General Alpha, gasping for breath from a dead sprint. "Sir, he is fading, he wants to see you.... You too Ahaz."

"Okay lets go, can you make it to the East Wing?"

"I'll do my best." Ahaz gingerly arose to his feet and they all began briskly walking across the front of the room to the east wall and then towards the tall, vaulted, wooden door. Ahaz was limping and needed the soldier to help him make it.

Uzziah was kneeling down with eyes locked on General Alpha keeping him alert. "Sir you're gonna make it, I know. You just can't go out like this." Amos had his hand on General Alpha's chest and blood was gushing, he did everything he could to stop the bleeding. Shaphan was there with a suture light and mended the wound to form a searing line that welped up after he administered the light.

The bleeding did stop and General Alpha had something to say, "Where is my wife?...and my daughter? Get them here immediately. Can you do that for me Uzziah?"

"We just talked to them and they are getting closer, you just have to stay with us sir, you lost a lot of blood." Uzziah answered the General although things didn't look good as his eyes were inadvertently moving around.

In his barely conscience state he was able to see Colonel Grant and he welled up with joy as he saw him. "Grant, listen I have called a stand down, no takeover, go tell the men this war is over, General Omega was telling the truth. I was in the wrong here. It must end now."

Zeke had been talking to Cody in the Central Control room and they were now operational on the South's side of the equation. Now Matt and Cody were both working to get the DTR available to the North as well. Colonel Grant tested his transcom and it didn't work so he decided he and some others must go tell the soldiers in the standoff.

Ahaz wiped an intermittent tear from his cheek and asked Uzziah, "How did this all happen?"

"When General Alpha got here there was a skirmish going on between the Alpha soldiers and the Omega soldiers over a reluctant Senator..."

His boots made no noise as he sprinted up the marble steps of the Capitol buliding, swiftly he moved with ambition and intention. His AIIA suit had the words, "Stand down" zooming in and out. He was there for one thing and one thing only, to tell the men to stand down, and that this war was over.

Barging through the front doors he went brashly and brazen, ball to ball he tapped out a sprint down to where the skirmish was going on over the decline of the slick, polished, marble floor. He knew he could stop this thing and he only needed to talk to one man to make it happen. The same man that made all of this standoff happen in the first place, Colonel Grant.

Halfway down he noticed that the Colonel was right in the middle of the skirmish that was going on between opposing sides. The Alpha Colonel pushed the Omega soldier and General Alpha put his arm in between the two men and shoved the Senator down to the ground. "What is going on here?"

"This Senator managed to get a disrupter from one of our soldiers and shot him at Max Stun in the leg. He's over there." Colonel Grant points to a man crumpled up on the cold marble floor. "This Omega over here tried to stop me from getting the disrupter from the Senator. I wasn't having any of that so I punched his lights out got the disrupter and thats when this Omega came up and started talking smack to me. I am just about ready to shoot the Senator and the Omega if they don't get off it."

"Grant, you can't do this. Don't you see I have decided to call a stand down we are no longer fighting against the South." The General attempted to calm down the Colonel and seek out some sort of solution to this whole debacle.

"You tellin' me to get off it punk? I'll have you for dinner. We never fired on your so called precious mountains. Its not our fault that your resources were depleted."

"Another word from you and I am going postal on your sorry grump."

"Oh, really so you think that you can just kill me just like that? Do it I dare you."

Colonel Grant's disrupter was set to kill and General Alpha knew it. The Colonel then buried the discharger into the chest of the Omega soldier.

"What do you got in there? A blood-magnet?"

"By the time this kills you, you would wish it were a blood-magnet."

"Don't do this Grant there are other ways out of this, you know that." General Alpha attempted to take the disrupter from the Colonel to no use.

"Stand back General." Colonel Grant reached for his hip and pulled out another disrupter that General Alpha noticed was set to stun.

The Colonel then pointed it at the General's face. "Don't get involved in this General. I am telling you I will light you up for a few minutes while I kill this invalid Omega." All the while digging further into the temple of the Omega soldier.

"If you kill me, my men will kill you in a matter of nano-seconds. Got it?"

"Don't do it Grant. Why would you do something like this it was just a misunderstanding leave it at that."

"My wife died because one of you idiot Omega's decided to bomb the Zeus Mountains. No one knew where she was for weeks. Then one day they found this." Colonel Grant moved his neck around and some charred dog-tags emerged that had his wife's name on them. "While they were scanning for deposits of Nivio, cremated, incinerated, burned alive. Can you imagine the pain that she went through all because of your idiot General deciding to call the shots and start this war."

"Don't do anything dumb here Grant there is a way out and this is not the answer. I know what its like to lose a loved one."

"My children cry themselves to sleep every night since she passed. Do you know what it was like to tell them that their mom had been incinerated? You weren't there, you didn't see the look on their faces, you didn't hold them in your arms while they wept like babies. They didn't hit you screaming why Daddy why? Dont tell me you know what its like."

"Just don't end this mans life because your wife died Grant its not the right thing to do." General Alpha held the disrupter that was pointed at his face and tried to push it to the side, but Colonel Grant was too strong.

"She's gone now and my children are without a mother to raise them. What do you think it's like for them? There is nothing I can do about that until now!" An Omega soldier heard the Colonel say this and bull rushed him from the right side next to General Alpha. At the same time General Alpha backed out of the way grabbing the disrupter that was pointed at him, so now he was safe.

Before the Omega soldier could tackle the Colonel he got off a shot that hit the soldier in the shoulder and then in an attempt to kill the Omega soldier that was charging at him, he fires off an early round while sweeping the disrupter across his body, fires several shots and then hits the Omega soldier in the back.

General Alpha then started screaming for help as he starts bleeding from the chest. His AIIA protective suit was disabled in the melee and the shot from Colonel Grant's disrupter hit him squarely in the chest at full blast on a killshot.

Uzziah finished the story by saying, "And that is when the our soldiers picked him up and took him to the East wing for safety."

Sharon Alpha could see General Alpha from the doorway and quickly covered the eyes of her daughter Esther as they walked in to spend some time with Aaron before he died. "Honey, are you okay?" With tears in their eyes Sharon and Esther knelt beside Aaron and grasped his hand. "Can you talk?"

"You made it. Honey, I am sorry that this has happened. I love you and Esther so much."

"I love you too daddy. You're going to be okay. I saw Jesus and he said that you would be fine."

"Sweety, when did you see Jesus?"

"In the Shuffle Cruiser when I was closing my eyes praying. I talked to Jesus."

The steps of Colonel grant were precise and littered with emotion as he now knew what he had to do to set all of this straight. He had to act and fast as there were a ton of soldiers that needed to hear from him, and being a man of his word he would keep it with the General, for his sake. A few short steps away from the main entrance to the Senate floor he was praying, knowing God would hear his petition and make his current mission a success. Imagining the tons of men that he had to talk to, he decided to start in the back right corner of the floor and work his way forward from there. He stepped through the grand doorways, knowing the vote was about to take place, and found a scene that made his whole heart jump into his throat.

There was a shootout, plasma bursts were going every which direction, so Colonel Grant ducked behind the back right wall just behind the last row of seats on the Senate floor. Cold smooth marble chilled a frost on his hands as he inched towards the back right corner where a few Alpha soldiers were gathered to take refuge from the warfare. Over his head a plasma burst sailed hitting the wall, spreading trinkets of energy onto the floor beside his right hand. It was a close one, if he had not been ducking it surely would have landed, where?

God only knows, perhaps his chest, like the inadvertent shot that hit the General. Maybe worse, in the head, he didn't want to think about this so to keep from getting plasma spray on his hands he lifted them up in front of himself about chest high and waddled forward to the awaiting men.

"You got your suit set to anti-gravity landing pal?" Eddie was doing something on his Scroll Datapad and looked over for Tregg's response.

"You know it buddy."

"Just set mine, sure wish we had these things back in the states."

"I saw this Sci Fi flick in the theaters once and they had this same technology. Kindda funny that we're actually about to use it."

"Yeah and if it doesn't work we'll be toast."

"I'd prefer to be the ones making a toast after all is said and done."

"Sparkling grape, to all the girls I've loved before."

"Now you're showing some country in your roots. I am sure your melifluisims never failed you once."

"This smooth talker had a beginning you know. I learned from the best."

"Yeah, I am sure you did, but we just met once we got to Ionious."

"I would sit and watch my Dad twirl my Mom across the living room floor as he sweet talked her. Now that's a cassanova. Taught me everything I know. He helped me on my first date, at a football game, hold hands with the girl that I loved, and I've never looked back once. Always listening to everything he said to my lovely Mom."

"I think we're getting close."

They were about 1,000 feet up from the Senate Building and approaching fast. The back platform opened, they looked at each other and jumped. Sailing through the air Tregg's anti-gravity suit kicked in first as his descent slowed to a halt on the beautiful, white granite dome on the top of the Senate roof. Eddie followed to a safe landing about ten feet away on the other side of the Oculus.

The Oculus was an enormous flat circle that peaked at the top of the dome that had a shield over it that let sunlight in and kept the birds out. Jeter was already inside and was part of the shootout that was going on inside the Senate. Eddie and Tregg peered into the

Oculus crouching just over the rim and noticed a starburst had been fired that lit up the whole place inside. This gave them the signal to setup the Shield Cage emitter, so the two soldiers began unpacking the components as Eddie began to pray.

"Dear Lord, in the name of Jesus, you are so amazing and I worship all that you have done and all that you are about to do for us. My request is that you make our plans go through without any obstructions with no casualties in the process. Proverbs 33:20 says that Our soul waits for the Lord, He is our help and our shield. I know that you will help us and meet our needs."

"Eddie, I am with you always, the Alpha and the Omega, remember what I said to Abraham in Genesis 15:1, 'Do not be afraid, Abram, I am your shield, your exceedingly great reward.' And I the LORD shall help you and deliver you; I shall deliver you from the wicked, And save you, Because you trust in me."

They worked tirelessly and with tenacity and had the Shield Cage up and ready with no problems. On their Scroll Datapads they could see and hear the Senate leader calling to action a vote for free Vionium for the North. They knew that they had to stop the obstruction of justice that was just about to take place so Tregg hit the pad and the Shield Cage emitter went to work.

The discharge point was enveloped in energy that burst forth, forming a ball of bright sparkling green plasma that stored up and then released hundreds of streaming energy bursts. They all hit their targets and formed transparent, green tinted, energy shields around all of the Alpha soldiers disabling them and putting the vote to a standstill.

An Alpha soldier that was in the foyer saw this happen and he immediately boosted himself up to the roof. "We have an operation to run here and you're not part of it. I am going to have to ask you to turn the shields off."

Eddie said, "No, can do compadre. We have our orders too."

"Well then I guess I am just going to have to make you."

"I don't think you want any of us. I'll drop you in a New York minute."

"Enough of the words."

The Alpha soldier pulled out his disrupter as did Eddie and Tregg. They balsted each other and their suits just absorbed the hits. Getting frustrated the Alpha threw down his disrupter and charged right at

Tregg in a dead heat, tackling him, as Eddie pounced his back. It was a flagrant fistfight with Tregg on the bottom graveling with the Alpha as they inched closer to the Scroll Datapad that held the key to turning off the shields. Eddie held him back as he reached forward within an arms grasp of the Datapad. The Alpha then tucks his chin and rares back and headbutts Eddie jolting him loose which gave him a free path to the Datapad.

The Alpha soldier lunged forward and grasped the Datapad and searched for the turnoff key while Tregg wrestled him down to the ground again. The Alpha kneed Tregg sending him to his back as the Alpha stood to his feet and found the key on the Datapad. Eddie was already running towards him and did a jumping superman punch that landed right on his loose jaw. The Alpha soldier fell over the Shield Cage emitter and tumbled down it through the Oculus to his death with the Scroll Datapad in his hand the whole way down.

"Tregg, you alright?"

"Tingling pain." Tregg grimaced through all of the overwhelming sensations struggling to make it to his feet. "Flesh wound, yeah, I guess I'll live."

"Don't think that guy will be though."

"What happened? Where did the Alpha go?"

"I punched the idiot and he fell through the Oculus."

"Yeah, don't think he'll be helping out with the vote." They were now crouched over the rim looking at him on the cold marble floor through the Oculus.

"It looks like he already has." They began to survey the situation.

"What?"

"The shields are down and they're all voting."

"Now that's dying for your planet."

"Cody, listen man, you've been doing good, but we have to have this whole thing up and running."

"Just about got it."

"Ezekiel says they're voting."

"Will this effect the vote if its not up for the North?"

"Just get it running."

"I just need to get energy to the transmitter in Olympia."

"Well don't just talk about it."

"Energy is there Matt, now its your turn."

"Okay I am working on it."

"Come on we need the communications up and running."

"I think I know what to do."

"Ezekiel says they are almost done with the vote."

"Okay, I figured it out."

"We don't have all day, brainless."

"There I got it, knucklehead."

"I knew you would. I just had to give you a hard time."

"I knew what you were doing brainless."

"You mean I didn't irritate you?"

"I was working."

On the Senate floor the vote was done and the results were being generated and sent to the DTR. On the Scroll Walling behind the speaker the numbers for those in favor of free Vionium began racking up. Colonel Grant had not been able to talk to very many Alpha soldiers so the firefight was still going on.

The vote was final, 68 to 32, in favor of the free Vionium, and the Alpha soldiers were ecstatic. Colonel Grant left to go tell General Alpha that it had passed. His transcom hadn't been working so he made it quick and got there as soon as possible. There were several gathered around General Alpha including Sharon and Esther, he spoke to all in attendance, "It passed, we have free Vionium."

They all just looked at the Colonel and said nothing.

"What's wrong? This is great, the war might be over."

"Aaron died." Sharon said to the Colonel.

"What? No, this can't be."

"About ten minutes ago."

"I will avenge his death, I am General now I will give the orders."

"Grant you can't do this, this isn't what he would have wanted."

"We have the Vionium and now we can fight."

"Don't use it for war Grant."

"I will do what I have to do."

The new General left and began speaking orders to the soldiers that were in the Senate.

Chapter 17
Revelation from God

"Things to Consider"

Have you ever wondered what it would be like to be face to face with God? In this chapter I describe what it might be like if God were to come down from Heaven and talk to His people. God's presence is inside you and He is never far and is always with you no matter what you are going through. To see God for yourself will be an even greater thing than just having the presence of God inside you. I do my best to describe what that might be like.

Chapter 17
Revelation from God

All of the Senators that were wounded began to pile in the room in the West wing where Aaron was now. There were several medical technicians that tended to the Senators and other soldiers that were also wounded. Aaron was still on the marble floor and Esther began to pray for him.

"Father, in the name of Jesus, I know what you said to me while we were in the Shuffle Cruiser, and I know the promise in your word. All things are possible for you. Lazarus' death was not so much that Jesus couldn't bring him back to life and neither is the death of my Daddy. Please God have mercy on us and bring my Dad back to life. We need him at home and this planet needs him as a General. The spirit that brought Christ back from the dead lives in me, and in my Dad, and I know that nothing is impossible to you God. I ask this in, Jesus name."

Above the Senate building clouds were gathering scattered amidst a beautiful day highlighted by a sun that gleamed in the mid-day sky. This created silver linings on the brilliant borders of the obscrucated gray moisture developing. Sparks inside the main thunderhead high inside the upper atmosphere ignited a daunting lightning bolt that jolted towards the Oculus of the Senate Building. The towering antennas retrieved the bolt before it could get to the Oculus. Seconds later thunder is felt inside the West Wing vibrating the Walls and shaking the hearts of the people gathered around General Alpha.

The strike of lightning could be seen from the windows in the West Wing and the combination of the intense resplendent light and the shaking thunder temporarily disables the peoples senses not being able to see. The grand thunderhead gray and daunting began to take the shape of a face with a break in the eye that allowed silvery shafts of light to stream down on the Senate Building. Inside the light a host of angels appeared and in the center of the light a brilliantly reflective chariot emerges with white stallions leading the charge.

The cart of the chariot then arises in glory with the holy stature of Jesus glistening with silvery borders around his long brown hair and beard with shafts of light gleaming from the sides of his grand white clothes. The cloud moves with the charging angels and chariot toward the Senate Building as Sharon Alpha is speaking in tongues praying for her husband General Alpha. Esther is the first to notice the emerging cloud in the distance. "Mom, look, its the cloud."

"Okay, honey." She closes her eyes and continues to pray.

"Mom, look in the clouds, its Jesus. I knew he would save Daddy."

"What?"

"Sharon in the clouds do you see the light?" Uzziah pointed to the cloud for Sharon to see.

"My goodness that's a chariot." Sharon is thoroughly amazed.

"Mom, in the chariot is Jesus."

"Oh sweety, I have been praying that he would heal your Dad."

The windows began to shake and rumble as the host of angels encircling Jesus could now be heard and their praises sounded out. Closer and closer the cloud began to form the face of Jesus as the chariot enters the atmosphere. The angels land on the front lawn of the Senate West wing singing praises to the king as the white stallions hoofs dig into the grass and the golden wheels touchdown on the green grass and Jesus makes his entrance.

The angels then hover around Jesus as he steps down from the chariot and begins walking right towards the west wing window. The angels then fly over to the west wing window and supernaturally pass through the window walls as Jesus divine presence gleams amidst the green background of the front lawn, and He supernaturally walks through the wall. He enters the room and sees General Alpha laying dead on the floor. The soldiers and other people in the room hide their eyes bowing before the sights of the resplendent light emitting from Jesus and the sounds of the singing angels resounding praises for the son of God.

Esther immediately runs up to Jesus and knees at his feet and grasps his white clothes, "Thank you, I knew you would be here when I saw you in my vision. Please Jesus heal my Dad, he is dead."

The eyes of mercy and grace emit a love that changes the hearts of all that gaze in his presence. With the most gentle voice with concern and faith Jesus spoke, "My children, do not be afraid, fear not for I am with you. I have heard your prayers and your faith has made you whole. Aaron rise up and walk for you were dead and now you have arisen."

The hand of the General moves then his AIIA suit starts beating as his heart comes to life. His eyes then open and start moving around the room as he sees his wife Sharon, and his daughter Esther. His blank face suddenly sparks alive into an emotional smile complimented by tears that streams from both eyes. Finally he speaks, "Honey I was in Heaven with Jesus and I was just talking to my Grandfather and now I am here. What happened?"

"Aaron, you were shot and you died and Jesus brought you back to life." Sharon ran her fingers through his short brown hair.

"Jesus, its you, we were just talking, I can't thank you enough. I want to go back its indescribable. Why did you bring me back?"

"It is like a bird that goes away for a short while from his nest to gather food for his family. They do not know if he will return and when he finally returns he brings the food and it invigorates his family with strength for life and they rejoice in his presence. Rejoice, my child, you are needed here by your family and your planet, they need you now. I will see you again someday so fear not I am with you always. Listen for my calling on your life, there are great things on the way for you, your family, and your people. Keep your trust in God and seek Him and his righteousness first and love Him with your whole heart and all things that pertain to life and Godliness shall be added unto you. Go forth and live in peace and love."

"Jesus, there are more here that love you and follow you, they are wounded and need healing. They have all been praying that you would heal them." Sharon humbly points to the gathered soldiers that are scattered about the room.

"Their prayers will not go unanswered. My child, your faith has made you whole." Jesus went to one soldier knelt down and touched his wound and it was miraculously sealed and smooth, He healed the man. He did this until all wounded in the room were healed and made whole.

When Jesus was through healing the lame and sick he said to Aaron, "There are some people who want to see you."

General Omega walked in with General Lambda and Daniel Delta at his sides, General Alpha's eyes grew large. General Omega smiled and extended his right hand as he approached Aaron. "You have been brought back from the dead, and I am so glad to see that you are okay."

"Isaiah? Is that really you? Daniel, John, I thought..."

"We were always one step ahead of you, we had your direct view and allowed you to assassinate us. Only we weren't even there, we have been watching you and praying that God would reveal himself to you, and now he has."

"Thank you, God, I was the one who was in the wrong, Ezekiel explained everything to me and he had some help from Esther and Sariah. I did everything I could to stop them from taking control of the Senate."

"We know Aaron, all is in the past, now is when you can make a difference and bring peace to Ionious and stop this war."

"I can do nothing without my savior, I put all my trust in God, and ask that He will bring peace. There is only so much I can do I am only one man. Through Jesus all things are possible."

"Then let us pray that God will bring peace, there is a firefight on the Senate floor after the vote. They need His presence now or this war will never end. Isaiah will you pray?"

"Father, in the Holy name of Jesus, bring heaven to this world, you have given us your word and our thanks and faith will never cease, forgive us for our sins against one another, deliver us from the evil one, for you alone have the power to accomplish all and we humbly ask that you bring peace to Ionious. Yours is the kingdom of Heaven and in all things we give you all the glory for as long as we have breath we will praise your mighty name, in your glory and magnificent splendor. Amen."

Simultaneously all that were in the Senate building received the same voice in their transcom, which was now working thanks to Matt and Cody. The voice was the Holy Spirit saying, "I have seen it from the Heavens God is on His way, so do not be afraid, just prepare your hearts for what He has to tell you."

Outside the West Wing, where Jesus and all of the leaders of Ionious were gathered, a great cloud began to give off multiple strikes of lightning that stuck to the side of the building creating a great light emitting from the center of the cloud. Jesus saw this and said, "I must go, I will return so be ready, and listen to my voice. You will be witnesses throughout the Universe and testify for the sake of my Father."

In the center of the dark gray cloud a great ball of energy and light extended one tentacle out that reached into the room and it touched Jesus and he immediately disappeared in a flash of great light and colors. More tentacles reached out to all of the angels and they too disappeared in a flash. The cloud then ascended with great speed into the Heavens and met with another greater cloud that was gathering size. After melding with the new cloud the singular cloud began to grow in energy and bright light at the center.

The firefight on the Senate floor was escalating and suddenly the great cloud dropped through the Oculus hovering in the center of the four story room and blinded all that were there. All those that were fighting now were covering there eyes and recovering from their temporary blindness. As they regained their sight they all hid their eyes from the great ball of lightning and energy. The dynamic ball of light emitted lightning tentacles that touched the Scroll Wallings of the room. When this happened God's angels appeared at the point of contact, and they began to fly around they room in patterns around the cloud and light until there were thousands of angels in the room.

Hovering around the cloud the angels began to sing, "Glory to God in the highest, praises to His name, Glory to God the greatest, to Him alone we will sing. Hallelujah, He has come. Hallelujah, He is here. Hallelujah, his will be done. Hallelujah, lend your ear. To the sound of His Glory, His name alone is Holy, Holy, Holy is the Lord Almighty."

The great light in the center of the cloud began to grow, pulsating with colors with each gain in size. The angels began to sing, " Hallelujah God is here." They repeated this several times and then the cloud rose into the ceiling and out the Oculus until there was an enormous sphere of light in the center of the room that began to take the form of a human. An arm separated itself from the torso and a tentacle of lightning was sent out to the man that had fallen from the Oculus and he was healed and brought back to life. Another arm separated and then the fingers separated forming tentacles of lightning emitting out from each, which hit several wounded soldiers that were miraculously healed.

His face then began to take form into a masculine shape with a beard and white hair. His robe was pearl white, long, and flowing. He was now in the full shape of a human standing up, and hovering over the soldiers and Senators. It was God himself and as he began to get ready to talk, looking over the people, the angels began to sing much softer until he spoke.

"My people of great faith and trust, you have honored me in some things and for that you will be eternally blessed. You must choose to honor me in all things. When I send a dream or a vision to one of my servants and you turn your back on me and make the choice to wage war against one another, does this honor me? Some of you do not listen when I speak to you, and like fools you run to do your next act of war out of your own ignorance. Why do you not seek me first and my wisdom for you know that I will guide you in the right direction? Yet you choose your selfish ways and want to do what you feel is best. Do you not know that you are not doing My will but your own? How can I allow you to sin against me like this?"

"Never do what you feel is best, do what you know to be right according to my word given to you through the prophets. When I sent the dream to Ezekiel and you did not take heed to my signs, you chose to turn your back on me, oh Aaron. And out of your own anger you started a war that cost many their lives. You should have listened to my servant Isaiah, yet you did not, and when you died I sent my son Jesus to save you. Did you deserve this? For all of the lives that were under your name that died I could have sent you to hell, and instead I gave you mercy and gave you back your life again. Am I not a merciful God? Can you not see my unconditional grace?"

"When you pray do I not answer you? Aaron it was almost too late before you finally decided what you were doing was wrong. Are you not thankful to me for forgiving you of your evil actions? I sent you my servant Ezekiel and you finally believed, but at what cost to your people? I could decide to create a new race of people, ones that will listen to me and serve me all of their days. Ones that will not turn their backs on my chosen people. However, during this war I saw a faith and trust in you people that I have never seen before, and for that I have chosen to extend my blessings to you and grant you the answers to your prayers for peace."

"Mark 10:27 It's impossible for people to save themselves, but it's not impossible for me to save them. Everything is possible when you trust in me. You must turn away from evil and do good. You must seek peace and pursue it. Romans 15:13 May Jesus, the source of hope, fill you with joy and peace through your faith in Him. Then you will overflow with hope by the power of the Holy Spirit. 2 Peter 1:1 May good will and peace fill your lives through your knowledge about Jesus. Jesus is the light of the world. Light allows us to see in the physical and Jesus allows us to see in the spiritual to the obedience of My word."

"Go forth, in peace and listen with your spiritual ears when I talk to you, for there is a new thing that I will bless you with. Which will help you sustain your peace, I have already sent the plans and blueprints for the construction of a new being. This being will be made in my image and will serve me and my will alone on Ionious. This new being is called SHIFT, Synergy Holographic Intelligent Force Technology Being that look and feel real just like humans only they are a combination of Holographic projections and Energy Fields that make them indistinguishable to humans. They are my gift to you. Go forth and create them according to my plan and glory. Remember to always seek me first and my righteousness and I shall give you all things pertaining to life and Godliness and when you pray my glory shall be revealed to you."

Chapter 18
The ReQUEST

"Things to Consider"

When I was young I was good friends with Michael Philbrick and we loved to play with GI Joes. One day when we were playing he said that he liked one of my GI Joes so I gave it to him. A week later my mom was cleaning my room and noticed that several of my GI Joes were missing and she asked me where they went. So I told her I gave them away to Michael. She said that it is good to have a giving heart but not to give all of my toys away because my parents worked hard to earn the money to buy them for me. I said that I just wanted for him to have it because he didn't have very many toys. So she said that would be alright just as long as I didn't give all of them away.

In this chapter Prime Minister of Ionious Jacob is asked for help to bring peace to the USA by the President and just like I gave away my toys to my friend so does Jacob. Think about ways that you could be a blessing to others by giving things that you already have to them.

Chapter 18
The ReQUEST

Several months back a vote was put to Congress, in the United States, for the permission to allow a DTR system of communication to be installed in the US. This vote went down to the wire and passed by a narrow margin. Due to the passing of this vote the President Jonathan Houston and Vice-President Ed Young have traveled to Ionious and are in the ready room awaiting the presence of the Prime Minister of Ionious, Jacob.

"Men, how are you?" Jacob enters the room and greets them with handshakes and hugs.

"Just great, Jacob. Thanks." President Houston shakes Jacobs hand and they all sit to talk.

"So, we are at peace, finally,... I wish the same could be said of you."

"I am glad to hear it sir. Actually, our peace is the reason why we are here. A vote was approved from our Congress to allow a DTR to be installed in our country. Available to all who want to use it, and we wanted to ask for your permission to install it in Washington."

"That is just great that you would want this for your people too. It has been an indescribable help to us in all areas of life."

"Will you?"

"Of course, there is something else that I think that you might be interested in."

"This sounds exciting."

Jacob calls into another room, "Rachel! Could you please come in here for a moment?"

A beautiful voice answers, "Of course, sir." Rachel was a stunningly beautiful woman with a professional plaid skirt up to her knees on, showing off her toned atheletic legs. She was wearing a blue silk blouse that matched her plaid skirt. She was typing something into her Scroll Datapad poised about chest high when she entered the room. She was tall for a woman and had amazing brown hair and astonishingly brilliant brown eyes.

"Rachel there are some people that I want for you to meet." As she stepped forward extending her hand to the GQ looking President Houston he arose as did the Vice President. "This is President Jonathan Houston of the planet Earth, this is my secretary Rachel."

The President shook her hand with a smile thinking what a beautiful woman to have as a secretary. "Nice to meet you." She said with a warm smile that displayed her elegance and grace."

"Nice to meet you, too Rachel."

Prime Minsiter Jacob also introduced Rachel to Vice-President Ed Young and they exchanged handshakes and gestures.

"What kind of new Scroll is it sir?

"It is not the Scroll that I was wanting for you to see.

"What is it then sir?"

"Actually it is Rachel. She is God's latest creation."

"Aren't we all God's creation?" Vice-President Ed Young asked.

"This is different, she is different. Can you notice anything about her that might set her apart from other people?"

"She is very beautiful, I am sorry, you are quite beautiful ma'am."

"That's not what I was wanting for you to notice. Actually you might have heard that we got a visitation from God Himself."

"We haven't heard all about what he said."

"Well, he instructed Ezekiel Epsilon and Daniel Delta as well as many other to undertake a project that would lead to the creation of a new being."

"A new being?"

"Yes, and Rachel is the first of these new beings of her kind. It is called a SHIFT being. Standing for Synergy Holographic Intelligent Force Technology being."

"She is a holographic projection?"

"You could say that."

"Rachel could you log off?"

"Sure, Prime Minister."

She typed something into her Scroll Datapad and the beautiful Rachel instantaneously vanished leaving only a metallic sphere hovering where her stomach was.

"This is the brains and holographic field synergy projection device that emits her. She is virtually indistinguishable from regular humans."

President Houston was in awe. "This is absolutely amazing."

"They will help you keep the peace and attain it in your efforts toward winning the war."

"You're giving this technology to us?"

"I think you need all the help from God that you can get. We will be sending several of them over to you as you install the new DTR system in the US. Consider it a thanks to you for sending your people to us."

"I don't know what to say. Thank you."

"You can also express your thanks to the men and women that will be helping you install the DTR they will be leaving shortly and we have you leaving with them so is there anything else that you would like to discuss?"

"What does God look like?"

"I'll let Rachel answer that she has a perfect access memory chip or PAM and she has several videos and pictures of God installed, and she can project all of them. Rachel?"

Her amazing figure suddenly reappeared with a pleasant smile. "President Houston you wish to see God?"

"Yes, can you display Him?"

She did some more typing into her Scroll and tossed her beautiful brunet hair over her shoulder. "Here he is."

Instantaneously she disappeared and God appeared right in front of the President and Vice-President to their utter amazement.

In God's distinct voice He said, "Blessed are the pure in heart, for they shall see God."

Dictionary of Terms

ACT 1 and ACT 3: These are classes of an Argos String Transport that are used to transport soldiers to the battlefield and for various operations. The South has an ACT 1 that is equipped with a Shield Cage emitter They are all equipped with various weapons.

AIIA Suit: Artificial Intelligence Interactive Armor Suit. This is the primary suit that is used by all branches of the military. It is capable of being an artificial intelligent camouflage that blends in with the environment around to be undetectable from any viewing angle. The suit can be equipped with cloaking and flying capabilities. Anything that can be generated on a Scroll Data Pad or Scroll Walling can be played or viewed on this suit.

Athenia: The capitol city of the planet Ionious located on the Southern continent.

Blood-Magnet: a cartridge that is used to be fired from a disrupter gun that sends an energy string to hit the chest of target and tethers back to create a rectangular shield that realigns all of the blood and bones to a liquid state and then pulls all of the liquid in the body to the shield from the pores and orifices in the target body.

Cloak: Holographic projection to change or alter the appearance of a person or ship.

Direct View: This is the seeing and sensing side of the DTR that allows other people with the proper clearance to see and sense all that a person is experiencing. This includes their vision, thoughts, and all of their senses.

Disrupter: This can be hand held or in rifle form for sniper operations. It looks like a cell phone and uses cartridges to fire various forms of energy ammunition that can be set to stun a person or kill someone.

Dreamstream Interactive: This is an entertainment platform that allows users to relive their dreams after they dream them.

DTR: Digital Trinity Republic: This is a supercomputer that serves as the government for the Ionious people through the Trinity composed of God, Jesus, and Holy Spirit. In combination of the citizens taking a pill that creates an implant of receivers and transmitters in their brain that allows the DTR to see and sense all that happens to a person 24 hours a day. After the DTR sees and senses all that a person is going through in their day it is able to have God talk to them as they face an obstacle. Jesus and the Holy Spirit also talk to the citizens of Ionious.

Eye 2 Eye Interactive: This is a sporting and training platform used for leisure and gaming and also by the military that allows users to compete and learn using the mind and their eyes as controls.

Interactive Bible: This is an application that is used with Dreamstream that allows users to go to and interact with all events and things that happened in the bible. In 200 AD God sent dreams to all peoples of Ionious that were from God's omnipresent eye view of all of the scriptures of the bible. These dreams were sent to the DTR and complied to create a complete interactive bible.

Ionious: The planet in which all of the citizens live that is located in the Ephesial Galaxy. The majority of inhabitants of this planet are Christians and all hear directly from God as they go throughout their day. A race of ancient aliens once dwelt on this planet then the Ancient Greek slaves created a revolt that lead to them taking over this world.

Megaport: This is a large doorway PAST functioning gateway that allows Shuffle Cruisers and other vehicles to pass through to other Megaports on the planet.

Nivio: The first element found on the planet that was in use from 10,000 BC to 2033 AD. The deposits in the Zeus Mountain range were destroyed and the new element Vionium went into full prominence used by the South to power everything.

Odyssey: A planet in the Ephesial Galaxy that has vast deposits of a new element that the North pursues.

Olympia: This is the North's Capitol city.

ONOA: Oranos Nivos Omega Aircraft: Small one to two seater aircraft that is quick agile and can fire a range of weapons on the ground or at other aircrafts.

PAST: Personal Argos String Transport. The primary means of travel for all people on the planet of Ionious. It is a doorway that when activated an energy stream appears that allows you to travel from one doorway to any other on the planet in the PAST system.

QUEST Starship: Quantum Universal Energy String Transport. This is a starship developed for interstellar travel instantaneously through String Theory that has been proven and is used by the String Drive Engine that creates a bending of space in front of the ship that it passes through for instantaneous travel from one place in the universe to any other.

Scroll Data Pad: It is a FOLED flexible organic light emmiting diode that is much like a foldable or flexible display that rolls out to be a laptop computer.

Scroll Walling: Is an OLED panel used over the existing structures of all walls that are able to generate any image in 2D and 3D holographic. They are touch sensitive and can be used with either a Scroll Data Pad or by touching the OLED wall.

Shield Cage: this is a peaceful weapon that is used to be fired from an ACT 1 from the South that will simultaneously send out shield cages to over a thousand soldiers on the ground that immobilizes the soldier so that they cannot get out until the South soldiers take them prisoner.

SHIFT Beings: Synergy Holographic Intelligent Force Technology Beings that look and feel real just like humans only they are a combination of Holographic projections and Energy fields that make them indistinguishable to humans. The Force fields work in conjunction to the projected image from the holographic sphere heart that emits both energy fields and holograph projections with real time reality. The synergistic function of the brainpower in the transmitting sphere heart allows for infinite detail to be projected holographically and emit force fields that are felt congruent to the seen image down to the last .0001 thousandth of an inch. Every folical, pore, hair, fingerprint, and skin tone that make humans humans can be seen and felt with the synergy dynamic transmitter.

Shuffle Cruiser: Primarily used by the North for special operations. It has jet blowers underneath that allow it to hover and move across the land or sea.

SWORD: Systemic World Objects Replication Dynamatom. This is used when programmed by a Scroll to replicate food or any other object through the arrangement of molecules and atoms to create any element that in turn creates any object: food, liquid, gas or solid.

Vionium: This is an element that when used with a Vionium generator can provide energy to all of the inhabitants of the planet or continent. This element is the life blood of the planet and was refined and developed after vast amounts were found in the Southern Universal mountains. This element powers everything from QUEST Starships to ACT 1's and Disrupters, as well as electricity to the the cities and Army bases.

Xum: ex-u-m This is the next step up in the type of transmissions that were once digital and before that analog. While digital is 1's and 0's Xum is iconic embedded transmissions sent in constant stream packets. No more 1's and 0's pure icon symbol representation of the precise data packet. Program files can be saved and categorized as one icon giving more space for storage on the DTR. One extension on all files, .xum.

Zyahth: A race of reptile-like aliens that live mostly on the planet Zythica.

Zythica: The home world planet of the Zyahth in the Ephesial Galaxy.

Index of Characters

General Aaron Alpha: He is the General of the North's military operations and has a wife named Sharon and a daughter named Esther.

Sharon Alpha: wife of the Northern General Aaron Alpha. Plays an integral role in allowing her friend Kedar Kappa and General Omega to access the Direct View of General Alpha.

Daniel Delta: The Shield engineer for the South married to Zeph Delta with a daughter named Sariah.

Ezekiel Epsilon: The creator of the DTR instructed by God to program the consciousness of the Trinity into the DTR so that all could have a direct communication with God.

President Jonathan Houston: The President of the United States from the years 2028-2036. He is a conservative Christian Republican that loves the Lord and does all that he can to protect his people and he serves God with all his heart.

Kedar Kappa: Northern woman and wife of Tophet Tau Kappa. She is used to gain access to General Alpha's Direct View.

General John Lambda: General of the South along side General Omega.

General Isaiah Omega: He is the General of the South military operations and has a wife named Ruth.

Vice President Ed Young: The Vice President of the United States from the years 2028-2036. He is a conservative Christian Republican that loves the Lord like Jonathan and he too does all that he can to protect his people and he serves God with all his heart.